A First Course in Aerial Robots and Drones

A First Course in Aerial Robots and Drones

Yasmina Bestaoui Sebbane

CRC Press
Taylor & Francis Group
Boca Raton London New York

CRC Press is an imprint of the
Taylor & Francis Group, an **informa** business

A CHAPMAN & HALL BOOK

First edition published 2022
by CRC Press
6000 Broken Sound Parkway NW, Suite 300, Boca Raton, FL 33487-2742

and by CRC Press
2 Park Square, Milton Park, Abingdon, Oxon, OX14 4RN

CRC Press is an imprint of Taylor & Francis Group, LLC

© 2022 Yasmina Bestaoui Sebbane

Library of Congress Cataloging-in-Publication Data

Names: Bestaoui Sebbane, Yasmina, author.
Title: A first course in aerial robots and drones / Yasmina Bestaoui
Sebbane.
Description: First edition. | Boca Raton, FL : CRC Press, 2022. | Series:
Chapman & Hall/CRC artificial intelligence and robotics series |
Includes bibliographical references and index.
Identifiers: LCCN 2021044896 | ISBN 9780367631383 (hbk) | ISBN
9780367640828 (pbk) | ISBN 9781003121787 (ebk)
Subjects: LCSH: Drone aircraft--Textbooks. | Airplanes--Radio
control--Textbooks.
Classification: LCC TL685.35 .B469 2022 | DDC 629.133/39--dc23/eng/20211103
LC record available at https://lccn.loc.gov/2021044896

ISBN: 978-0-367-63138-3 (hbk)
ISBN: 978-0-367-64082-8 (pbk)
ISBN: 978-1-003-12178-7 (ebk)

DOI: 10.1201/9781003121787

Typeset in CMR10 font
by KnowledgeWorks Global Ltd.

Publisher's note: This book has been prepared from camera-ready copy provided by the authors.

This textbook was nearly completed, prior to the untimely and tragic death of the author, Yasmina Bestaoui Sebbane. The book is being published posthumously and the Publisher apologizes for any gaps that may appear in the content.

To my family.

Contents

CHAPTER 6 ▪ Theory   137

CHAPTER 7 ▪ Flight Operations   147

List of Figures

CHAPTER 1

Introduction

1.1 INTRODUCTION

This book prepares readers to the field of **unmanned aircraft systems** (UAS), also known as **remotely piloted aircraft systems** (RPAS) or drones. The term unmanned aircraft includes very large aircraft similar in size and complexity to manned aircraft, but also very small drones. The smaller ones have the size of an insect. Even small UAS may be equipped with advanced features that allow the drone operator to operate out of their **visual line of sight** (VLOS), relying on the guidance and navigation control system of the drones. The UAV performance capabilities coupled with the installation of cameras and other sensors make small UAVs very attractive for both commercial and not commercial operations. The remote pilot keeps the UAV close enough to be capable of seeing it with vision unaided by any device other than corrective lenses, and seeing and avoiding all threats and hazards. Drones can hover or reach a speed of more than 1000 Km/h, be controlled by a computer, a smartphone, a tablet or satellite communication, and carry all kinds of material.

The civil operation of UAS is a rapidly growing area of aviation as technical developments are booming. New actors compared to those of manned aviation are appearing and different uses be commercial or leisure are being found. UAVs mostly perform services and tasks considered by humans as dull, dirty or dangerous. Drones that can fly closer to the ground than manned aircraft are considered well-suited for risky flights to accident areas. During the hurricane season in the US of 2017, drones came to the rescue in many different locations and scenarios. Drones were used to identify the location of hurricane survivors that needed to be rescued, to assess damage, to evaluate routes toward saving those caught up in flood conditions, and to collect vital information on the status of places that would otherwise be impossible to reach. They can help in fire-fighting, survey of flooded areas or areas affected by chemical, biological or nuclear accidents, help in various domains of science research, and also finding missing persons.

Drone applications in agriculture are booming, and new agriculture focused drone companies and products are being announced all the time. UAVs allow farmers to collect more actionable data about their crops. Also, new data-focused platforms are helping to analyze and use the data gathered to better pinpoint crop damage. By helping to create detailed maps, aerial robots UAV can assist in detecting illegal logging operations, as well as tracking and monitoring overall tree count and the health of a forest. Using **Normalized Difference Vegetation Index** (NDVI) imagery, areas of dry vegetation can be monitored, which can assist with forest fire prevention. NDVI quantifies vegetation by measuring the difference between near-infrared (which vegetation strongly reflects) and red light (which vegetation absorbs). Maps can also help identify dead trees, revealing whether a disease might be affecting the forest.

UAVs can also provide commercial services, such as delivery of packages, infrastructure maintenance and monitoring, aerial mapping, and so on. For example, as drones become cheaper, they are becoming a viable tool for countries with fewer resources to use for mapping projects. The Zanzibar mapping initiative has the goal of creating a high resolution map of the islands of Zanzibar and Pemba, covering an area of over 2,000 square kilometers, by using low-cost drones instead of satellite images or manned planes. Zipline announced a partnership with the government of Rwanda to deliver blood and other crucial medical supplies to rural areas that are difficult to reach by land. Drones are helping archaeologists to create detailed 3D maps of important sites so that even if they do fade with time, an accurate replica will persist that can be studied and used as a resource for future generations. As time passes, archaeological sites can become degraded and even fall into danger of disappearing beyond recognition.

Drones can also provide complete coverage of telecommunications and help authorities in security. For example, the FAA has officially approved the use of drones to restore cell service in Puerto Rico, following the devastation brought by Hurricane Maria. The Sea Shepherd Conservation Society has been using drones to help in stopping poachers on the open oceans. Police Departments around the world are starting to incorporate drones into their operations. Police officers are using drones to help assess damage following floods, fires, and other natural disasters; to create detailed orthomosaic maps of crime scenes, and even of places where a crime might be likely to happen so that they can use that knowledge to respond more quickly to potential threats; for accident reconstruction; and for fugitive apprehension, among others. Using aerial thermography, a drone can fly over the sight of a fire that is almost out to identify smoldering hot spots that might not be visible to the naked eye. Aerial thermography can also help to quickly find potential fire victims who need immediate medical attention in fires that are still smoldering.

UAVs are an option of inspection that continues to improve with collision avoidance possibility, higher levels of autonomy, higher payloads and alternative imaging sensors. Time is crucial in search and rescue scenarios. If someone is lost in the woods in harsh conditions, the chances of survival all come down to how long they are out there before someone finds them. Drones help search and rescue teams find people quickly using aerial thermography to identify heat signatures. Drones can also be helpful for getting an aerial view of an area where a search and rescue mission needs to take place in order to help guide the work being done by people on the ground. In Canada, a search and rescue team found a group of five missing snowboarders and skiers that had been missing for two days using UAVs with infrared cameras.

Some advantages of UAVs over conventional manned aircraft include:

1. It is programmable such that the UAV does not exceed its limits. The on-board computer uses the information given by the sensors and can calculate the limits of the aircraft. Thus the UAV will not undertake a maneuver that will cause it to stall.

2. Drones tolerate wider environmental ranges, greater ranges of pressure, temperature, and turbulence.

3. UAVs are also able to operate in areas that would prove hostile to humans, such as **Nuclear, Biological, or Chemical** (NBC) radiated areas.

4. UAVs save weight as there is no pilot and no-pilot related equipment on-board.

5. UAVs have lower operational costs. The reduction in weight and size allows the vehicles to operate on far less power.

Remark 1 *UAVs generally possess shorter flight endurance than manned aircraft which limits their overall operations and work area.*

Fundamental safety requirements are the same for manned or unmanned aviation. The basic principles are:

1. UAVs should be as safe as manned aviation;

2. UAVs operations should not exclude other airspace users;

3. UAVs should adapt to Air traffic management (ATM) and to existing regulations. UAVs should be transparent to Air traffic control (ATC) and to other airspace users;

Definition 2 *Air traffic management (ATM) consists primarily of air traffic control ensuring that aircraft are safely separated in the sky and at airports), air traffic flow management (sending flight paths to a central repository, analyzing and computing them) and aeronautical information services (compilation and distribution of aeronautical information needed by airspace users). Air traffic control (ATC) is responsible for providing the safe, orderly and expeditious flow of air traffic at airports where the type of operations and/or volume of traffic requires such a service.*

The current chapter begins by introducing common UAV categories, and then it describes some current regulations.

1.2 UAV CATEGORIES

An **Unmanned Aircraft System** (UAS) includes an unmanned aircraft, the human element (UAV operator, payload operator, flight technician, etc.), payload, control elements (autopilot and ground control stations) and data link communication (line-of-sight, satellite).

Definition 3 *Remote pilot or operator: person who is in control of the flight part of the aircraft.*

UAVs can be remotely controlled or fly autonomously based on pre-programmed flight plans or more complex dynamic automation systems. Unmanned does not imply fully autonomous flight.

Definition 4 *The **payload** is the equipment a UAV carries during the flight that is necessary to accomplish the mission. There are various types of payloads that are mounted according to the mission type. They describe the capability of the airframe structure to resist expected flight loads and provide test data/ or analysis. External load operations are allowed if the object being carried by the UAS is securely attached and does not adversely affect the flight characteristics or controllability of the aircraft.*

For classification according to size, the following sub-classes can be presented: Micro or Nano UAVs, Mini UAVs, Very small UAVs, Small UAVs, Medium UAVs, Large UAVs. UAVs also can be classified according to the ranges they can travel and their endurance in the air using the following sub-classes: Very low close range UAVs, Close range UAVs, Short Range UAVs, Mid-range UAVs, Endurance UAVs.

Definition 5 *Unmanned aerial vehicle (UAV): aircraft with no on-board pilot, from a few grams to hundreds of kilograms. The term drone is more common for military use, whereas UAV or aerial robot is more common in universities.*

They also be of different types: fixed wing-airplane; lighter than air-airship; rotary wing-helicopter or quadcopter (quadrotor); Bird or insect-like.

Definition 6 *the **lift** is the carrier effect of the combined actions of the pressures and depressions that the air exerts on a body. **Pressure** is the application of a force on a surface.*

A rotor craft is heavier than aircraft that depends principally for its support in flight on the lift generated by its rotors. The lift of the fixed-wing type is created mainly by the wings. Lighter than air drones rely on low-density gas inside the envelope to balance its own weight and the weight of the payload. It uses buoyancy to float in the air. Flapping wings drones fly like birds, and they mimic avian flight. They are expected to better navigate in rugged, unpredictable environments. They seem to be more efficient and wind-tolerant than inert wings.

Remark 7 *Among the various types of UAS, the one with highest units worldwide is the rotor-craft or rotary-wing type followed by the fixed-wing category. Fixed-wing UAVs are able to carry more equipment on less power. These features determine that fixed-wing UAVs suit perfectly long missions. However, airplanes are not the best option to perform a precision mission. Due to the air moving over their wings to generate lift, they cannot hover in one spot and, as a result, cannot provide the precise camera positioning, while rotary-wings vehicles can do this perfectly.*

The ongoing improvement of cost-effective multirotors symbolizes game-changing technological breakthrough. Even though drones seem at first look to be an easy application of simple physics—air gets pushed down, craft gets pushed up—in fact, they represent an intersection of numerous advancements in electronic miniaturization, applied computing, robotics, imaging and satellite navigation.

UAVs being susceptible to weather conditions, the remote pilot should use accurate and timely weather information to make informed decisions, to plan and execute effective fuel management, diversions and alternate route planning. Many UAVs often fly at lower altitudes, causing them to be directly affected by the weather. The UAVs can be more sensitive to wind or precipitation than large aircraft, but they may also be able to adapt to the weather changes with more agility due to their lower operating altitudes. Information on wind speed and direction, cloud ceiling, visibility, precipitation, humidity and temperature is crucial for flight plan preparation and execution. **Visibility** is the greatest horizontal distance at which prominent objects can be viewed with the naked eye. The remote pilot must be able to see the UAV at all times during flight.

Even small UAS may be equipped with advanced features that allow the user to operate the UAS out of their VLOS (visual line of sight), relying on the guidance and navigation control system of the unmanned aircraft, which usually provides self-stabilization and some automated functions. Navigation determines the location of the UAV, then allows the UAV to navigate to its intended destination.

Drones are used to survey cell sites when engineers are not able to safely access sites to visually survey them. In specific situations, drones can save time by surveying multiple sites during one flight and by sharing information in real-time. For example, after Hurricane Matthew, a small UAS was able to both record and livestream HD video and high-resolution photographs of a cell site.

With using drones in the aftermath of an emergency situation, challenges include gaining approval to fly, coordinating with government agencies and having companies ready to go.

Skyward assisted with the coordination with the FAA during Hurricane Irma. Skyward was recently approved by the FAA to give commercial drone operators fast access to controlled airspace with the Low Altitude Authorization and Notification Capability (LAANC), which will allow to respond to disasters in these areas without lengthy approval processes in the future. LAANC enables businesses to access airspace that previously required the submission of a manual request for authorization, and it will automate the approval process, reducing the wait time from months to seconds.

Another challenge occurred during the response to the California wildfires. To do an aerial survey, close coordination was necessary for mission safety with the amount of helicopters and other aircraft actively fighting the fires. For emergency response, utilizing a "flying cell site" in an area where no wireless service may be available.

In the energy sector, drones enable automation of the field inspection work and can do a task quickly and more accurately. Improvement in safety, reduction in hazardous field hours, cost savings, revenue enhancement and digital asset management are some of the important factors that are driving the adoption of this technology.

Other companies have developed specialized drone services for inspecting solar farms, wind turbines, power lines, power generation assets like coal plants, providing actionable data to inform asset management and business decisions. To a larger extent, the wind industry relies on corrective maintenance rather than predictive mitigation steps. Corrective maintenance is expensive; unnoticed defects can result in catastrophic failure, resulting in expensive repairs, extended downtime of the turbine, and associated lost revenues. A single catastrophic failure on a wind farm can wipe out the savings of not budgeting regular predictive maintenance.

Predictive maintenance today relies on ground inspection methods, which involve shutting off the turbines and hiring contractors who either need to physically climb the turbines to inspect them or take pictures from the ground. In addition to the significant safety risk associated with physical climbs, but needing to shut off the turbines for a long duration greatly reduces the output and revenues. Ground inspection with cameras can take upwards of two hours per turbine, which can be reduced to 15–30 min with drones, reducing the downtime of turbines by 75 percent and making the inspection cost-effective.

Drones follow a pre-planned automated flight to capture images at regular overlap. This automation reduces the chances of missing small cracks and defects, and produces highly accurate reporting. Ground inspections require manual or semi-automated data capture, and picture-taking can only be done hundred's of feet away from the blade, introducing human error and inaccuracy in data collection.

Drone imagery enables storing of digital signatures of the asset health. Information from past inspections can be conveniently presented to show asset performance over time. Digital dashboards with key performance indicators can enable an asset manager to perform comparative portfolio analytics.

The drone inspections more than pays for the cost of services when evaluated against these benefits.

Besides 3D and robot vision, embedded vision is one of the latest hot topics in machine vision. This is because without real-time machine vision, there would be no such thing as autonomous transport systems and robots in the Industry 4.0 environment, self-driving cars, or unmanned drones. Classic machine vision systems, however, do not enter the equation due to space or cost limitations, while the functionality of so-called smart cameras is usually very limited. Only by combining a miniaturized camera, a compact processor board, and flexibly programmable software can tailor-made machine vision applications be developed and embedded directly in machines or vehicles.

Drones can be put to a variety of uses, such as taking water samples, casting down life belts, or providing geodata and images from areas that are difficult or even impossible for people to access. It can deliver maps in real-time, which the rescue teams can use immediately to help them with their mission planning. The multicopter operates autonomously. Its area of operation is defined using an existing georeferenced satellite image. A waypoint list is generated from this automatically depending on the size of the area and the required ground resolution. The multicopter then flies over this using GNSS technology (Global Navigation Satellite System) or GPS. The multicopter also takes off and lands automatically.

The real-time requirements exclude remote sensing methods, such as photogrammetry, which are currently available on the market. These methods do not deliver results until all images have been captured and combined based on algorithms that usually require considerable processor power. Although the maps created using this method are extremely precise, precision is not a top priority for gaining an initial overview in a disaster situation and only delays the rescue operations unduly. In contrast, the principle of image mosaicing, or stitching, is a proven method of piecing together a large overall image from many individual images extremely quickly. To put this principle into practice on board a multicopter, however, the images provided by a camera must be processed by a computer quickly and nearby.

Drone deliveries drastically reduce the cost of last-mile deliveries while meeting customers' demand for receiving their orders as quickly as possible.

Regulatory authorities are understandably concerned about the safety and other implications of widespread usage of drones, especially autonomous drones that go beyond the line of sight. These concerns remain the biggest barrier to widespread drone deliveries.

Drones have the technology to navigate obstacles like trees and buildings in real-time. They are equipped with technology capable of navigating rural as well as urban environments through smart mapping surroundings and navigation routes based on existing landscapes. In fact, drone deliveries are safer than regular deliveries, as they decrease the number of courier bikes and delivery cars on the road, resulting in fewer accidents (and a cleaner environment).

Safety and security are of utmost importance to create safe and secure systems. Built into a cloud technology, a failsafe system whereby all drones can be programmed to land immediately upon detection of a hack. Both domestically and internationally, there are differences in regulatory bodies and their particular concerns. Iceland, for example, has an exceptionally progressive regulatory body, which is keen to make drone deliveries a reality, provided all precautions are taken, and they are proven to be safe. Another significant difference is that in Iceland, there are no line-of-sight restrictions, unlike in the U.S., where strict line-of-sight restrictions prohibit delivering items further than a few hundred meters.

> Items falling from drones – recently, there has been a lot of media attention surrounding instances of items being dropped by personal use drones. Drones must have a number of fail-safes that prevent items from being dropped.

> Collision: Regulators only allow one drone company to operate per each approved flight path, ensuring that there are no collisions. Moreover, as drones can be tracked simultaneously, they are suited with technology that prohibits collision between them. With regards to third party objects and other aerial vehicles, only the highest quality tracking and area mapping are deployed, reducing the threat of collision significantly.

> Hacking: As mentioned, regulators are justifiably concerned by the possibility of drones being hacked. To satisfy this concern, companies must build a secure system to prevent hacking, which includes the fail-safe opportunity to land the drone upon recognition of a hack—which includes a change in the operator or a simple course diversion.

1.3 REGULATIONS

Multiple incidents have been observed across the globe in terms not only of safety but also of security; for example, incidents such as the drone that flew into the White House grounds in 2015 and also of a drone being piloted into a major tennis match (US Open) in 2015. These issues stem from a multitude of grey areas that are currently part of the regulations.

There is a pressing need for drones to be regulated, compliant and licensed. The media reports issues with drones on a regular basis. If an aircraft is impacted during flight, the blame is on the drone operator. This is an interesting concept since if a drone does impact an aircraft, the drone itself will generally be completely destroyed, leaving little or no evidence. Therefore, the impact damage itself, together with eyewitness accounts, are often the only evidence available. However, it is important to question what distinguishes a drone impact from various other FOD (foreign object damage) impacts? Testing is being undertaken to analyse the damage profile of impacts with drones, together with the physics behind the impacts. Eyewitness accounts are often unreliable as the pilot may have seen something but is unsure what it was. A drone is generally not very large, and the pilot is in mid-air flying an aircraft at high speed. The chance of actually getting a proper visual on the drone is highly improbable.

Drones pose various risks. In some cases, drones have narrowly missed commercial manned aircraft, flown over or landed on the residence of public figures, nuclear power station, embassies and tourist attractions, obstructed fire-fighting and injured people. Drones are small and generally hard to see when they are in the air. To be licensed under the Geneva Convention, it is required that the aircraft's licensing number is written on the aircraft. While it can be written on the drone, it probably will not be visible. Therefore, regulators and safety professionals must face these issues. Tracking in the form of a GPS chip would be beneficial. This would allow investigators to know which drones were airborne when an accident occurred and also be alerted to drones that are not adhering to regulations. However, this may be hard to implement today. The millions of drones currently in circulation would need to be microchipped. The regulators would also have to come to an agreement on what size drones need chipping? Drones literally come in every shape and size. Going too far and microchipping all of them would mean an enormous cost and use of resources.

Under 2kg drones are generally accepted to not have the potential kinetic energy in a fall or while flying to cause death to an individual. However, they possess very sharp propellers which have the potential to slice. There are very specific areas of the human anatomy to which they can cause considerable harm and injury, for instance the eyes. Another problem is that many of these drones are equipped with a lithium battery, which has the potential of blowing up or causing fire when impacted. So even a drone of under 2kgs has the potential, even though highly unlikely, to impact an aircraft engine or propeller blades. This could cause considerable danger.

The potential to negate these issues may not lie with the drones themselves but rather with protection of other objects. For instance, there is a booming industry alongside drone development for anti-drone products. These can prevent drones from entering an area or can even disable drones. This technology within these anti-drone products may be the solution. If that technology could be installed into aircraft or buildings using a computer program, then there would be established a "bubble" around them of anti-drone air-space. If a drone were to enter, the computer program would be able to push it back. Unfortunately, the technology is not yet available at the level required.

People are also concerned about their privacy. Drones usually carry video cameras to allow the remote pilot to fly them. These may record images and include technologies such as zoom, microphones and many sensors as well as GPS systems recording the location of persons filmed. All this can make drones highly intrusive.

Global rules covering unmanned aircraft are established at United Nations level by the Convention of International Civil Aviation (the Chicago Convention). It prohibits all unmanned aircraft from flying over another state's territory without its permission. It also obliges states to ensure that flights without a pilot on board in regions open to civil aircraft are controlled so as to eliminate danger to civil aircraft. NASA and EASA are currently studying a UAS traffic management (UTM) system that could develop airspace integration requirements for enabling safe, efficient low-altitude operations.

1.4 LABORATORIES

The title of the labs associated with this book are:

1. UAS airframe assembly

2. Install external pilot controls, range test

3. Bench test and install motor and power system

4. Ground control station software

5. Setup and hardware in the loop simulation, tune autopilot

6. Bench test, install video payload

7. Install, test autopilot telemetry modem

1.5 CONCLUSIONS

Even just within the civilian side of things, the list of unmanned aerial devices seems to be constantly expanding. These days, the term encompasses everything from what is essentially a cheap, multi-bladed toy helicopter, all the way up to custom-built soaring machines with incredibly adept artificial intelligence capabilities.

CHAPTER 2

Components of UAVs

2.1 INTRODUCTION

At the earliest stage of UAV conceptual design, some estimate of weight, propulsive power and efficiency, and aerodynamic performance is required. Custom methods are common.

2.2 TYPES

Classification can of different types, depending on the configuration, such as fixed-wing or rotary-wing drones.

2.2.1 Airplane

Fixed-wing UAV or airplane: This type of UAV consists of a fixed wing which surface generates the major lift of the aircraft. Due to that rigid wing the unmanned aircraft has natural gliding capabilities and is more forgiving in the air if facing piloting or technical errors. Control Surfaces are flaps, ailerons, elevators, and rudders. The control surfaces are steered using actuators.

2.2.2 Control surfaces

A fixed wing aircraft has four actuators: forward thrust, ailerons, elevator and rudder. Thrust provides acceleration in the forward direction and the control surfaces exert moments: rudder for yaw torque, ailerons for roll torque and elevator for pitch torque.

Moveable surfaces on an airplane's wings and tail allow a pilot to maneuver an airplane and control its attitude or orientation. These control surfaces work on the same principle as lift on a wing. They create a difference in air pressure to produce a force on the airplane in a desired direction. Ailerons are hinged control surfaces attached to the trailing edge of the wing of a fixed-wing aircraft. The ailerons are used to control the aircraft in roll. The two ailerons are typically interconnected so that one goes down when the other

DOI: 10.1201/9781003121787-2

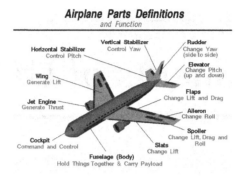

Airplane Parts Definitions
and Function

FIGURE 2.1 Airplane parts definition

goes up: the downgoing aileron increases the lift on its wing while the upgoing aileron reduces the lift on the other wing, producing a rolling moment about the aircraft's longitudinal axis.

Elevators are control surfaces, usually at the rear of an aircraft, which control the aircraft's orientation by changing the pitch of the aircraft, and so also the angle of attack of the wing. An increased wing angle of attack will cause a greater lift to be produced by the profile of the wing, and a slowing of the aircraft. A decreased angle of attack will produce an increase in speed (a dive). The elevators may be the only pitch control surface present (and are then called a stabilator), or may be hinged to a fixed or adjustable surface called a stabilizer.

On an aircraft, the rudder is called a "control surface" along with the rudder-like elevator (attached to horizontal tail structure) and ailerons (attached to the wings) that control pitch and roll. The rudder is usually attached to the fin (or vertical stabilizer) which allows the pilot to control yaw in the vertical axis, i.e. change the horizontal direction in which the nose is pointing.

To help make turning easier, an airplane is usually less stable along its roll axis than along its pitch and yaw axes. Several factors help the pilot keep the wings level: the inclined mounting of the wings, the position of the wings above or below the fuselage, the swept-back shape of the wings, and the vertical stabilizer. As an airplane rolls, it tends to slip to the side; changing the direction of relative wind on the wings and tail. These design features help the pilot restore the airplane to its upright position.

Maintaining stablity: The main purpose of the tail is to provide stability. If tilted by a gust of wind, a stable airplane tends to recover, just as a ball lying at the bottom of a bowl will roll back to the center after being disturbed. Lift differentials are calculated by subtracting the inner wing's slower speed from the outer wing's higher speed. This difference in speed slowly establishes a bank and entry into a turn.

Airplane UAVs have the following characteristics:

1. Launched by hand, runway or catapult, and generally lands on relatively flat grass or a runway.

2. Requires a large open space in which to fly since the airplane's maneuverability is limited.

3. Wings / airfoils create the lift. The airfoil section and wing planform of the lifting surface are critically important to the performance of all airplanes.

4. Higher potential payload capacity.

5. Foam models can be forgiving in the event of a crash, and most can be repaired.

6. Models with a $0.5m$ to $1.8m$ wing span are most common.

7. In case of an engine failure, there is still the potential to land without damaging the aircraft.

An average, medium-sized electric airplane will provide around $20-60$ minutes under normal use (i.e. not full throttle). Mapping and long-range flights are better with an airplane. Common applications include **First-person-view** (FPV) flight, mapping. For autonomous flight, a flight controller with GPS is needed, as well as some additional sensors.

Flight simulation training devices: For training extensively, to use a simulator allows to get a feel for its handling to avoid potentially expensive crashes. There is a growing potential of free simulator to help master the vehicle. There are two types of drone simulator: those designed to help practice first person view racing and those for refining handling of camera drones to help achieve better video and photos. The best simulators offer a variety of scenarios being indoors or outdoors, variable weather conditions and realistic physics. Some allow also the control of real licensed drone models. All the free simulators allow the use of the remote control transmitter and game controllers. The environments can be in virtual reality (realistic but computer-generated) and real-world.

Common wing types UAV airplanes may have different forms as in the following figure.

1. **Delta wing UAV**: By far the simplest design is a flying or delta wing as in Figure 2.2. A simple and rudimentary frame can be made using inexpensive foam board. These classically have only two control surfaces, meaning all turns are banked. The resulting stepped wing can have improved performance and flying characteristics compared to the even simpler flat plate wing used in some radio-controlled models. The propeller

FIGURE 2.2   Delta wing

FIGURE 2.3   Motorized sailplane/glider

is commonly found at the rear (to allow a camera to be mounted at the front), but flies just as well with the motor placed in the center or at the front, provided the center of gravity is correct. These are great for their simplicity and tend to need to fly at higher speeds.

2. **Motorized sailplane/glider**: For longest flight time, this design is the best choice. These tend to have a mid-wing or high wing design, and the tail is T or V-shaped, as in Figure 2.3. These are not meant to be the fastest (and are often the slowest) nor carry the greatest payload (they need to be as lightweight as possible), but a good design can stay in the air for many hours. Almost all have the propeller mounted at the front, so applications which require a camera normally need to have it mounted on the underside/belly of the fuselage.

3. **Skywalker UAV**: the propeller is mounted just behind the wings, and the tail support is mounted just below so as not to interfere, as in Figure 2.4. The fact that the propeller is at the rear means the front can be equipped with a camera (unobstructed view). Having the propeller mounted quite high makes it easy to hand launch, and the propeller should never touch the ground in a normal landing (with or without landing gear). These designs tend to be good for payload capacity, decent speed and decent flight time, and offer the greatest versatility.

FIGURE 2.4   Skywalker

▲ Close-range UAV

FIGURE 2.5 Conventional UAV

4. **Conventional UAV**: Almost all have the propeller mounted at the front (puller), as in Figure 2.5. The wings have a generally straight leading / trailing edge (rectangular). These designs are not the easiest designs to work with when choosing an unobstructed mounting location for a camera and many of the designs use wood, which is not forgiving at all in a crash.

Takeoff and landing performance   Takeoff and landing performance is a condition of accelerated and decelerated motion. For instance, during takeoff, an aircraft starts at zero speed and accelerates to the takeoff speed to become airborne. During landing, the aircraft touches down at the landing speed and decelerates to zero speed. The important factors of takeoff or landing performance are:

1. The takeoff or landing speed is generally a function of the **stall speed** or minimum flying speed. In theory, it is possible to configure an autopilot to avoid approaching flight conditions where a stall/spin could occur. In practice, however, horizontal gusts, configuration errors, clogged static systems, poor launches, and pilot errors can lead to a stall or worse a spin.

2. The rate of acceleration/deceleration during the takeoff or landing roll. The speed (acceleration and deceleration) experienced by any object varies directly with the imbalance of force and inversely with the mass of the object. An airplane on the runway moving at 75 knots has four times the energy it has traveling at 37 knots. Thus, an airplane requires four times as much distance to stop as required at half the speed.

3. The takeoff or landing roll distance is a function of both acceleration/deceleration and speed.

Runway conditions affect takeoff and landing performance. Typically, performance chart information assumes paved, level, smooth, and dry runway surfaces. Since no two runways are alike, the runway surface differs from one runway to another, as does the runway gradient or slope. The gradient or slope of the runway is the amount of change in runway height over the length of the runway. The gradient is expressed as a percentage such as a 3 percent gradient. This means that for every 100 feet of runway length, the runway height changes by 3 feet. A positive gradient indicates the runway height increases, and a negative gradient indicates the runway decreases in height. An up-sloping runway impedes acceleration and results in a longer ground run during takeoff. However, landing on an upsloping runway typically reduces the landing roll. A down-sloping runway aids in acceleration on takeoff resulting in shorter takeoff distances. The opposite is true when landing, as landing on a down-sloping runway increases landing distances. Water on the runways reduces the friction between the tires and the ground, and can reduce braking effectiveness. The ability to brake can be completely lost when the tires are hydroplaning because a layer of water separates the tires from the runway surface. This is also true of braking effectiveness when runways are covered in ice.

2.2.3 Rotary-wings Types

Rotary-wing UAV is an unmanned aircraft with means of propulsion which derives the whole or a substantial part of its lift from a rotary-wing system. The best quality of this type is the ability for takeoff and land vertically, which allows the user to operate within a smaller space. The **frame** is like the skeleton of the aircraft and holds all of the parts together. Simple frames have motors connected to aluminum or other lightweight extrusions (arm) which then connect to a central body. A good size range which offers the most versatility and value is between $0.350m$ to $0.700m$. This measurement represents the diameter of the largest circle which intersects all of the motors. The capacity to hover and perform maneuvering makes rotary-wing UAVs well suited to applications where precision maneuvering is necessary to the operation. On the other hand, this type of UAVs requires longer and more complicated maintenance and repair processes.

Remark 8 *The key factor when choosing between fixed-wing, rotary-wing or multi-rotor types is the application to which the UAV is selected. Each application requires different type of operations, thus a different type of UAV. The more important qualities are the ability of speed and distance, or precision and stability.*

UAV Rotary-wings may have different forms as in the following figures.

Definition 9 *Multi-rotor: means an aircraft with multiple rotors. These UAVs consist of several rotor blades that revolve around a fixed mast. There are a wide range of setups: 3 rotors (tricopter), 4 rotors (quadrotor), 6 rotors (hexacopter), 8 rotors (octocopter). There are also more unusual setups like 12 or 16 rotors.*

Multi-rotor UAVs have the same qualities as rotary-wings, but they are even more stable and easier to control. They come in use in an accurate and precise missions. They are perfect for filming, aerial mapping or infrastructure monitoring. But multi-rotors usually have short flight time and ranges.

FIGURE 2.6 Tricopter

Definition 10 *Size (mm): Size represents the greatest point to point distance between two motors on a UAV. Size can also determine the class of UAV.*

Tricopter has three motors/propellers, and three support arms, each connected to one motor, as in Figure 2.6. The front of the UAV tends to be between two of the arms (Y3). The angle between the arms can vary but tends to be 120 degrees. In order to move, the rear motor normally needs to be able to rotate in order to counteract the gyroscopic effect of an uneven number of rotors, as well as to change the yaw angle. **Advantages**: it flies more like an airplane in forward motion. **Disadvantages**: Since this UAV is not symmetric, the design uses a normal RC servo to rotate the rear motor and as such, the design is less straightforward than many other multi-rotors. The rear arm is more complex since a servo needs to be mounted along the axis. Most, not all flight controllers support this configuration.

Quadcopter or quadrotor has four motors/propellers and four support arms, as in Figure 2.7. Each arm is connected to one motor. The front of the UAV tends to be between two arms (x configuration), but can also be along an arm (+ configuration). Quadrotors are essentially a system where counteracting forces work to simplify the control system. In particular, there are two pairs of rotors which spin in opposite directions, so the angular momentum of each propeller cancels out with the propeller which spins the opposite direction. An average medium sized quadrotor will remain in the air for around $10 - 15$ minutes. **Advantages**: It is the most popular multi-rotor design, simplest construction and quite versatile. In the standard configuration, the arms / motors are symmetric about two axes. **Disadvantages**: There is no redundancy, so if there is a failure anywhere in the system, especially a motor or propeller, the aircraft is likely going to crash.

Remark 11 *V-Tail has four arms, the rear two are at an angle to form a V, as in Figure 2.8.*

FIGURE 2.7 Quadrotor

FIGURE 2.8 Hunter-vtail

Hexacopter has six motors / propellers, each arm being connected to one motor. The front of the UAV tends to be between two arms, but can also be along one arm, as in Figure 2.9. **Advantages**: It is easy to add two additional arms and motors to a quadrotor design, increasing the total thrust available, meaning this UAV can lift more payload. Also, should a motor fail, there is still a chance the UAV can land rather than crash. Hexacopters often use the same motor and support arm, making the system modular. Almost all flight controllers support this configuration. **Disadvantages** : This design uses additional parts, so compared to a quadrotor which uses a minimum number of parts, the equivalent hexacopter using the same motors and propellers would be more expensive and larger. These additional motors and parts add weight to the UAV, so in order to get the same flight time as a quadrotor, the battery needs to be larger (higher capacity) as well.

FIGURE 2.9 Hexacopter

FIGURE 2.10   y6

FIGURE 2.11   Octocopter

Y3/Y6 are UAV configurations with three support arms; Y3 configurations have one motor at the end of each arm, whereas Y6 have two motors per arm (one facing up, the other facing down). A Y6 design is a type of hexacopter but rather than six arms, it has three support arms, with a motor connected to either side of the arm (for a total of six motors). The propellers mounted to the underside still project the thrust downward.**Advantages**: A Y6 design actually eliminates a support arm (as compared to a quadrotor), for a total of three. This means the UAV can lift more payload as compared to a quadrotor, with fewer components than a normal hexacopter. A Y6 does not have the same issue as a Y3 as it eliminates the gyro effect using counter-rotating propellers. Also, should a motor fail, there is still a chance the UAV can land rather than crash. **Disadvantages**: The thrust obtained in a Y6 as opposed to normal hexacopter is slightly lower, likely because the thrust from the top propeller is affected by the lower propeller. Not all flight controllers support this configuration.

Octocopter   has eight motors / propellers, each arm connected to one motor, as in Figure 2.11. The front of the UAV tends to be between two arms. **Advantages**: More motors give more thrust, as well as increased redundancy. **Disadvantages**: More motors lead to higher price and larger battery pack. Most users are looking at very heavy payloads such as DSLR (digital single-lens reflex) cameras and heavy gimbal systems. Added redundancy is really important.

Definition 12 *Digital Single-lens Camera: is a digital camera that combines the optics and the mechanisms of a single-lens camera with a digital imaging sensor, as opposed to photographic film.*

Definition 13 *Almost Ready to Fly (ARF): a UAV which comes assembled with almost all parts necessary to fly. Components like the controller and receiver may not be included.*

Definition 14 *Bind and Fly (BNF): the UAV comes fully assembled and includes a receiver. A compatible transmitter must, however, be chosen.*

Definition 15 *Do It Yourself (DIY): This normally involves using parts from a variety of different suppliers and creating or modifying parts.*

Definition 16 *A tube clamp is a device normally used on a round tube in order to connect it to another device (such as a motor mount or a UAV's body).*

Definition 17 *Ready To Fly (RTF): a UAV which comes fully assembled with all necessary parts.*

2.3   MOTORS AND PROPELLERS

2.3.1   Motors

Motors have an important impact on the payload (or maximum load) which the UAV can support, as well as the flight time. Even if a pair of motors are the same brand and model, their speeds may vary slightly. Motors can be of two types: brushed and brushless. Brushed motors spin the coil inside a case with fixed magnets mounted around the outside of the casing. Brushless motors do the opposite; the coils are fixed either to the outer casing or inside the casing while the magnets are spun. Brushless electric motors are the most common type of electric motor used in present-day UAVs. While brushed motors use brushes to mechanically switch the phase of the windings in order to keep the motor running, brushless motors require the use of an **Electronic Speed Controller** (ESC) board to do this task. However, they provide various advantages over traditional brushed motors including better thrust-to-weight ratios, higher efficiencies, increased reliability, higher torque per weight, and lower noise. For the typical behavior for a brushless motor at a given operating voltage, if no load is placed on the motor it will run at its maximum speed, where the input current is a very small value. As a torque load is applied, the speed decreases and the input current and power increase. If the torque load reaches a certain level (called the stall torque) the motor would slow down to a halt, increasing the input power and current to its maximum value. The motor delivers its maximum power when operating at half of its maximum speed, and operates at maximum efficiency when running at a speed that is close to its maximum speed. Increasing the operating voltage has the effect of increasing the output power and torque, as well as the input current and power. However, brushless motors also have a maximum current limit. If this current is exceeded, overheating may occur leading to complete failure of the motor. It is, therefore, important to ensure that this value is not exceeded in operating conditions.

Brushless motors can be classified into outrunner motors and inrunner motors:

1. **Inrunner** has the fixed coils mounted to the outer casing and the magnets are mounted to the armature shaft which spins inside the casing. Their rotational core is contained within the motor's can, much like a standard ferrite motor.

2. **Outrunner** has the magnets mounted on the outer casing, which is spun around the fixed coils in the center of the motor casing (the bottom mounting of the motor is fixed).

3. **Hybrid outrunner** has a static outer shell around them to make them look like they are inrunners.

Remark 18 *Inrunner brushless DC motors tend to be used in RC cars, airplanes and helicopters because of their high KV. They may also be geared down to increase the torque. Outrunners tend to have more torque.*

KV: The KV rating / value of a motor relates to how fast it will rotate for a given voltage. KV refers to the constant velocity of a motor. It is measured by the number of **revolutions per minute** (rpm) that a motor turns when 1V (one volt) is applied with no load attached to that motor. The KV rating of a brushless motor is the ratio of the motor's unloaded revolutions per minute to the peak voltage on the wires connected to the coils. The KV rating of a motor determines how fast that motor will rotate when a given voltage is applied to it. For most multirotor, a low KV is desired (between 500 and 1000 for example) since this helps with stability. For acrobatic flight however, a KV between 1000 and 1500 should be considered and smaller diameter propellers. If the KV rating for a particular motor is 650rpm/V, then at 11.1V, the motor will be rotating at $11.1V \times 650 = 7215$rpm (revolutions per minute). Using a lower voltage tends to mean that the current draw will be higher ($power = current \times voltage$).

Thrust kg, Lbs or N.: Some brushless motor manufacturers give an indication of a motor's thrust corresponding to several propeller options. For a quadrotor, if a specific motor can provide up to $0.5Kg$ of thrust with an $0.28m$ propeller, that means that four of these motors can lift $0.5Kg \times 4 = 2Kg$ at maximum thrust. Therefore, if the quadrotor weighs just less than $2Kg$, it will only take off at maximum thrust, either choose a motor + propeller combination which can provide more thrust, or reduce the weight of the aircraft. If the propulsion system (all motors and propellers) can provide a maximum of 2Kg of thrust then the entire UAV should be at most about half this weight ($1Kg$, including the weight of the motors themselves). The same calculation can be done for any given configuration. Let's assume a hexacopter's weight (including frame, motors, electronics, battery, accessories) to be $2.5Kg$. Each motor should, therefore, be capable of providing $(2.5Kg/6motors) \times 2 = 0.83$ kg of thrust (or more).

Remark 19 *With multirotors it is important to make sure that the motors can produce around 50 percent more thrust than the total weight of your drone. The UAV should be able to hover at just over half throttle. The motors will have enough extra thrust to control the multirotor in wind and during aggressive flight maneuvers. Some motors are better suited for racing while others are better for stability.*

2.3.2   Propellers

Propeller performance is often characterized by curves that illustrate the variation of thrust and torques with revolutions per minute and forward speed. Propellers are either designed to rotate clockwise (CW) or couter-clockwise (CCW). It is important to know which part of the propeller is intended to face upwards (the top surface is curved outward).

2.3.2.1   Blades and Diameter

Most multi-rotor aircraft have two rotor blades, as in Figure 2.12. Adding more blades will automatically mean more thrust; each blade must travel through the wake of the one which precedes it, so the more blades, the more prevalent the wake will be. A smaller diameter propeller has less inertia and is, therefore, easier to speed up and slow down, which helps in acrobatic flight. There are a number of factors that should be taken into consideration when choosing the right propeller blades. They have a significant influence on power and can affect how smoothly a drone flies. Therefore, one of the most important considerations is flight efficiency. When selecting new drone propeller blades, the following factors are important:

1. The number of blades required per propeller will vary depending on the platform, usage and payload requirements. Smaller blades, are most frequently used for racing drones and those used for acrobatics. Smaller blades are generally paired with smaller motors with high kV ratings. Larger blades, are paired with motors that have low KV ratings and can be used to carry heavier payloads, such as video equipment or spraying containers for agriculture.

2. Pitch is defined as the traveling distance per a single revolution of the propeller. The correct pitch will often depend on the specific application for a UAV platform. Lower pitch often results in more torque and less turbulence for lifting, and as a result the motors do not have to work as hard to carry heavy payloads which can result in increased flight time (as the motors will draw less current from the battery). Propellers with higher pitches move more air, but generally create more turbulence and less torque.

FIGURE 2.12   Propellers

3. Typically, a larger diameter propeller blade allows greater contact with the air. This relates directly to flight efficiency, as a small increase or decrease in diameter can change how efficiently a drone performs. Larger propellers tend to be more stable when hovering than smaller propellers. However, smaller propeller blades require less effort to speed up or slow down than larger ones, making them more responsive than larger propellers.

4. Other factors to be considered include: Blade material, Power revolution per minute, Air density and Maximum noise.

In summary, selecting the most appropriate propeller blades for a VTOL UAV will vary depending on the planned usage and there are a number of factors that need to be taken into consideration. For example, in heavy lift applications larger blades with low pitches will be more suitable.

2.3.2.2   Efficiency/Thrust

The thrust produced by a propeller depends on the density of the air, on the propeller's revolutions per minute, on its diameter, on the shape and area of the blades and on its pitch. A propeller's efficiency relates to the angle of attack. The efficiency itself is a ratio of the output power to the input power. Most well-designed propellers have an efficiency of 80 percent.

Definition 20 *The **angle of attack** is defined as the angle between the chord of an airfoil and the direction of the surrounding undisturbed flow of fluid. It is the angle formed by the wing (or propeller) and the relative wind, relative wind being the opposite of travel of the UAV.*

The angle of attack is affected by the relative velocity, so a propeller will have different efficiency at different motor speeds. The efficiency is also greatly affected by the leading edge of the propeller blade, that should be as smooth as possible.

2.3.3 Material

The material used to make the propellers can have a moderate impact on the flight characteristics, but safety should be the primary consideration.

1. **Injection-Molded Plastic** propeller is the most popular choice for multi-rotor aircraft, because of their low cost, decent flight characteristics and respectable durability. A plastic propeller which has been reinforced with carbon fiber is arguably the best overall choice because of its high rigidity and low cost.

2. **Fiber-Reinforced Polymer** propeller is cutting edge technology. Carbon fiber parts are still not very easy to produce.

Folding: Folding propellers have a central part which connects to two pivoting blades. When the center which is connected to the motor's output shaft spins, centrifugal forces act on the blades, forcing them outwards and essentially making the propeller rigid, with the same effect as a fixed propeller. Because of lower demand and higher number of parts required, folding propellers are less common than fixed propellers.

Propeller guards are material which surround a propeller to prevent the propeller from contacting other objects. They are implemented as a safety feature and a way to minimize damage to the UAV. Propeller guards connect to the main frame and provide a fixed ring/cushion around the propeller.

2.3.4 Electronic Speed Controller

Electronic Speed Controller (ESC) allows the flight controller to control the speed and direction of a motor, Figure 2.13. The ESC must be able to handle the maximum current which the motor might consume, and be able to provide it at the right voltage. These small components known as electronic speed controllers are what produces the three phase AC current needed to drive your motors. The flight controller sends a signal to the ESC to let it know how fast it wants it to spin the motor at a given point in time. One ESC is needed for each motor, either get four separate ESCs to mount them on the arms or get an all in one board that sits inside the frame.

1. **Power input**: The two thick wires normally black and red are to obtain power from the power distribution board/harness which itself receives power directly from the main battery.

FIGURE 2.13 Electronic Speed Controller

2. **3 bullet connectors**: These pins connect to the three pins on the brushless motor.

3. **3-pin R/C servo connector** accepts remote control signals.

2.4 BATTERY

The advantages of the Lithium-ion polymer (Li-Po) battery is not only its light weight, but its discharge rate is high, allowing to see immediate reaction when the UAV is given full throttle. Multirotors need this because they are dependent on instant thrust as they change the speed of the propellers many times per second to keep it level or moving in the same direction, etc. However, they are relatively fragile and also highly flammable:

1. **Chemistry:** almost exclusively Lithium polymer (LiPo), with some being Lithium-Manganese or other Lithium variations.

2. **Voltage** should correspond with the motors. Almost all batteries incorporate a number of 3.7V cells, where 3.7V = 1S. Therefore, a battery which is marked as 4S is $4 \times 3.7V = 14.8V$ nominal. Providing the number of cells, however, will help determine which charger to use.

3. **Capacity** is measured in amp-hours (Ah). Small battery packs can be in the range of 0.1Ah(100mAh) though battery packs for medium sized UAVs are $2 - 3$Ah. The higher the capacity, the longer the flight time, but the heavier the pack will be.

4. **Discharge Rate** is measured in C, where 1C is the capacity of the battery. The discharge rate of most LiPo batteries is at least 5C (five times the capacity), but since most motors used in multirotors consume high current, the battery needs to be able to discharge at high current, which is often in the order of 30V or more.

Endurance or flight time values assume a constant current draw and linear relation to the battery capacity:

$$t = \frac{Q}{I} \tag{2.1}$$

where t is the endurance, Q the battery capacity and I the current draw.

Peukert effect: as the current draw increases, the battery capacity becomes less effective. The endurance calculation adjusted for the Peukert effect is:

$$t = \frac{R_t}{I^n} \left(\frac{Q}{Rt} \right)^n \tag{2.2}$$

where R_t is the battery hour rating (discharge time over which the capacity was determined) and n is a constant discharge parameter dependent on the temperature and type of battery.

FIGURE 2.14 Power distribution

Definition 21 *A **flight mode** is the way the flight controller uses sensors and RC input in order to fly and stabilize the aircraft.*

GUI: A GUI (Graphical User Interface) is what is used to visually edit the code (via a computer) which will be uploaded to the flight controller. More recently flight controller GUIs use interactive graphical interfaces to help configure the necessary parameters.

2.5 ADDITIONAL EQUIPMENT

Payload: any added weight reduces flight time. To have a payload, the mounting should be as lightweight as possible (while still being secure) and the load itself should not shift in flight. A UAV's payload is more specific than a typical aircraft's payload. Factors such as how the payload will detect objects or how to position a camera system so that it may best capture video, must be considered. Good locations depend on payload type.

Gimbal: A gimbal is often used to stabilize a camera, as in Figure 2.15. Connecting a camera directly to a UAVs frame means it is always pointing in the same direction as the frame itself, which does not provide the best video experience. Most gimbals are mounted beneath the frame, in line with the UAV's center of weight. Gimbals are either connected directly to the bottom of a UAV, or to a rail system. The gimbal system, therefore, means the UAV needs longer landing gear so it does not touch the ground. Mounting the gimbal or camera to the front of the UAV can also be done, and the weight can be offset by placing the main battery further aft in the aircraft. A gimbal system comprises a mechanical frame, two or more motors (normally up to three for pan, tilt and roll), as well as sensors and electronics. The camera should be positioned in the belly of the UAV in such a way that the wings do not block the camera's view and should be mounted in such a way that the motors do not need to provide a torque to keep the camera at a fixed angle (balanced).The most popular design involves a two motor setup which controls the camera's tilt and roll. The camera, therefore, always faces the front of the UAV. For rotations in three dimensions, pan is the horizontal angle (0..360 degrees) about the upright Z axis, tilt is the vertical angle $(-90.. + 90)$ degrees about the rotated Y axis, and roll is the angle (0..360) degrees about the rotated and tilted X axis.

Light Emitting Diode (LED) are used to make the UAV visible, primarily at night or low lighting conditions.

FIGURE 2.15 Gimbal

FIGURE 2.16 UAV roll, pitch, and yaw

Transmitter/Remote Control – The hand-held device that allows to maneuver the UAV and adjust its settings.

Camera – Many UAVs either come with a camera or allow the pilot to attach a camera to them

Throttle: Throttle gives the propellers on the quadrotor enough power to get airborne. This adjusts the altitude, or height, of the quadrotor. **Trim** – Buttons on the remote control that help to adjust roll, pitch, yaw, and throttle if they are off balance. **Roll** – Done by pushing the right stick of the RC to the left or right, maneuvers the quadrotor left or right. **Pitch** – Done by pushing the right stick forwards or backwards. Tilts the quadrotor, which maneuvers the quadrotor forwards or backwards. **Yaw**– Done by pushing the left stick to the left or to the right. Rotates the quadrotor left or right. Points the front of the UAV different directions and helps with changing directions while flying. Euler angles are shown in Figure 2.16.

Rudder – it's the same as the left stick. However, it relates directly to controlling yaw (as opposed to the throttle).

Bank turn – A consistent circular turn in either the clockwise or counterclockwise direction.

Hovering – Staying in the same position while airborne. Done by controlling the throttle.

Flight modes:

1. **Manual** – Once the multi-rotor is tilted (roll) it will not auto-level itself back to its original position.

2. **Attitude (Auto-level)** – Once the sticks are centered, the multi-rotor will level itself out.

3. **GPS Hold** – Returns the multi-rotor's position once the sticks have been centered. The same as attitude mode (auto-level) but using a GPS.

2.6 UAV MATERIALS

1. **Wood**: Inexpensive, wood will greatly reduce build time and additional parts required. Wood is fairly rigid and has been a proven material time and time again. Replacing a broken arm after a crash is relatively easy. Wood should straight (no twisting or warping).

2. **Foam**: Foam is rarely used as the sole material for the frame and there tends to be some form of inner skeleton or reinforcement structure. Foam can also be used strategically; as propeller guards, landing gear or even as dampening. There are also many different types of foam, and some variations are considerably stronger than others.

3. **Plastic**: Plastic tends to flex and as such is not ideal. Used strategically (such as a cover or landing gear), plastic can be a great option. 3D printing parts (or the entire frame) has so far been more successful on smaller quadrotors. Using plastic extrusions may also be an option for small and medium sized UAVs.

4. **Aluminum** comes in a variety of shapes and sizes: sheet aluminum for body plates, or extruded aluminum for the support arms. Aluminum may not be as lightweight as carbon fiber or G10, but the price and durability can be quite attractive. Rather than cracking, aluminum tends to flex. Working with aluminum really only requires a saw and a drill.

5. **G10** (variation of fiberglass): This is a material commonly used instead of carbon fiber to make a UAV's frame since it is very rigid and lightweight, but significantly less expensive. G10 is mostly available in sheet format and is used largely for top and bottom plates, while tubing in carbon fiber (as compared to G10) is usually not much more expensive and is often used for the arms. Unlike Carbon Fiber, G10 does not block RF signals.

6. **PCB**: Printed Circuit Boards are essentially the same as fiberglass, but , PCBs are always flat. Frames smaller than $600mm$ sometimes use PCB material for top and bottom plates, since the electrical connections integrated into the PCB can reduce parts (for example the power distribution board is often integrated into the bottom plate). Small quadrotor frames can be made entirely out of a single PCB and integrate all of the electronics.

7. **Carbon Fiber**: is the most used building material due to its light weight and high strength. The process to manufacturer carbon fiber is still quite manual, meaning normally only straightforward shapes such as

FIGURE 2.17 Shell

FIGURE 2.18 Dampener

flat sheets and tubes are mass produced, while more complex 3D shapes are normally "one off". However, Carbon fiber impedes RF signals.

8. **Shell**: This is an aesthetic / functional cover used to improve resistance to the elements and sometimes improve aerodynamics, as shown in Figure 2.17. **Aerodynamics** is the study of forces and the resulting motion of objects through the air. Aerodynamics affects the motion of airplanes, helicopters, airships, rockets, and drones. Some production UAVs only have a plastic shell which also acts as the frame.

9. Dampeners: These are molded rubber parts used to minimize vibration transmitted throughout a UAV.

2.7 LAUNCHING SYSTEMS

Implementing a high-energy launching system delivers better stability, accuracy and reliability. UAVs with high-energy launching capabilities remain intact and provide longer useful life spans. The method of launching the drone may be considered within three types, each with an appropriate means of recovery:

1. A **horizontal take-off and landing** (HTOL), with a wheeled undercarriage, where there is a length of prepared surface (runway or strip) available. The length of run required to achieve launch is dependent upon the acceleration of the aircraft to lift-off speed. The thrust available to accelerate the aircraft is a major issue which depends upon the

power available for thrust and the efficiency of the propulsion from stationary to lift-off speed. The speed at which the aircraft is safe to lift off is a function of the wing's aircraft mass/area ratio (wing loading) and lift coefficient.

2. A catapulted or zero-length rocket-powered launch when the aircraft has no vertical flight capability and where the operating circumstances or terrain preclude availability of a length of runway: The solution adopted is to catapult the aircraft into the air with sufficient acceleration to achieve flight speed on release. The catapult must be positioned where it can launch the aircraft sensibly into the wind. A shift in the wind direction may mean a repositioning of the launcher.

3. A **vertical take-off and landing** (VTOL): A controlled VTOL enables the drone system to be operated from almost any type of terrain, requiring no runway, airstrip or catapult equipment. The launch is totally independent of wind direction and the aircraft can be airborne within minutes of the system arriving on site. It is merely required , after initial start-up and check-out via the UAV on-board monitoring system display on the ground control system (GCS) for the controller to input height (or altitude) and rate of climb.

Recovery of the drone requires not only a safe landing, but the return of the drone to its base or hangar. A process for recovering a UAV at the end of a flight is one difficult challenge. Recovery involves the return of the aircraft to make a controlled touch-down onto its undercarriage at the threshold or runway, deceleration along the runway, followed by taxiing or the UAV being towed back to its base point, see Figure 2.19.

1. **Launch and recovery element**: A UAV may take-off and land vertically from a port that has enough space or horizontally that has enough length of runway, or a catapult launching and hand-launching may be used.

2. **Landing gear**: Multirotor landing gear normally does not have wheels as on an airplane, as in Figure 2.19. Using landing gear can be beneficial for:

   (a) Providing clearance between the bottom of the UAV and a non-flat surface such as grass (or small rocks)

   (b) Providing clearance between the battery pack / gimbal and the ground

   (c) In the event of a hard landing, it's ideally the landing gear which will break (and be replaced) rather than the frame

   (d) The right landing gear can also provide flotation

FIGURE 2.19 Landing-gear

3. **Retractable**: landing gear which has two positions: one for landing and takeoff, and another, which takes up less room or improves visibility, during flight.

Although the take-off is relatively easy, the landing approach and touch-down at the correct position and airspeed require considerable judgment. Some popular recovery options are:

1. **parachutes** carry UAV down as a fail-safe recovery system. However, parachutes add weight to UAVs. Additionally, high winds cause parachutes and their UAVs to drift great distances.

2. During **deep stall** recovery, the UAV falls quickly, which minimizes wind drift; Much energy is absorbed in order to bring the UAV to a stop. Positioning batteries beneath the belly of the UAV absorbs force on impact, minimizing wear and tear on other UAV components.

3. **Belly landings** is fitting for smaller UAVs if onboard cameras are well protected, although not suitable for UAVs carrying payloads positioned under the belly.

4. **wheeled landings** are appropriate for large and long-range UAVs that use runways.

5. **Net recovery** capture require extremely accurate postioning information.

The recovery of a VTOL is simple, the control arrangement will descend the drone at a vertical rate of descent proportional to its height above ground to an arrest at a nominal contact.

2.8 LAB: UAS AIRFRAME ASSEMBLY

1. The first step is to gather the drone parts: a frame is needed with four motors and propellers, a flight controller, four electronic speed controllers and a lithium polymer (LiPo) battery, a power-distribution board and, depending on the requirements, a 5V regulated power supply

for the FPV camera. A common battery size is 1300 mAh; too large and it will be too heavy to take off. Finally, straps and zip ties are needed to keep it all in place.

2. The second step is to assemble the controller. To control the quadcopter, a handheld transmitter (TX) and a radio signal receiver unit (RX) attached inside the drone are needed. The RX is wired to the FC unit, which commands the motors via the ESCs. FPV hardware is fairly simple, comprising a camera and video transmitter on the drone and a receiver and display on the ground.

3. The third step is to build the frame. The kit may consist of two layers of carbon fibre attached together with screws and standoffs. It is a basic kit assembly, without the wiring or motors. Motors are generally attached with screws as well. Install propellers on each motor (to be removed before testing); two will need to use clockwise propellers (front-left and back-right), and the other two anti-clockwise propellers.

4. The fourth step is to wire the motors. Starting with the battery LiPo, each ESCs must be attached so that the red wire goes to the positive battery wire, and the black to the negative. Each is powered in parallel, so the red and black from the battery can be connected to four separate wires to power each ESC. The other end of each ESC will have three connections that are hooked to the three wires of each motor.

5. The fifth step is to configure the controls. Each of the ESCs must be connected to the flight control board using a three-wire connector, then the connectors must be plugged from the FC into the RX. The camera should be attached. The ESC and transmitter should be wired to the proper voltage supply; for example, this is a 5V, drawing power of the main battery. Zip ties can be used to keep errant wiring in place, and shorten wires to fit the frame. Before testing, remove the blades until you're ready to fly. Turn the unit on, and if everything connected, you should hear the ESCs beep. The motors may also twitch.

6. the sixth step is to calibrate and test with the propellers still removed and power supplied, plug a USB cable into the FC, and into your computer. Boot up your ground-station software, then calibrate the maxim um and minimum throttle positions for your ESCs. You should be able to spin up and stop your motors with the computer. Disconnect the USB cable and bind your TX to the quadcopter RX. Assign the correct channels to each quadcopter action and test the function on a bench. Once you're confident the drone is working, it's time to reinstall the rotors and take it to a clear outdoor area to fly.

7. The last step is then to take a flight test. At first, the quadcopter should be flown without using FPV equipment. At second, one can then try out the FPV gear.

2.9   CONCLUSIONS

This chapter describes the various components of UAVs including motors and propellers, launching systems and batteries. It also reviews the various type of materials UAVS ant their components are made off.

CHAPTER 3

Flight Mechanics

3.1 INTRODUCTION

At the earliest stage of UAV conceptual design, some estimate of weight, propulsive power and efficiency, and aerodynamic performance is required. Custom methods are common.

The aerodynamic issues important to UAVs are similar to those for manned aircraft. However, certain classes of UAVs operate quite differently from manned aircraft and present different aerodynamic design problems. Aerodynamic development for UAVs relies strongly on linearized aerodynamics, especially for aeroelasticity studies. In most cases the particular demands on UAVs are reflected in changes in the relative importance of aerodynamic performance parameters. (P.A. Wells) Newton's three laws involve the classical concepts of mass, length, time, force, and the rules of geometry, algebra and calculus. The basic laws of dynamics can be formulated in several ways: Newton's law and the principal of virtual work, D'Alembert's principle, Lagrange equation, Hamilton's principle. All are basically equivalent, and imply some frame of reference with respect to which position and its derivatives, the co-ordinate axes are fixed relatively to the average of the 'fixed' start or moving with uniform linear velocity and without rotation relative to the start. In either case, the frame of reference is referred to as inertial frame and corresponding coordinate as inertial coordinates. A frame that has linear acceleration is rotating in any maner is non-inertial. One must be able to recognize inertial and non-inertial frames by inspection.

3.2 MODELING PRESENTATION

Modeling is a crucial stage in designing flight control and also for simulation purposes. UAV configuration is defined by three spatial dimensions and one time dimension. In general, the motion of a UAV involves both translation and rotation. The translations are in direct response to external forces. The rotations are in direct response to external torques or moments (twisting forces). The motion of an aircraft is particularly complex because the rotations and translations are coupled together; a rotation affects the magnitude and direction of the aerodynamic forces which affects the translation.

Definition 22 *Aerodynamic forces directly depend on the air density. The* **aerodynamic force** *is the force generated by all the over-pressures on the underside and the depressions on the extrados. It increases with speed and angle of incidence.*

It is in general assumed that the aircraft translates from one point to another as if all the mass of the aircraft were collected into a single point called the center of gravity. The motion of the center of gravity can be described by using Newton's laws of motion. There are four forces acting on the aircraft; the lift, drag, thrust, and weight. Depending on the relative magnitudes and directions of these forces, the aircraft climbs (increases in altitude), dives (decreases in altitude), or banks (rolls to one side and turns). The magnitude of the aerodynamic forces depends on the attitude of the aircraft during the translations. The attitude depends on the rotations about the center of gravity. A rotation is caused by a force being applied, at some distance from the center of gravity. When the aircraft is trimmed, rotations caused by several forces are balanced and the aircraft does not rotate.

Flight dynamics is the science of air vehicle orientation and control in three dimensions. The three critical flight dynamics parameters are the angles of rotation in three dimensions about the vehicle's center of mass, known as pitch, roll and yaw. Each class of UAVs is driven by aerodynamic considerations that are either unique or very important for the future development of UAVs. Airspeeds: slowest speed attainable, stall speed (if applicable), nominal cruise speed, max cruise speed. Wind speed limitations: headwind, crosswind, gusts, turbulence.

Definition 23 *Viscosity: As an object moves through a gas, the viscosity (stickiness) of the gas becomes very important. Gas molecules stick to any surface, creating a layer of air near the surface, called a boundary layer that, in effect, changes the shape of the object. The boundary layer may lift off or "separate" from the body and create an effective shape much different from the physical shape of an object. The flow conditions in and near the boundary layer are often unsteady (changing in time) and may become randomly turbulent. The boundary layer is very important in determining both the drag and lift of an object.*

The drag of an aircraft moving through a fluid of any kind is a viscous force. The design of small UAVs is dominated by problems associated with very low Reynolds number flows. The focus is on low Reynolds number, low aspect ratio (LAR) wing aerodynamics.

Definition 24 *Stall speed is slowest speed a plane can fly to maintain level flight. Stalls depend only on angle of attack, not airspeed. However, the slower an airplane goes, the more angle of attack it needs to produce lift equal to the aircraft's weight.As the speed decreases further, at some point this angle will be equal to the critical (stall) angle of attack.*

Low Reynolds numbers are the result of the low speeds in combination with the small wing chords while the low aspect ratio (< 4) is the result of high wing loadings due to high aircraft weight, stall speed requirements and limits on the wing span.

1. Low Reynolds number and airspeed, The Reynolds number is the ratio of inertial forces to viscous forces within a fluid, which is subjected to relative internal movement due to different fluid velocities

$$Re = \frac{\rho u L}{\mu} = \frac{uL}{\nu} \tag{3.1}$$

   where ρ is the density of the air (Kg/m^3), u is the velocity of the air with respect to the aircraft (m/s), L is a characteristic linear dimension (for the aircraft, it is the length) (m), μ is the dynamic viscosity of the air $(kg/m.s)$ and ν is the kinematic viscosity of the air (m^2/s).

2. Increased dynamic rates due to decreased mass and moments of inertia,

3. Dominance of propulsion dynamic forces and moments versus aerodynamic body forces and moments,

4. Asymmetric or atypical designs, Acrobatic maneuvers not possible by manned aircraft ....

Definition 25 *Compressibility: As an object moves through a gas, the compressibility of the gas also becomes important. Gas molecules move around an object as it passes through. If the object passes at a low speed (typically less than 350 Km/h), the density of the fluid remains constant. But for high speeds, some of the energy of the object goes into compressing the fluid, moving the molecules closer together and changing the gas density, which alters the amount of the resulting force on the object. This effect is more important as speed increases. Near and beyond the speed of sound, shock waves are produced that affect both the lift and drag of an object.*

Definition 26 *The Earth's atmosphere is an extremely thin sheet of air extending from the surface of the Earth to the edge of space, about 100 Km above the surface of the Earth. Gravity holds the atmosphere to the Earth's surface. Within the atmosphere, very complex chemical, thermodynamic, and fluid dynamics effects occur. The atmosphere is not uniform; fluid properties are constantly changing with time and place. This is the weather.*

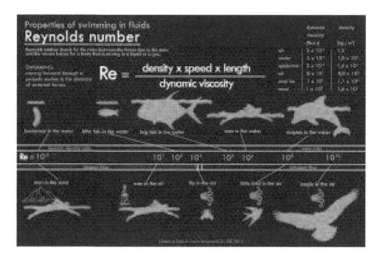

FIGURE 3.1 Reynolds number

Definition 27 *Troposphere, the lower stratosphere, the upper strato-*
sphere The atmosphere has three zones with separate curve fits. The tropo-
sphere runs from the surface of the Earth to 11 Km. In the troposphere, the
temperature decreases linearly and the pressure decreases exponentially. The
rate of temperature decrease is called the lapse rate. The lower stratosphere
runs from 11 Km to 25 Km. In the lower stratosphere the temperature is con-
stant and the pressure decreases exponentially. The upper stratosphere model
is used for altitudes above 25 Km. In the upper stratosphere the temperature
increases slightly and the pressure decreases exponentially. Because the grav-
ity of the Earth holds the atmosphere to the surface, as altitude increases, air
density, pressure, and temperature (for lower altitudes) decrease. At the edge
of space, the density is almost zero.

Earth's atmosphere is composed of air. Air is a mixture of gases, 78 percent
nitrogen and 21 percent oxygen with traces of water vapor, carbon dioxide,
argon, and various other components. Air is usually modeled as a uniform
(no variation or fluctuation) gas with properties that are averaged from all
the individual components. Pressure and temperature of the air depend on
location on the Earth and the season of the year. Pressure and temperature
change day to day, hour to hour, sometimes even minute to minute during
severe weather. All of the variables will change with altitude, which is why
the typical values are given at sea level, static conditions. The variation of the
air from the standard can be very important since it affects flow parameters.
From poor lift-to-drag ratios to low values for the maximum lift coefficient
and related control problems, the design of efficient, small vehicles represents a
significant aerodynamic challenge. **Friction**: Without friction, the air particles

would not stick to any surface and would not create the well-known boundary layer, responsible for the lift force.

Navier-Stockes equations are a set of Partial Differential Equations. They can be separated in two regions: the Boundary Layer, where all the vorticity is assumed to be confined, and the outer layers, assumed to be a inviscid potential flow. Essentially the flow around an airfoil separates at the nose and joins again at the trailing edge: the vorticity causes the fluid to change its velocity (direction and magnitude), thus resulting in a net force on the body (action/reaction). The pressure distribution along the airfoil contour shows a strong suction on the upper side, that eventually integrated all over the profile leads to the Lift Force (sum of all the forces normal to the air stream). The Drag force instead is the sum of all the forces along the main stream, both due to friction and pressure. Lift is the component acting perpendicularly to the air-relative velocity vector. Drag is in the opposite side of the motion.

The four forces acting on an airplane are: Lift (upward force); Thrust (forward force); Weight (downward force); Drag (backward force).

1. **Weight**: Weight is a force that is always directed toward the center of the earth. The weight is distributed throughout the UAV. In flight, it rotates about the center of gravity. Flying encompasses two major problems; overcoming the weight of an object by some opposing force, and controlling the object in flight. Both of these problems are related to the object's weight and the location of the center of gravity.

2. **Lift**: To overcome the weight force, UAVs generate an opposing force called lift. Lift is generated by the motion of the aircraft through the air and is an aerodynamic force. Lift is directed perpendicular to the flight direction. The magnitude of the lift depends on several factors including the shape, size, and velocity of the aircraft. As with weight, each part of the aircraft contributes to the aircraft lift force. Most of the lift is generated by the wings. Aircraft lift acts through a single point called the center of pressure. The center of pressure is defined just like the center of gravity, but using the pressure distribution around the body instead of the weight distribution. The distribution of lift around the aircraft is important for solving the control problem. Aerodynamic surfaces are used to control the aircraft in roll, pitch, and yaw. The **Lift** force can be modeled as the product of the lift coefficient, the density, the square of the velocity and wing area. It can be expressed in terms of a non dimensional value, named Lift coefficient (C_L) that contains all the complex dependencies and is usually determined experimentally, as:

$$L = q \times S \times C_L \tag{3.2}$$

where $q = 0.5\rho V^2$ is the dynamic pressure, ρ is the air density, V is the air velocity, S is a reference surface in 3D or a reference length in 2D The lift coefficient C_L is linear with the angle of attack up to a value

FIGURE 3.2 Airfoils

known as stall at which the boundary layer begins to separate from the airfoil. Increasing the angle of attack beyond the stall leads to a small increase of the C_L up to the $C_{L_{max}}$, but suddenly it drops together with a strong increase of total drag:

$$C_L = C_{L0} + C_{L\alpha}\alpha \tag{3.3}$$

C_{L0} being the zero incidence lift coefficient and $C_{L\alpha}$ the slope coefficient.

3. **Drag**: As the airplane moves through the air, the air resists the motion of the aircraft and the resistance force is called drag. Drag is directed along and opposed to the flight direction. Like lift, there are many factors that affect the magnitude of the drag force including the shape of the aircraft, and the velocity of the aircraft. Like lift, drag acts through the aircraft center of pressure. For low speed aircraft, drag can be divided into the following components:
$Drag = SkinFrictionDrag + ViscousPressuredrag + invisciddrag.$
Drag, is a function of a Drag Coefficient C_D that contains all the complex dependencies and is usually determined experimentally,

$$C_D = C_{D0} + kC_L^2 \tag{3.4}$$

where C_{D0} is due to the friction and k is a proportional coefficient. Thd shpae of an object has a very great effect on the amount of drag.

4. **Thrust**: To overcome drag, UAVs use a propulsion system to generate a force called thrust. The direction of the thrust force depends on how the engines are attached to the aircraft. The magnitude of the thrust depends on many factors associated with the propulsion system including the type of engine, the number of engines, and the throttle setting. If the forces are balanced, the aircraft cruises at constant velocity.

The rotation is what makes the fluid change its velocity,

Definition 28 *Mean sea level (MSL) is the true altitude or the average height above standard sea level where the atmospheric pressure is measured in order to calibrate altitude.*

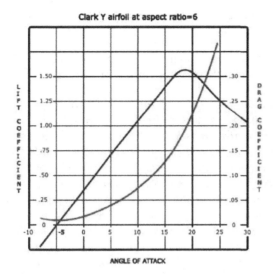

FIGURE 3.3 Lift coefficient vs angle of attack

Given a certain surface S and a flight velocity V, the altitude allowing the calculation of q and knowing the UAV's weight, the C_L needed to fly and the corresponding angle of attack can be evaluated:

$$\alpha_{flight} = \frac{C_L}{C_{L\alpha}} \tag{3.5}$$

and

$$C_{L_{flight}} = C_{D0} + kC_{L_{flight}}^2 \tag{3.6}$$

When flying at a constant altitude, if thrust and drag are equal, aircraft holds constant airspeed. If thrust is increased, aircraft accelerates thus airspeed increases and as drag depends on airspeed, drag increases. When drag is again equal to thrust, aircraft no longer accelerates but holds a new, higher, constant airspeed.

There exists an angle of attack at which the airplane will fly at maximum efficiency: the angle where the ratio $\frac{C_L}{C_D}$ is maximum. Different types of altitude exist:

1. **Absolute Altitude**: The height **above ground level** (AGL).

2. **True Altitude**: The height above **mean sea level** (MSL).

3. **Density Altitude**: is the altitude relative to the standard atmosphere conditions at which the air density would be equal to the indicated air density at the place of observation. It is the vertical distance above sea level in the standard atmosphere at which a given density is to be found.

4. **Indicated Altitude**: The indicated altitude is directly read on the altimeter as the height.

5. **Pressure Altitude**: The indicated altitude when the barometric pressure scale is set to 29.92 inHg (inches of mercury).

Remark 29 *The aerodynamics of rotary-wing aircraft are by nature, more complex than the aerodynamics of fixed-wing aircraft. The same basic mechanism applies for rotary wings as for fixed wings, the difference merely being that the fixed wing moves on a sensibly linear path in order to encompass the air, whilst the hovering rotary wing moves on a circular path. The latter therefore draws in new air from above in order to add energy to it and accelerate it downwards, compared with the former which receives it horizontally to accelerate it downwards. In forward flight, the rotor is able to entrain a greater mass of air and so, as with the fixed wing, it becomes more lift-efficient and the induced power rapidly reduces with increasing speed. For a quadrotor, low pressure is on the top of the blades and high pressure at the bottom of the blades. It is actually the difference between these high and low pressures that allows the drone to generate thrust. The pressure ripples accross the body of the drone as the blades pass over; this is pivotal for aerodynamics. When the blades pass over the arms, the body produces a downward force that reduces thrust. Making more efficient drones is about carefully calibrating the shape of the arms. The blades are cutting their own vertices.*

3.3 FRAMES

In guidance and control of aircraft, reference frames are used often- They describe the relative position and orientation of objects Aircraft relative to direction of wind Camera relative to aircraft Aircraft relative to inertial frame Some things most easily calculated or described in certain reference frames Newton's law Aircraft attitude Aerodynamic forces/torques Accelerometers, rate gyros GPS Mission requirements.

There exist at least a dozen frames in the aerospace domain,but for UAV modeling, the most important are the inertial frame, In navigation, guidance and control of an aircraft, there are several coordinate systems (or frames) intensively used in controller design and analysis. One of the first steps in the treatment of any problem is that of selecting the appropriate coordinates. For some missions, certain coordinates may be more suitable than others. Hence the quantities chosen in any particular case are those that appear to be most advantageous for the problem in hand.

1. The geodetic coordinate system

2. The Earth-Centered-Earth-Fixed (ECEF) coordinate system

3. The local North-East-Down (NED) coordinate system

4. The vehicle carried NED coordinate system

5. The body coordinate system

The relationship among these coordinate system, i.e. the coordinate transformations are also introduced.

3.3.1   Geodetic coordinate system

The longitude measures the rotational angle (ranging from $-180\circ$ to $180\circ$) between the prime meridian and the measured point. The latitude measures the angle (ranging from $-90\circ$ to $90\circ$) between The equatorial plane and the normal of the reference ellipsoid that passes through the measured point. The altitude is the local vertical distance between the measured point and the reference ellipsoid.

3.3.2   Earth-centered, Earth fixed

Earth-centered, Earth fixed (ECEF) is a geographic cordinate system. The point $(0, 0, 0)$ is defined as the center of mass of the Earth. The ECEF rotates with the Earth, and therefore coordinates o a pont fixed on the surface of the Earth do not change. The ECEF coordinate system rotates with the Earth around its Spin axis. As such, a fixed point on the Earth surface has a fixed Set of coordinates The origin and axes of the ECEF coordinate system:

1. The origin O_e is located at the center of the Earth

2. The Z-axis, Z_e, is along the spin axis of the Earth, pointing to the North Pole

3. The X-axis, X_e, intersects the sphere of the Earth at $0\circ$latitude and $0\circ$longitude

4. The Y-axis, Y_e, is orthogonal to the Z- and X-axes with the usual right hand rule

3.3.3   North-East-Down frame

The local NED is also known as navigation or ground coordinate system. It is a coordinate frame fixed to the Earth's surface. Based on the WGS-84 ellipsoid model, its origin and axes are

1. The origin, O_n, is arbitrarily fixed to a point on the Earth's surface

2. The X-axis, X_n, points toward the ellipsoid north (geodetic north)

3. The Y-axis Y_n point toward the ellipsoid east (geodetic east)

4. The Z-axis, Z_n, points downward along the ellipsoid normal

The local NED frame plays an important role in flight control and navigation. Navigation of small scale UAV is normally carried out within this frame

3.3.4 Vehicle carried NED coordinate system

The vehicle-carried NED system is associated with the flying vehicle. Its origin and axes are given by:

1. The origin O_{nv}, is located at the center of gravity (CG) of the UAV

2. The X-axis, X_{nv}, points toward the ellipsoid north (geodetic north)

3. The Y-axis, Y_{nv}, point toward the ellipsoid east (geodetic east)

4. The Z-axis, Z_{nv}, points downward along the ellipsoid normal

An inertial frame fixed with respect to the ground (North-East-Down or East-North, Up frames).

3.3.5 Body based frame

The body coordinate system is vehicle carried and is directly defined on the body of the UAV. Its origin and axes are given by:

1. The origin O_b is located at the center of gravity of the aircraft

2. The X-axis, X_b, points forward, lying in the symmetric plane of the aircraft

3. The Y-axis Y_b, is starboard (the right side of the aircraft)

4. The Z-axis Z_b, points downward to comply with the right hand rule

3.3.6 Air relative frame

The air relative frame: relative to the surrounding air.

3.4 KINEMATIC MODELING

Direction cosine matrix (DCM) or Rotation matrix $\mathbf{R}$ is function of $\eta_2 = (\phi, \theta, \psi)^T$:

$$\mathbf{R}_{GB} = \mathbf{R}(\eta_2) = \mathbf{R}_z(\psi)\mathbf{R}_y(\theta)\mathbf{R}_x(\phi) \tag{3.7}$$

with

$$\mathbf{R}_x(\phi) = \begin{pmatrix} 1 & 0 & 0 \\ 0 & \cos\phi & -\sin\phi \\ 0 & \sin\phi & \cos\phi \end{pmatrix}$$

$$\mathbf{R}_y(\theta) = \begin{pmatrix} \cos\theta & 0 & \sin\theta \\ 0 & 1 & 0 \\ -\sin\theta & 0 & \cos\theta \end{pmatrix}$$

$$\mathbf{R}_z(\psi) = \begin{pmatrix} \cos\psi & -\sin\psi & 0 \\ \sin\psi & \cos\psi & 0 \\ 0 & 0 & 1 \end{pmatrix}$$

Thus the Direction cosine matrix (DCM) is given by

$$\mathbf{R}_{GB} = \mathbf{R}_{BG}^T = \mathbf{R}(\eta_2) = \begin{pmatrix} \cos\psi\cos\theta & \mathbf{R}_{12} & \mathbf{R}_{13} \\ \sin\psi\cos\theta & \mathbf{R}_{22} & \mathbf{R}_{23} \\ -\sin\theta & \cos\theta\sin\phi & \cos\theta\cos\phi \end{pmatrix} \quad (3.8)$$

with

$$\mathbf{R}_{12} = -\sin\psi\cos\phi + \cos\psi\sin\theta\sin\phi$$
$$\mathbf{R}_{13} = \sin\psi\sin\phi + \cos\psi\sin\theta\cos\phi$$
$$\mathbf{R}_{22} = \cos\psi\cos\phi + \sin\psi\sin\theta\sin\phi$$
$$\mathbf{R}_{23} = -\cos\psi\sin\phi + \sin\psi\sin\theta\cos\phi$$

Kinematic relationship between the different velocities can be written as:

$$\begin{pmatrix} \dot{\eta}_1 \\ \dot{\eta}_2 \end{pmatrix} = \mathbf{R}\mathbf{V} = \begin{pmatrix} \mathbf{R}_{GB} & 0_{3\times3} \\ 0_{3\times3} & \mathbf{J}(\eta_2) \end{pmatrix} \begin{pmatrix} V \\ \Omega \end{pmatrix} \quad (3.9)$$

where

$$\mathbf{J}(\eta_2) = \begin{pmatrix} 1 & 0 & -\sin\theta \\ 0 & \cos\phi & \sin\phi\cos\theta \\ 0 & -\sin\phi & \cos\phi\cos\theta \end{pmatrix}^{-1} =$$

$$\quad (3.10)$$

$$= \begin{pmatrix} 1 & \sin\phi\tan\theta & \cos\phi\tan\theta \\ 0 & \cos\phi & -\sin\phi \\ 0 & \frac{\sin\phi}{\cos\theta} & \frac{\cos\phi}{\cos\theta} \end{pmatrix}$$

$V = (u, v, w)^T$ and $\Omega = (p, q, r)^T$ expressed in the body-fixed frame. $\mathbf{J}(\eta_2)$ presents a singularity for $\theta = \pm\frac{\pi}{2}$.

Remark 30 *Euler angles are kinematically singular since the transformation from their time rate of change to the angular vector is not globally defined.*

The relationship between the body-fixed angular velocity vector $\Omega = (p, q, r)^T$ and the rate of change of the Euler angles $\dot{\eta}_2 = (\dot{\phi}, \dot{\theta}, \dot{\psi})^T$ can be determined by resolving the Euler rates into the body fixed coordinate frame:

$$p = \dot{\phi} - \dot{\psi}\sin\theta$$
$$q = \dot{\theta}\cos\phi + \dot{\psi}\sin\phi\cos\theta \quad (3.11)$$
$$r = -\dot{\theta}\sin\phi + \dot{\psi}\cos\phi\cos\theta$$

The complete rotation from body to wind axes is given by

$$\begin{bmatrix} x_W \\ y_W \\ h_W \end{bmatrix} = \underbrace{\begin{bmatrix} \cos\alpha\cos\beta & \sin\beta & \sin\alpha\cos\beta \\ -\cos\alpha\sin\beta & \cos\beta & -\sin\alpha\sin\beta \\ -\sin\alpha & 0 & \cos\alpha \end{bmatrix}}_{C_B^W = C_B^S \cdot C_S^W} \begin{bmatrix} x_B \\ y_B \\ h_B \end{bmatrix} \quad (3.12)$$

3.5 FIXED-WING AIRCRAFT DYNAMIC MODELING

Dynamics is the effect of force on mass and flight dynamics is the study of aircraft motion through the air, in 3D. Newton's second law governs the translation degrees of freedom and Euler's law controls the attitude dynamics. Both must be referenced to an inertial reference frame, which includes the linear and angular momenta and their time derivative.

Definition 31 *The acceleration of a rigid body is represented by means of the linear acceleration of a specified point in the body and the angular acceleration vector which applies to the whole body. The center of mass is the point around which the frame can be placed so there is equal weight on all sides. The center of lift is the point where the sum total of all lift generated by the wings and control surfaces and is usually located at the highest point of the airfoil. The center of mass should correspond with the center of lift. The center of mass moves as if the entire mass was concentrated at this point with all forces transferred, without change in magnitude or direction to this point. The center of pressure is the average location of the pressure. It moves with angle of attack. Pressure varies around the surface of an object. Aerodynamic force acts through the center of pressure*

Definition 32 *Degree of freedom are independent coordinates required to specify completely the position of each and every particle or component part of the system. A particle free to move in space has three degrees of freedom in translation and three degrees of freedom in rotation. The equations governing the translational and rotational motion of an aircraft can be divided into the following two sets:*

1. *Kinematic equations giving the translational and rotational position relative to the earth reference frame. Euler angles (roll, pitch and yaw)*

2. *Dynamic equations relating forces to translational acceleration $\left(\overrightarrow{F} = m\overrightarrow{a}\right)$ and moments to rotational acceleration $\left(\overrightarrow{M} = I\overrightarrow{\omega}\right)$. Models determined from Newton-Euler laws for rigid-body dynamics, or energy-oriented approach such as the Lagrange formulation.*

These equations are referred to as six degree of freedom (6DOF) equations of motion. The rigid-body equations of motion can be expressed in the body-frame or the inertial frame, and can have different model structures and parameterizations.

With P the linear momentum vector and f the external force vector, the time rate of change of the linear momentum equals the external force, time derivative is taken with respect to the inertial frame I:

$$[f]_I = \left[\frac{dP}{dt}\right]_I \qquad (3.13)$$

If the reference frame is changed to the aircraft's body frame B, Newton's law is

$$[f]_B = \left[\frac{dP}{dt}\right]_B + [\Omega]_B \times [P]_B = \left[\frac{dP}{dt}\right]_B + [Sk(\Omega)]_B [P]_B \qquad (3.14)$$

$Sk(\Omega)$ skew symmetric form of Ω expressed in body coordinates, $\mathbf{R}_{BI}$ transformation matrix of the body coordinates wrt the inertial coordinates.

speed/impact relationship is important in flying a UAV:

1. if traction increases, speed increases, lift increases, aircraft goes up

2. if the incidence increases, the lift increases, the plane goes up

3. if the traction decreases, the speed decreases, the lift decreases, the plane descends

4. if the incidence decreases, the lift decreases, the plane descends

5. To fly at a constant altitude, if speed increases, incidence must decrease. To maintain the altitude at a constant speed, it is necessary to increase the lift while keeping the incidence and increasing if possible the power

6. an upward burst has the effect of increasing the angle of attack and consequently the lift. But if, before the gust takes place, the aircraft was already flying at an indication close to the maximum incidence (minimum speed and coefficient of maximum lift): there is a risk of stalling.

7. The load factor has the effect of weighing down the plane which then loses altitude. To keep the altitude at constant power, it is necessary to increase the lift by increasing the incidence, and consequently the speed decreases.

The turn is a permanent change of trajectory in a horizontal plane. Dynamics of position (m mass and V linear velocity of the aircraft)

$$m\dot{V} + \Omega \times mV = F \qquad (3.15)$$

Dynamics of orientation (Ω angular velocity of the body relative to the inertial frame, $\mathbf{I}$ inertia matrix and M torque)

$$\mathbf{I}\dot{\Omega} + \Omega \times \mathbf{I}\Omega = M \qquad (3.16)$$

When the wind is included, velocity of the center of gravity with respect to the air:

$$V_R = V_B - \mathbf{R}_{BG} \begin{pmatrix} W_N \\ W_E \\ W_D \end{pmatrix} \qquad (3.17)$$

Equations of motion can be explicited as:

$$m(\dot{u} + qw - rv) = mg \sin\theta + X$$
$$m(\dot{v} + ru - pw) = mg \sin\phi \cos\theta + Y$$
$$m(\dot{w} + pv - qu) = mg \cos\phi \cos\theta + Z$$
$$I_{xx}\dot{p} + I_{xz}(\dot{q} - pr) + I_{xz}(\dot{r} + pq) + I_{yz}(q^2 - r^2) + (I_{zz} - I_{yy})rq = L$$
$$I_{yy}\dot{q} + I_{xy}(\dot{p} + qr) + I_{yz}(\dot{r} - pq) + I_{xz}(r^2 - p^2) + (I_{xx} - I_{zz})pr = M$$
$$I_{zz}\dot{r} + I_{xz}(\dot{p} - qr) + I_{yz}(\dot{q} + pr) + I_{xz}(p^2 - q^2) + (I_{yy} - I_{xx})pq = N$$

$$(3.18)$$

When this equation is added to the flat Earth equation, the wind components must be supplied as inputs. Then, V_R rather than V_B must be used in the calculation of aerodynamic forces and moments.

Stability and control: An aircraft is stable if it returns to its initial equilibrium flight conditions when it is perturbed. There are two main types of aircraft instability:

1. An aircraft with static instability uniformly departs from an equilibrium condition.

2. An aircraft with dynamic instability oscillates about the equilibrium condition with increasing amplitude

There are two modes of aircraft control: one moves the aircraft between equilibrium states, the other takes the aircraft between equilibrium states, the other takes the aircraft into a non-equilibrium (accelerating) state.

n_z is the load factor. Aircraft load factor n_z is defined as lift L divided by the weight W.

In aerodynamics, the maximum load factor (at given bank angle) is a proportion between lift and weight and has a trigonometric relationship.The load factor is measured in Gs (acceleration of gravity). Any force applied to an aircraft to deflect its flight from a straight line produces a stress on its structure. The amount of this force is the load factor. For example, a load factor of 3 means that the total load of on an aircraft's structure is 3 times its weight.

Lift to drag ratio: $\frac{L}{D} = \frac{C_L}{C_D}$ The aerodynamic efficiency is primarily determined by the lift-to-drag ratio

Translational motions can be expressed as

$$\begin{pmatrix} \dot{x} \\ \dot{y} \\ \dot{z} \end{pmatrix} = \mathbf{R}_{BG} \begin{pmatrix} u \\ v \\ w \end{pmatrix} \tag{3.19}$$

$$\dot{u} = rv - qw - g\sin\theta + \frac{\bar{q}S}{m}C_x + \frac{X_T}{m} \tag{3.20}$$

$$\dot{v} = pw - ru + g\cos\theta \sin\phi + \frac{\bar{q}S}{m}C_y + \frac{Y_T}{m} \tag{3.21}$$

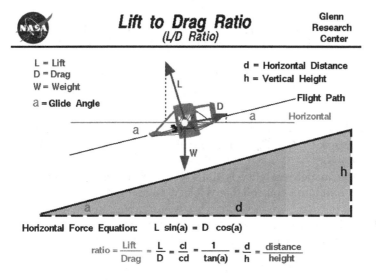

Lift to Drag Ratio
(L/D Ratio)

L = Lift
D = Drag
W = Weight
a = Glide Angle

d = Horizontal Distance
h = Vertical Height

Flight Path
Horizontal

Horizontal Force Equation: L sin(a) = D cos(a)

$$\text{ratio} = \frac{\text{Lift}}{\text{Drag}} = \frac{L}{D} = \frac{cl}{cd} = \frac{1}{\tan(a)} = \frac{d}{h} = \frac{\text{distance}}{\text{height}}$$

FIGURE 3.4 Lift-to-drag ratio

$$\dot{w} = qu - pv + g\cos\theta\cos\phi + \frac{\bar{q}S}{m}C_z + \frac{Z_T}{m} \tag{3.22}$$

u, v, w 3 velocity components, C_x, C_y, C_z aerodynamic force coefficients in the body axes x_b, y_b, z_b, S wing area, $\bar{q}$ dynamic pressure.

Rotational dynamic model:

$$\mathbf{I}\dot{\Omega} = \mathbf{I}\Omega \times \Omega + M \tag{3.23}$$

M moment created by the gravity, the aerodynamic moments, the propulsion and control moments, the aerologic disturbances .... Or

In another form, the dynamic equations can be written as:

$$\dot{V}_B = -Sk(\Omega)V_B + \mathbf{R}_{BE}g_0 + \frac{F_B}{m} \tag{3.24}$$

$$\dot{\Omega} = -\mathbf{I}^{-1}Sk(\Omega)I\Omega + \mathbf{I}^{-1}T_B \tag{3.25}$$

F_B and T_B applied force and torque on the center of gravity.

Rotational equations:

$$\dot{p} = \frac{I_{xz}(I_x - I_y + I_z)}{I_xI_z - I_{xz}^2}pq - \frac{I_z(I_z - I_y) + I_{xz}^2}{I_xI_z - I_{xz}^2}qr + \frac{\bar{q}Sb}{I_x}C_l \tag{3.26}$$

$$\dot{q} = \frac{I_z - I_x}{I_y}pr + \frac{I_{xz}}{I_y}\left(r^2 - p^2\right) + \frac{\bar{q}S\bar{c}}{I_y}C_m \tag{3.27}$$

$$\dot{r} = \frac{(I_x - I_y)I_x + I_{xz}^2}{I_x I_z - I_{xz}^2} pq - I_{xz}\frac{I_x - I_y + I_z}{I_x I_z - I_{xz}^2} qr + \frac{\bar{q}Sb}{I_z}C_n \tag{3.28}$$

$$\dot{\phi} = p + (q\sin\phi + r\cos\phi)\tan\theta$$
$$\dot{\theta} = q\cos\phi - r\sin\phi \tag{3.29}$$
$$\dot{\psi} = \frac{1}{\cos\theta}(q\sin\phi + r\cos\phi)$$

I_x, I_y, I_z, I_{xz} components of the aircraft inertial matrix, b wing span aerodynamic chord, C_l, C_m, C_n rolling, pitching and yawing aerodynamic moment coefficient.

Airplane maneuverability is limited by several constraints such as stall speed and minimum controllable velocity, engine limitations, structural limitations ....

Physical limitations mean that the maximum specific lift is limited by maximum lift coefficient $C_{L,max}$ and load factor constraints (n_{min}, n_{max}):

$$|C_L| \le C_{L,max} \qquad n_{min} \le n_z \le n_{max} \tag{3.30}$$

The velocity is saturated to prevent stall as follows:

$$0 < V_{stall} \le V \le V_{max} \tag{3.31}$$

The flight path angle rate is saturated to prevent stall and ensure commanded paths stay within physical limits.

$$|\dot{\gamma}| \le \dot{\gamma}_{max} \tag{3.32}$$

3.5.1 Dynamic modes in longitudinal mode

Longitudinal variables $X_{long} = (x, z, u, w, \theta, q)^T$,

$$\dot{x} = V\cos\gamma$$
$$\dot{z} = -V\sin\gamma$$
$$\dot{\theta} = q \tag{3.33}$$
$$\alpha = \theta - \gamma$$

$$\dot{V} = \frac{1}{m}(T\cos\alpha - D - mg_D\sin\gamma) \tag{3.34}$$

$$\dot{\gamma} = \frac{1}{mV}(T\sin\alpha + L - mg_D\cos\gamma) \tag{3.35}$$

$$\dot{q} = \frac{M}{I_y} \qquad M = \frac{1}{2}\rho V^2 S_c C_M + \frac{1}{2}\rho V^2 S_c C_z \tag{3.36}$$

Or

$$m\dot{V}_T = F_T\cos(\alpha + \alpha_T) - D - mg_D\sin\gamma$$
$$m\dot{\gamma}V_T = F_T\sin(\alpha + \alpha_T) + L - mg_D\cos\gamma$$
$$\dot{\alpha} = q - \dot{\gamma} \tag{3.37}$$
$$\dot{q} = \frac{m}{I_y}$$

V_T, α, β: magnitude and direction of the relative wind. Thrust vector lies in the $x_b - z_b$ plane but is inclined at an angle α_T to the fuselage reference line. In load factor coordinates, the resultant aerodynamic force posseses lift and drag as its two components:

$$f_a = \bar{q}S \begin{pmatrix} -C_D & 0 & -C_L \end{pmatrix}^T \qquad (3.38)$$

Eigenvalues analysis of the longitudinal stability matrix allow the determination of the stability of the airplane. The system is stable if all eigenvalues λ have negative real part. The natural frequency is given by: $\omega_n = \sqrt{\lambda_{real}^2 + \lambda_{im}^2}$ while the damping ratio is given by $d = -\frac{\lambda_{real}}{\omega_N}$. Natural frequency is how fast the motion oscillates. Damping ratio is how much amplitude decays per oscillation. The half-life if the time taken for the amplitude to decay by half: $\frac{0.693}{|\lambda_{real}|}$

The period is the time take to complete one oscillation: $\tau = \frac{2\pi}{\omega_n}$

Static stability is the initial tendency to return to trim while dynamic stability is the long-term tendency to return to trim. The **dynamic stability** of an aircraft refers to how the airplane behaves after it has been disturbed following steady non-oscillating flight. It has longitudinal modes and lateral-directional modes **Longitudinal modes**: range has no dynamic effect and altitude effect is minimal (air density variation). Neglecting range and altitude, the following fourth-order nonlinear dynamic equations are obtained:

$$\begin{aligned} \dot{u} &= f_1 = X/m - g\sin\theta - qw \\ \dot{w} &= f_2 = Z/m + g\cos\theta + qu \\ \dot{q} &= f_3 = M/I_{yy} \\ \dot{\theta} &= f_4 = q \end{aligned} \qquad (3.39)$$

The state vector x_{long} has four components: u axial velocity m/s, w vertical velocity m/s, q pitch rate rad/s and θ pitch angle rad. Replacing Cartesian body components of velocity by polar inertial components:

$$\begin{aligned} \dot{V} &= f_1 = [T\cos(\alpha + i) - D - mg\sin\gamma]/m \\ \dot{\gamma} &= f_2 = [T\sin(\alpha + i) + L - mg\cos\gamma]/(mV) \\ \dot{q} &= f_3 = M/I_{yy} \\ \dot{\theta} &= f_4 = q \end{aligned} \qquad (3.40)$$

where V is the velocity, γ the flight path angle and i is the incidence angle of the thrust vector with respect to the centerline.

Replacing pitch angle by angle of attack: $\alpha = \theta - \gamma$

$$\begin{aligned} \dot{V} &= f_1 = [T\cos(\alpha + i) - D - mg\sin\gamma]/m \\ \dot{\gamma} &= f_2 = [T\sin(\alpha + i) + L - mg\cos\gamma]/(mV) \\ \dot{q} &= f_3 = M/I_{yy} \\ \dot{\alpha} &= \dot{\theta} - \dot{\gamma} = f_4 = q - f_2 = q - [T\sin(\alpha + i) + L - mg\cos\gamma]/(mV) \end{aligned} \qquad (3.41)$$

Trim condition: $\dot{X} = f(X)$ become $\dot{X} = f(X)$

Longitudinal stability matrix

$$
M_{lon} = \begin{bmatrix}
-D_V & -g\cos\gamma_N & -D_q & -D_\alpha \\
L_V/V_N & g\sin\gamma_N/V_N & L_q/V_N & L_\alpha/V_N \\
M_V & 0 & M_q & M_\alpha \\
L_V/V_N & -g\sin\gamma_N/V_N & (1 - L_q/V_N) & -L_\alpha/V_N
\end{bmatrix} \tag{3.42}
$$

where D_V is represented by the stability derivatives.

Velocity and flight path angle typically have slow variations while pitch angle and angle of attack typically have quicker variations. Coupling is typically small.

1. **Phugoid (longer period) oscillations** is slow, light damped while pitch and velocity vary: relating to, or representing variations in the longitudinal motion or course of the center of mass of an airplane in flight. The phugoid is a constant angle of attack but varying pitch angle exchange of airspeed and altitude. This long period motion is a characteristic oscillations of the aircragt after a small disturbance of the steady flight (due to small horizontal surface motion or air gust). The airplane is traveling along the sinusoidal trajectory with small changes of the air speed and pitch angle.

   (a) It can be excited by an elevator pulse resulting in a pitch increase with no change in trim from cruise condition

   (b) as speed decays, the nose will drop below the horizon

   (c) light aircraft typically shows a phugoid period of 15-25 seconds

2. Short period mode is quick, high frequency and well damped. Pitch and angle of attack vary.

3.5.2 Dynamic modes in lateral model

The lateral variables are $X_{lat} = (y, v, \phi, \psi, r)^T$:

$$
\begin{aligned}
\dot{y} &= u_N \sin\psi + v\cos\phi\cos\psi \\
\dot{\psi} &= r\cos\phi \\
\dot{\phi} &= p
\end{aligned} \tag{3.43}
$$

$$
\dot{v} = \frac{Y_b}{m} + g\sin\phi - ru_N \tag{3.44}
$$

$$
\dot{p} = \frac{I_{zz}L + I_{xz}N}{I_{xx}I_{zz} - I_{xz}^2} \tag{3.45}
$$

$$
\dot{r} = \frac{I_{xz}L + I_{xx}N}{I_{xx}I_{zz} - I_{xz}^2} \tag{3.46}
$$

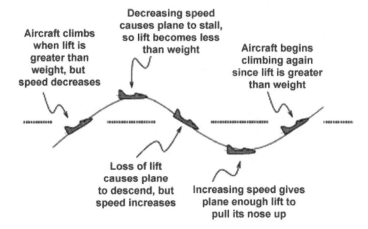

FIGURE 3.5 Phugoid

Eigenvalues analysis of the lateral directional stability matrix allow the determination of the stability of the airplane. The system is stable if all eigenvalues have negative real part.

Lateral-directional modes: 4-component lateral-directional equations of motion, neglecting crossrange and yaw angle, assuming steady, level longitudinal flight ($q_N = 0, \gamma_N = 0, \theta_N = \alpha_N$), dynamic pressure is constant,

$$\dot{v} = Y_B/m + g \sin\phi \cos\theta_N - r u_N + p w_N$$
$$\dot{p} = \frac{\left(I_{zz}L_B + I_{xz}N_B - \left\{I_{xz}(I_{yy} - I_{xx} - I_{zz})p + \left(I_{xz}^2 + I_{zz}(I_{zz} - I_{yy})\right)r\right\}q\right)}{I_{xx}I_{zz} - I_{xz}^2}$$
$$\dot{r} = \frac{\left(I_{xz}L_B + I_{xx}N_B - \left\{I_{xz}(I_{yy} - I_{xx} - I_{zz})r + \left(I_{xz}^2 + I_x(I_{xx} - I_{yy})\right)r\right\}q\right)}{I_{xx}I_{zz} - I_{xz}^2} \qquad (3.47)$$
$$\dot{\phi} = p + (s \sin\phi + r \cos\phi) \tan\theta_N$$

where v is the side velocity, p the body-axis roll rate, r the body-axis yaw rate, ϕ roll angle about body x axis.

Lateral dynamic stability matrix

$$M_{lat} = \begin{bmatrix} Y_V & -(Y_p + w_N) & (Y_r - u_N) & g\cos\theta_N \\ L_v & L_p & L_r & 0 \\ N_v & N_q & N_r & 0 \\ 0 & 1 & \tan\theta_N & 0 \end{bmatrix} \qquad (3.48)$$

1. **Roll subsidence mode and spiral** bank and sideslip angles steadily increase; they are primarily described by stability-axis roll rate and roll angle

2. **Dutch roll mode** bank and sideslip angles oscillate side to side. It is a type of aircraft motion consisting of an out-of-phase combination of tail-wagging and rocking from side to side. This yaw-roll coupling is one of

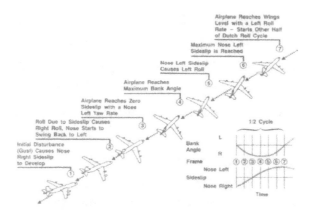

FIGURE 3.6 Accident dutch roll

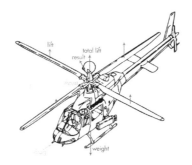

FIGURE 3.7 Helicopter

the basic flight dynamics modes. This motion is normally well damped. Dutch roll modes can experience a degradation in damping, decrease in airspeed and increase in altitude. Dutch-roll motion is primarily described by stability-axis yaw rate and sideslip angle.

3.6 QUAD-ROTOR DYNAMIC MODEL

In a **helicopter**, there are four different subsystems: rigid-body dynamics, force and torque generation mechanism, rotor aerodynamics and dynamics, and actuator dynamics, as show in Figure 3.7.

Quadrotor controls: A quadrotor needs two clockwise propellers, and 2 counter-clockwise propellers, otherwise it will continually yaw on itself. The reason for this is that the yaw control is done by speeding up or slowing motors. A quadrotor is considered as a rigid body with six degrees of freedom that incorporates a mechanism for generating the necessary forces and moments,,as shown in Figure 3.8.

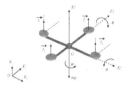

FIGURE 3.8 Quad rotor model

The equations of motion for a rigid body of mass m and inertia matrix $\mathbf{I} \in \Re^{3 \times 3}$ subject to external force vector $F \in \Re^3$, torque vector $\Gamma^b \in \Re^3$ are given by the following Newton Euler equations, expressed in the body fixed reference frame:

$$F = m\dot{V} + \omega \times mV$$
$$\Gamma = I\dot{\omega} + \omega \times I\omega \tag{3.49}$$

where $V = (u, v, w)^T$ and $\omega = (p, q, r)^T$ are respectively the linear and angular velocities in the body fixed reference frame. The translational force F combines gravity, main thrust and other body forces components. The orientation matrix is:

$$\mathbf{R} = \mathbf{R}_\psi.\mathbf{R}_\theta.\mathbf{R}_\phi \tag{3.50}$$

By considering the transformation between the body fixed reference frame and the inertial reference frame, it is possible to separate the gravitational force from other forces and write the translational dynamics as follows:

$$\dot{\eta}_1 = v$$
$$m\dot{v} = \mathbf{R}.F^b - mge_3^i \tag{3.51}$$

where $\eta = (x, y, z)^T$ and $v = (\dot{x}, \dot{y}, \dot{z})$ are the rotorcraft position and velocity in the inertial frame. In the above notation, g is the gravitational acceleration and F^b is the resulting force vector in the body frame (excluding the gravity force) acting on the airframe.

Definition 33 *The **airframe** describes the physical characteristics of the aircraft: mass (empty mass, maximum takeoff mass (MTOM)), center-of-mass (location and limits), dimensions (for fixed-wing specify wingspan, this means fuselage length, body diameter ... , for a rotor-craft this means length, width and height, propeller diameter ...).*

Different models have been proposed to represent the rotational dynamics like those based on Euler angles.

$$\dot{\eta}_2 = J(\eta_2)\omega$$
$$\mathbf{M}(\eta)\ddot{\eta}_2 + \mathbf{C}(\eta, \dot{eta})\dot{\eta} = \psi(\eta)\Gamma^b \tag{3.52}$$

Many small scale quad-rotors can be characterized by three main control torques $\tau = (\tau_\phi, \tau_\theta, \tau_\psi)^T$ and one main control force $F^b = (0, 0, F_z^b)$. We neglect the parasitic forces and moments that are induced by control inputs coupling and other small body forces and moments .

The collective lift F_z^b is the sum of the thrusts generated by the four propellers:

$$F_z^b = \sum_{i=1}^{4} T_i \tag{3.53}$$

The airframe torques generated by the rotors are given by:

$$\begin{aligned}
\tau_\phi &= \ell(f_2 - f_4) \\
\tau_\theta &= \ell(f_3 - f_1) \\
\tau_\psi &= (Q_1 + Q_2 - Q_3 - Q_4)
\end{aligned} \tag{3.54}$$

ℓ represents the distance from the rotors to the center of mass of the helicopter and $Q_i, i = 1..4$ is the fan torque due to air drag.

Propellers thrust and torque Q_i are generally assumed to be proportional to the square of the rotor angular velocity ω_r. The algebraic model for generating the force and control torques can be written as:

$$\begin{pmatrix} F_z^b \\ \tau_\phi \\ \tau_\theta \\ \tau_\psi \end{pmatrix} = \begin{pmatrix} \rho & \rho & \rho & \rho \\ 0 & -\ell\rho & 0 & \ell\rho \\ -\ell\rho & 0 & \ell\rho & 0 \\ \kappa_a & -\kappa_a & \kappa_a & -\kappa_a \end{pmatrix} \begin{pmatrix} \omega_{r_1}^2 \\ \omega_{r_2}^2 \\ \omega_{r_3}^2 \\ \omega_{r_4}^2 \end{pmatrix} \tag{3.55}$$

(ρ, κ_a) are positive propellers aerodynamics constants . These are valid approximations that are used in cases of hovering and low speed displacements.

The dynamical model considered for planning/control design is given by:

$$\begin{aligned}
m\ddot{\eta}_1 &= F_z^b R e_3^i \\
\mathbf{M}(\eta)\ddot{\eta}_2 + \mathbf{C}(\eta, \dot{eta})\dot{\eta} &= \psi(\eta)\Gamma^b
\end{aligned} \tag{3.56}$$

1. The rolling moments are composed of the body gyro effect, the propeller gyro effect, roll actuators action, the hub moment due to side-ward flight and the rolling moment due to forward flight.

2. The pitching moments consider the body gyro effect, the propeller gyro effect, the pitch actuators action, the hub moment due to forward flight as well as the rolling moment due to side-ward flight.

3. The yawing moments take into account body gyro effect, the inertial counter-torque, the counter-torque unbalance, the hub force unbalance in forward flight and the hub force unbalance in side-ward flight.

These considerations can be translated into the attitude equations:

$$\ddot{\phi} = \frac{I_{yy}-I_{zz}}{I_{xx}}\dot{\theta}\dot{\psi} + \frac{J_r}{I_{xx}}\dot{\theta}\Omega_r + \frac{\ell}{I_{xx}}(-T_2+T_4) - \frac{h}{I_{xx}}\sum_{i=1}^{4}H_{yi}+$$
$$+\sum_{i=1}^{4}\frac{(-1)^{i+1}}{I_{xx}}R_{mxi}$$

$$\ddot{\theta} = \frac{I_{zz}-I_{xx}}{I_{yy}}\dot{\phi}\dot{\psi} - \frac{J_r}{I_{yy}}\dot{\phi}\Omega_r + \frac{\ell}{I_{yy}}(T_1-T_3) + \frac{h}{I_{yy}}\sum_{i=1}^{4}H_{xi}+$$
$$+\sum_{i=1}^{4}\frac{(-1)^{i+1}}{I_{yy}}R_{myi}$$

$$\ddot{\psi} = \frac{I_{xx}-I_{yy}}{I_{zz}}\dot{\theta}\dot{\phi} + \frac{J_r}{I_{zz}}\dot{\Omega}_r + \sum_{i=1}^{4}\frac{(-1)^{i+1}}{I_{zz}}Q_i + \frac{\ell}{I_{zz}}(H_{x2}-H_{x4}) + \frac{\ell}{I_{zz}}(-H_{y1}+H_{y3})$$
$$\tag{3.57}$$

where ϕ, θ, ψ represent the Euler angles, respectively the roll, pitch and yaw. H represents the hub force, I_{xx}, I_{yy}, I_{zz} are the inertial moments, J_r is the rotor inertia, h is the vertical distance of the propeller center to the center of gravity, ℓ is the horizontal distance from the propeller center to the center of gravity, Ω is the propeller angular rate, T the thrust force, Ω_r is the overall residual propeller angular speed. The attitude dynamics are faster than the translational dynamics.

The forces along the x-axis take into account the actuators action, the hub force in x-axis and the friction. The same holds for the y-axis. The forces along the z-axis consider the weight and the actuators action. The position equations of motion are thus given by

$$\ddot{x} = \frac{1}{m}(\sin\psi\sin\phi + \cos\psi\sin\theta\cos\phi)\sum_{i=1}^{4}T_i - \frac{1}{m}\sum_{i=1}^{4}H_{xi} - \frac{1}{2m}C_xA_c\rho\dot{x}|\dot{x}| \quad (3.58)$$

$$\ddot{y} = \frac{1}{m}(-\cos\psi\sin\phi + \sin\psi\sin\theta\cos\phi)\sum_{i=1}^{4}T_i - \frac{1}{m}\sum_{i=1}^{4}H_{yi} - \frac{1}{2m}C_yA_c\rho\dot{y}|\dot{y}|$$
$$\tag{3.59}$$

$$\ddot{z} = g - \frac{1}{m}(\cos\psi\cos\phi)\sum_{i=1}^{4}T_i \tag{3.60}$$

where m represents the overall mass,

When only the most important phenomena are retained, the following nonlinear model is obtained:

$$\dot{X} = f(X,U) = \begin{pmatrix} \dot{\phi} \\ a_1\dot{\theta}\dot{\psi} + a_2\dot{\theta}\Omega_r + b_1U_1 \\ \dot{\theta} \\ a_3\dot{\phi}\dot{\psi} - a_4\dot{\phi}\Omega_r + b_2U_2 \\ \dot{\psi} \\ a_5\dot{\theta}\dot{\phi} + b_3U_3 \\ \dot{x} \\ \frac{\sin\psi\sin\phi+\cos\psi\sin\theta\cos\phi}{m}U_4 \\ \dot{y} \\ -\frac{-\cos\psi\sin\phi+\sin\psi\sin\theta\cos\phi}{m}U_4 \\ \dot{z} \\ g - \frac{\cos\psi\cos\phi}{m}U_4 \end{pmatrix} \tag{3.61}$$

where
$$U_1 = b\left(-\Omega_2^2 + \Omega_4^2\right)$$
$$U_2 = b\left(\Omega_1^2 - \Omega_3^2\right)$$
$$U_3 = d\left(-\Omega_1^2 + \Omega_2^2 - \Omega_3^2 + \Omega_4^2\right) \tag{3.62}$$
$$U_4 = b\left(\Omega_1^2 + \Omega_2^2 + \Omega_3^2 + \Omega_4^2\right)$$
$$\Omega_r = -\Omega_1 + \Omega_2 - \Omega_3 + \Omega_4$$

with $X = \left(\phi, \dot{\phi}, \theta, \dot{\theta}, \psi, \dot{\psi}, x, \dot{x}, y, \dot{y}, z, \dot{z}\right)^T$ and:

$a_1 = \frac{I_{yy} - I_{zz}}{I_{xx}}$, $a_2 = \frac{J_r}{I_{xx}}$, $a_3 = \frac{I_{zz} - I_{xx}}{I_{yy}}$, $a_4 = \frac{J_r}{I_{yy}}$, $a_5 = \frac{I_{xx} - I_{yy}}{I_{zz}}$

$b_1 = \frac{\ell}{I_{xx}}$, $b_2 = \frac{\ell}{I_{yy}}$, $b_3 = \frac{\ell}{I_{zz}}$ To achieve stability with respect to space, it is preferable to design the aircraft to have control surfaces which together with the aerodynamic shape of the remainder of the airframe, result in overall neutral, or near neutral aerodynamic stability characteristics. This will ensure minimum disturbance from air turbulence, but the aircraft will then need a system to ensure that it has positive spatial stability to prevent its wandering off course due to other influences, such as payload movement. This will require sensors to measure aircraft attitudes in the three axes of pitch, roll and yaw with altitude and height data input. These sensors are integrated into an automatic fligt control and stability system which will control the aircraft in flight as required for the mission. D.A. Wells "Lagrangian Dynamics", Schaum's outline series, Mc Graw-Hill book company 1967.

CHAPTER 4

Aircraft Performance

4.1 INTRODUCTION

At the earliest stage of UAV conceptual design, some estimate of weight, propulsive power and efficiency, and aerodynamic performance is required. Custom methods are common.

Due to the changing atmospheric pressure, a standard reference was developed.

Aviation weather sources and effects of weather on small unmanned aircraft performance

4.2 PRELIMINARIES

Performance is a term used to describe the ability of a UAV to accomplish certain things that make it useful for certain purposes. For example, its ability to land and take off in a very short distance is an important factor. The ability to carry heavy loads, fly at high altitudes at fast speeds, or travel long distances is essential performance for operators. The various items of UAVs performance result from the combination of aircraft and powerplant characteristics. The aerodynamic characteristics of the UAV generally define the power and thrust requirements at various conditions of flight, while powerplant characteristics generally define the power and thrust available at various conditions of flight. The matching of the aerodynamic configuration with the powerplant is accomplished by the manufacturer to provide maximum performance at the specific design condition (e.g. range, endurance, and climb). If the efficiency of the propulsion systems is known and the total energy content of the fuel or battery is given, the endurance may be estimated on energy considerations. Two major parameters are of particular interest: the maximum available thrust or power and the system efficiency. The overall efficiency is the product of the component efficiencies of the motor, control electronics, gear box and propeller.

DOI: 10.1201/9781003121787-4

Aircraft performance depends on:

1. The physical aspect: flight mechanics, aerodynamics, influence of external parameters on aircraft performance, flight optimization concepts. UAV performance parameters of interest may include stall speed, climb rate, maximum altitude, maximum sustained rates ... These parameters are determined by the aircraft weight, propulsion system performance and aerodynamic characteristics.

2. The operational aspect: description of operational methods, aircraft computer logic, operational procedures, remote pilot's actions

3. The regulatory aspect.

4.2.1 Atmospheric pressure

The atmosphere is a gaseous envelope surrounding the Earth. Its characteristics are different throughout the world. Though there are various kinds of pressure, aircraft are mainly concerned with atmospheric pressure. It is one of the basic factors in weather changes, helps to lift the aircraft, and actuates some of the most important flight instruments in the aircraft. Though air is very light, it has mass and is affected by the attraction of gravity. Since it is a fluid substance, this force is exerted equally in all directions, and its effect on bodies within the air is called pressure. The density of air has significant effects on the aircraft's performance. As air becomes less dense, it reduces:

1. Power, because the engine takes in less air.

2. Thrust, because the propeller is less efficient in thin air.

3. Lift, because the thin air exerts less force on the airfoils.

The pressure of the atmosphere varies with time and altitude. To help aircraft designers, it is useful to define a standard atmosphere model of the variation of properties through the atmosphere. There are actually several different models available: a standard or average day, a hot day, a cold day, and a tropical day. The models are updated every few years to include the latest atmospheric data.

Definition 34 *Atmosphere is composed of gases. In any gas, there is a very large number of molecules that are only weakly attracted to each other and are free to move about in space. When studying gases, the motions and interactions of individual molecules, or the large scale action of the gas as a whole can be investigated. Scientists refer to the large scale motion of the gas as the macro scale and the individual molecular motions as the micro scale.*

Definition 35 *The **standard atmosphere** at sea level is a surface temperature of 15 degrees Celsius and a surface pressure of 1013.2 millibars (mb).*

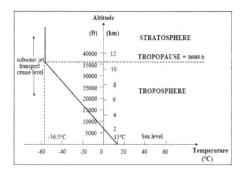

FIGURE 4.1   International standard atmosphere

International Standard Atmosphere (ISA): A standard temperature lapse rate is one in which the temperature decreases at the rate of approximately 2 degrees Celsius per thousand feet up to 11 Km. Above this point, the temperature is considered constant up to 24.5 Km.

Definition 36 *Fluid Dynamics* *involves the interactions between an object and a surrounding fluid, a liquid, or a gas. Fluid dynamics play a major role in the development of thrust in a gas turbine engine, and in the generation of aerodynamic drag for flight within the atmosphere.*

For any fluid system, mass is neither created nor destroyed (conservation of mass, continuity), momentum is neither created nor destroyed (conservation of momentum in 3 directions), energy is neither created nor destroyed: conservation of energy.

4.2.2   Pressure altitude

Pressure altitude is the height above the **standard datum plane** (SDP). The aircraft altimeter is essentially a sensitive barometer calibrated to indicate altitude in the standard atmosphere. If the altimeter is set for 29.92 "Hg SDP, the altitude indicated is the pressure altitude—the altitude in the standard atmosphere corresponding to the sensed pressure. Pressure altitude can have an effect on aircraft performance. It is used to figure density altitude, which is corrected for temperature, the higher the temperature, the higher the density altitude and the lower the performance of your engine and propeller. An altimeter does not measure altitude, it measures pressure change. As the pressure increases or decreases, so does the altimeter reading. The pressure altitude can be determined by either of two methods:

1. Setting the barometric scale of the altimeter to 29.92 and reading the indicated altitude.

2. Applying a correction factor to the indicated altitude according to the reported altimeter setting.

Table 2 Pressure altitude versus pressure [2].

Pressure (hPa)	Pressure altitude (PA)		FL= PA/100
	(feet)	(meters)	
200	38661	11784	390
250	34000	10363	340
300	30066	9164	300
500	18287	5574	180
850	4813	1467	50
1013	0	0	0

FIGURE 4.2 Pressure altitude versus pressure

FIGURE 4.3 Forces acting on an airplane

$pressureAltitude = (standardPressure - droneCurrentPressureSetting) \times 1000 + FieldElevation$

All of the principal components of flight performance involve steady-state flight conditions and equilibrium of the aircraft. For the aircraft to remain in steady, level flight, equilibrium must be obtained by a lift equal to the aircraft weight and a powerplant thrust equal to the aircraft drag. Thus, the aircraft drag defines the thrust required to maintain steady, level flight. While the parasite drag predominates at high speed, induced drag predominates at low speed. When an aircraft is in steady, level flight, the condition of equilibrium must prevail. The unaccelerated condition of flight is achieved with the aircraft trimmed for lift equal to weight and the powerplant set for a thrust to equal the aircraft drag.

Climb performance is a result of using the aircraft's potential energy provided by one, or a combination of two factors. The first is the use of excess power above that required for level flight. A second factor is that the aircraft can tradeoff its kinetic energy and increase its potential energy by reducing its airspeed. The reduction in airspeed will increase the aircraft's potential energy thereby also making the aircraft climb.

For a given weight of an aircraft, the angle of climb depends on the difference between thrust and drag, or the excess power. When the excess thrust is zero, the inclination of the flightpath is zero, and the aircraft will be in steady, level flight. When the thrust is greater than the drag, the excess thrust will allow a climb angle depending on the value of excess thrust. On the other

FIGURE 4.4 Climb performance

hand, when the thrust is less than the drag, the deficiency of thrust will allow an angle of descent.

The vertical velocity of an aircraft depends on the flight speed and the inclination of the flightpath. In fact, the **rate of climb** is the vertical component of the flightpath velocity. For rate of climb, the maximum rate would occur where there exists the greatest difference between power available and power required.

The climb performance of an aircraft is affected by certain variables. The conditions of the aircraft's maximum climb angle or maximum climb rate occur at specific speeds, and variations in speed will produce variations in climb performance. There is sufficient latitude in most aircraft that small variations in speed from the optimum do not produce large changes in climb performance. Climb performance would be most critical with high gross weight, at high altitude, in obstructed takeoff areas, or during malfunction of a powerplant. Then, optimum climb speeds are necessary.

If weight is added to an aircraft, it must fly at a higher **angle of attack** (AOA) to maintain a given altitude and speed. This increases the induced drag of the wings, as well as the parasite drag of the aircraft. Increased drag means that additional thrust is needed to overcome it, which in turn, means that less reserve thrust is available for climbing. A change in an aircraft's weight produces a twofold effect on climb performance. First, a change in weight will change the drag and the power required. This alters the reserve power available, which in turn, affects both the climb angle and the climb rate. Secondly, an increase in weight will reduce the maximum rate of climb, but the aircraft must be operated at a higher climb speed to achieve the smaller peak climb rate. The ability of an aircraft to convert fuel energy into flying distance is one of the most important items of aircraft performance. The problem of efficient range operation of a UAV appears in two general forms:

1. To extract the maximum flying distance from a given fuel load

2. To fly a specified distance with a minimum expenditure of fuel

A common element for each of these operating problems is the specific range; that is, **nautical miles** (NM) of flying distance versus the amount of fuel consumed. Range must be clearly distinguished from the item of endurance. **Range** involves consideration of flying distance, while **endurance** involves consideration of flying time. Thus, it is appropriate to define a separate term, **specific endurance**. If maximum specific range is desired, the flight condition must provide a maximum of speed per fuel flow. While the peak value of specific range would provide maximum range operation, long-range cruise operation is generally recommended at some slightly higher airspeed. The values of specific range versus speed are affected by three principal variables:

1. Aircraft gross weight

2. Altitude

3. The external aerodynamic configuration of the aircraft.

4.2.3 Density altitude

Density Altitude is the altitude relative to the standard atmosphere conditions (**International Standard Atmosphere**) at which the air density would be equal to the indicated air density at the place of observation, or the height when measured in terms of the density of the air rather than the distance from the ground. Pattern altitude, cruising altitude and field elevations do not change. However, Pressure altitude and Density altitude can change. Pressure altitude changes with air pressure, it is not a hard altitude but an altitude based on barometric pressure. Pressure altitude is directly related to air pressure. As air pressure increases so does the density of the air. This is due to the fact that pressure increases when more and more molecules of air are packed into the same area making the air more dense.

Density altitude, which takes into account several factors, including Pressure altitude, temperature, and humidity, is also an altitude number that changes. As the air becomes less dense the density altitude increases, as a result the aircraft performance will diminish. The wings produce less lift, the propeller loses forward thrust and the engine power output is reduced. Takeoff distance will be increased and vertical climb decreased making it more difficult to clear obstacles. A low density altitude does the opposite, denser cooler air allows for better performance, more airflow over the wings creates more lift, increased vertical climbs and better engine performance.

Atmospheric effects on density are the following:

1. Effects of pressure: Density is directly proportional to pressure. If the pressure is doubled, the density is doubled, and if the pressure is lowered, so is the density. This statement is true only at a constant temperature.

2. Effects of temperature: Increasing the temperature of a substance decreases its density. Conversely, decreasing the temperature increases the density. Thus, the density of air varies inversely with temperature. This statement is true only at a constant pressure. In the atmosphere, both temperature and pressure decrease with altitude, and have conflicting effects upon density. However, the fairly rapid drop in pressure as altitude is increased usually has the dominant effect.

3. Effects of Humidity (Moisture): in some conditions humidity may become an important factor in the performance of an aircraft. Water vapor is lighter than air; consequently, moist air is lighter than dry air. Therefore, as the water content of the air increases, the air becomes less dense, increasing density altitude and decreasing performance. It is lightest or least dense when, in a given set of conditions, it contains the maximum amount of water vapor.Expect a decrease in overall performance in high humidity conditions.

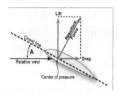

FIGURE 4.5 Lift vector

During a skid, the flow of air is not parallel to the plane of symmetry of the aircraft. This flow is said to be asymmetrical.

4.2.4 Configuration design

The design consists mainly in three phases:

1. The **conceptual phase**: This phase require the persons involved to have an appreciation of the market trends and either find a gap in the market or see means of producing a product offering better cost-benefit to the customer. It is necessary to establish its commercial viability at this early stage.

2. The **preliminary design phase**: Given the decision to proceed, the original outline design of the total system will be expanded in more detail. Optimization trade-offs within the system will be made to maximize the overall performance of the system over its projected operational roles and atmospheric conditions. This phase concludes with a comprehensive definition of the design of the complete system with its interfaces and a system specification.

3. The **detailed design phase**: There will follow a more detailed analysis of the aerodynamics, dynamics, structures systems of the aircraft and of the layout and the mechanical, electronic, and environmental systems of the control station and any other sub-systems such as the launch and the recovery systems.

   (a) Air vehicle- payload: The size and mass of the payload and its requirement for electrical power supplies is often the premier determinant of the layout, size, and all-up-mass of the drone. The necessary position of the payload may also be a significant factor in the configuration and layout of the airframe. Imaging payloads for surveillance may require a full hemispheric field of view and others a large surface area for antennae. Payloads which will be jettisoned must be housed close to the center of mass of the drone.

   (b) Air vehicle- endurance: The volume and mass of the fuel load to be carried will be a function of the required endurance and the reciprocal of the efficiency of the drone's aerodynamics and its powerplant

(c) Air vehicle- radius of action: The radius of action of the drone may be limited by the amount of fuel that it can carry, and the efficiency of its use, its speed or by the power, frequency and sophistication of its communication links.

(d) Air vehicle- speed range: The required speed range will be a dominant factor in determining the configuration and propulsive power of the aircraft.

(e) The method for launch and recovery will be significant in determining the aircraft configuration, its structural design and auxiliary equipments.

(f) A system which has been designed with only temperate conditions in mind, will fail if operated in more extreme conditions of altitude, temperature, solar radiation, precipitation, humidity and other atmospheric conditions. Lithium ion batteries rely on chemical reactions. Under cold conditions, these reactions slow down and the capacity of the battery is much lower than under normal conditions. The batteries will discharge much faster and might not recharge or very little. This have a direct effect on the performance of electronics.

(g) Wind strength and turbulence can be an important factor in the design of the structure of the ground control station and support equipment as well as the choice of air vehicle configuration.

To maximize endurance, most UAV designers minimize a vehicle's drag. UAV designers should to the maximum extent possible, design controls that affects only the intended axis.

Aircraft power model: for a conventional propeller-driven aircraft in level and unaccelerated flight, the power that is required for obtaining the maximum flight range is expressed in watts, by:

$$P_{rmr} = W \left(\frac{C_D}{C_L} \right)_{min} \times v_{TAS} \tag{4.1}$$

where W is the aircraft total weight, $\left(\frac{C_D}{C_L} \right)_{min}$ is the minimum obtainable ratio between the aerodynamic drag and lift coefficients and v_{TAS} is the true airspeed occurring at the $\left(\frac{C_D}{C_L} \right)_{min}$.

Aircraft range in normal operations: The Breguet range equation is a commonly used first-order approximation to determine the achievable maximum range of a conventional propeller aircraft. When assuming no wind and a parabolic drag polar, the resulting maximum range in normal operations (R_{no} in meters) is expressed by:

$$R_{no} = \frac{\eta_{pg}}{c} \left(\frac{C_L}{C_D} \right)_{max} \ln \left(\frac{W_0}{W_1} \right) \tag{4.2}$$

where η_{pg} is the complete propulsion efficiency of the system, c is the specific fuel consumption of the generator in Newtons per second per Watt, W_1 is the aircraft's current total aircraft weight in Newton, W_0 is the aircraft's total weight without fuel in Newton and $\left(\frac{C_L}{C_D}\right)_{max}$ is the maximum achievable ratio between the aerodynamic lift and drag coefficients in level and unaccelerated flight.

Aircraft range in battery-powered flight: taking into account the Peukert effect on the battery capacity and assuming no wind and a parabolic drag polar for the UAV airplane, the maximum range (R_{bp} in kilometers) for battery-powered small UAV in level and unaccelerated flight, without the influence of wind, is expressed by:

$$R_{bp} = \left(\frac{V \times C\eta_{pe}}{W\left(\frac{C_D}{C_L}\right)_{min}}\right)^n \left(\sqrt{\frac{2W}{\rho_\infty SC_L}}\right)^{1-n} R_t^{1-n} \tag{4.3}$$

W is the aircraft total weight, V is the battery bus voltage, C is the battery capacity, n is the battery-specific Peukert constant, R_t is the battery hour rating (i.e. the discharge period at which the rated capacity C was determined) and where η_{pe} is the propulsion efficiency of the battery-powered system.

Aircraft range in unpowered glide: this flight phase is modeled as pure unpowered glide, depending solely on the altitude h and maximum glide ratio $\left(\frac{L}{D}\right)_{max}$. When the aircraft's glide angle is moderate, the maximum range for unpowered glide in no-wind condition and for flat terrain is expressed by:

$$R_{ug} = h\left(\frac{L}{D}\right)_{max} \tag{4.4}$$

Effects of wind: Small UAVs are often operating in relatively high wind speeds, commonly exceeding half of the true air speed. Depending on the speed and direction, en-route winds may have a significant influence on the obtainable range of the aircraft, wind effects must be included. The optimum airspeed determined accounting head and tailwinds for propeller-powered aicraft is expressed by:

$$m_{br} = \frac{v_{TAS}}{v_{br}} = \frac{2m_{br} \pm \left(\frac{V_W}{v_{md}}\right)}{2m_{br} \pm 3\left(\frac{V_W}{v_{md}}\right)} \tag{4.5}$$

where m_{br} is the relative airspeed parameter between the true airspeed and v_{br} is the best-range airspeed, V_W is the wind speed, $\pm$ indicate a head or tailwind, v_{md} is the minimum-drag airspeed.

When assuming a flat and non-rotating Earth and flying in level and unaccelerated flight, the equations of motion through decomposed wind vectors are modeled as:

$$v_{GS} = v_{TAS}\begin{pmatrix} \cos\phi \\ \sin\phi \end{pmatrix} + V_W\begin{pmatrix} \cos\theta_w \\ \sin\theta \end{pmatrix} \tag{4.6}$$

v_{GS} is the aircraft's ground velocity vector, and θ_w is the direction of the wind, the aircraft's commanded heading ϕ is the sum of the course angle θ and the crab angle β defined as the angle between the TAS vector and the ground course angle.

The wind components perpendicular and parallel to the resulting ground track, in relation to the reference horizontal path, can be found by rotating the wind's x and y components through angle θ:

$$v_{parallel} = v_{WN} \cos\theta + v_{WE} \sin\theta$$
$$v_{perpendicular} = -v_{WN} \sin\theta + v_{WE} \cos\theta \tag{4.7}$$

4.3 ANALYSIS OF WEATHER FACTORS

4.3.1 Winds

High winds can make it harder and sometimes impossible to control or GPS-hold UAV. A battery will drain fast while holding in windy conditions or flying into a headwind. Higher wind speeds make it more difficult for the UAV to hold its positioning, which will result in shorter flight times, less accurate position holds, and more difficult maneuvering. The key is to not fly in conditions where gusts may exceed the UAV's top speed, not just the average wind speed.

The bigger the UAV the stronger wind it will be able to take off in, the pilot will understand its limitations.

The existing UAV platforms can measure the wind vector either while flying in patterns (fixed wing UAV) or by hovering (rotorcraft). Small UAV are equipped with meteorological sensors , which increases the minimum payload capacity required by the vehicle and shorten their flight time.

There are different kinds of wind estimation methods used currently.

1. Using GPS Velocity, local air mass velocity components can be obtained directly from vehicle kinematics and the GPS velocity:

$$\begin{pmatrix} W_x \\ W_y \\ W_z \end{pmatrix} = \begin{pmatrix} S_x \\ S_y \\ S_z \end{pmatrix} - \begin{pmatrix} V_x \\ V_y \\ V_z \end{pmatrix} \tag{4.8}$$

   where W is the wind speed over ground, S ground speed (GPS velocity) and V Air speed vector in Earth frame.

2. The method is based on autopilot module providing estimated components of airspeed and Euler angles. This method does not consider the changes in magnetic heading and turn rate while predicting the wind vector. This leads to inaccuracy in wind direction and velocity prediction.

3. Computing Wind from Vehicle Response is based on comparison of measurements of aircraft motion with respect to the Earth (GPS measurements) with predictions of aircraft motion obtained from UAV dynamic

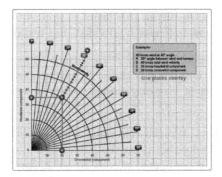

FIGURE 4.6   CrossWind

model (based on aircraft acceleration with respect to surrounding air). This method doesn't produce good results due to GPS uncertainty is of the order of 3 m.

4. Wind triangle method for wind estimation works on GPS ground track vector and true airspeed vector and considers turning rate (yaw rate) of aircraft. This method works on predicting wind vector (V_w) based on geometric transformation between true airspeed vector (V_a) and ground speed vector (V_g).

Strong winds have the capacity to affect the ground speed and flight path of a UAV. Wind speeds can easily surpass the maximum speed of the sUAV. Flying in a headwind with a greater velocity than that of the aircraft results in stationary or backward flight. Furthermore, flying in a crosswind can cause the small UAV to drift with the crosswind rather than at the intended heading.

Strong winds may result in the UAV to be blown over a populated, dangerous or unrecoverable area. Moreover, winds are often associated with gusts that can easily be a factor of two greater than the sustained wind speed.

Wind gusts are sudden increases in wind speed that typically last no longer than 20 seconds. Horizontal gusts affect the yaw of an airplane. Vertical gusts can roll an airplane if there is a gradient in the gust's magnitude from one wing to the other. For fixed-wing or multi-rotor UAV, a gradient between the front and the back of the aircraft can cause a pitching or a diving motion.

4.3.2   Wind Modeling

Wind modeling has a significant role in the design of UAVs. It helps to study and analyze the behavior of the aircraft facing the wind. We assume that the UAV flies in the troposphere layer. The air masses are in a constant motion and the region is characterized by gusty winds and turbulence.

As the movement of the air, in this layer, is similar to a fluid flowing over a solid object, the troposphere can be divided into two distinct regions.

1. In the first, the effect of the Earth's surface friction on the air motion is negligible, and it is known as the free atmosphere, while in the second one, the effect of viscosity cannot be neglected, and it is called the boundary layer.

2. The second region is typically extended over a several hundred meters to 2km roughly. It is depending on the landform and time of day/daytime, while the entire troposphere extends to 10–20 km approximately (it is larger in the tropics and shallower near the Polar Regions).

Definition 37 *The **static pressure** is the pressure exerted by the still air on the whole surface of a body at rest.*

Definition 38 *The **dynamic pressure** is the energy acquired by the air thanks to its speed, or pressure due to the speed of the relative wind applied on a surface perpendicular to the air streams. Its value is determined by Bernouli's law*

$$P_d = \frac{1}{2}\rho V^2 \tag{4.9}$$

Aerology characteristics (Atmosphere): wind profile, gust model:

1. A Pitot tube mounted on the nose of a fixed-wing UAV could be used to measure and calculate the horizontal wind. The Pitot tube uses Bernoulli's equation to relate wind speed to static and total pressure of the incoming air flow. It consists of a tube pointing into the fluid flow. The moving flow stagnates, giving a value of the total pressure. The static pressure is measured using an additional hole located at the side of the tube. The dynamic pressure can then be calculated and thus the wind speed. Its limitation is the necessity of being pointed directly into the fluid flow.

2. A propeller anenometer uses a propeller mounted on a horizontal axis to measure wind speed. It is often combined with a wind vane so the propeller always keep facing the wind, making possible to measure both wind speed and direction. Miniaturization of these sensors could be mounted on top of a sUAV.

3. Multi-hole proble extend the operating principle of Pitot tubes to 3D flow measurements, by using several holes at the tip of th probe.

In order to measure wind vector, a UAV can perform a spiral flight trajectory. When the quadrotor hovers at a certain position in space, the drag force of the wind acting on it tends to push it. If the autopilot system forces the quadrotor to keep the position, the quadrotor will tilt, compensating the drag

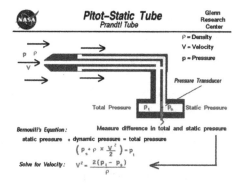

FIGURE 4.7 Pitot tube. This figure came from NASA web site, please reference   properly   https://www.grc.nasa.gov/www/k-12/airplane/pitot.html

force with a horizontal component of the thrust force generated by the rotors. The stronger the wind, the more tilted the quadrotor. Under steady state conditions, the wind vector can be estimated by knowing the drag coefficient of the vehicle and the area exposed.

In general, the wind speed can be modeled as a sum of two components: a nominal deterministic component, and a stochastic component, representing deviations from the nominal one. In the following, two classical mathematical models of gusts will be presented.

1. Discrete Gusts: The most used approximation, representing a sharp edged gust, is one minus cosine formulation, see Fig. 4.7. The gust velocity is defined as,

$$V_{wind} = \frac{1}{2}V_m \left[1 - cos\left(\frac{\pi x}{H}\right)\right] \tag{4.10}$$

where V_m denotes the gust amplitude, H is the distance from the start point to the point at which the gust reaches a maximum value and x represents the traveled distance. This formulation can be considered as a single representative section of the broader spectrum of continuous turbulence. However, in order to represent random continuous gusts that an UAV may encounter, it became necessary to use statistical methods, particularly the method involving the power spectral density.

2. Power Spectral Density (PSD): It is based on the frequency representation for describing the square of a random variable, which is originally considered in time domain. The turbulence model using this technique is assumed to be stationary, Gaussian, random process. There are two particular approximations for the PSD function of atmospheric turbulence: the von Karman and Dryden formula, each proposing a separate

function for gusts in the longitudinal, lateral and vertical directions. Dryden PSD function is simpler:

(a) Longitudinal wind velocity

$$\Phi_u(\omega) = \frac{2\sigma_u^2 L_u}{\pi V} \cdot \frac{1}{1 + \left(L_u \frac{\omega}{V}\right)^2} \tag{4.11}$$

(b) Lateral wind velocity

$$\Phi_v(\omega) = \frac{\sigma_v^2 L_v}{\pi V} \cdot \frac{1 + 3\left(L_v \frac{\omega}{V}\right)^2}{\left[1 + \left(L_v \frac{\omega}{V}\right)^2\right]^2} \tag{4.12}$$

(c) Vertical wind velocity

$$\Phi_w(\omega) = \frac{\sigma_w^2 L_w}{\pi V} \cdot \frac{1 + 3\left(L_w \frac{\omega}{V}\right)^2}{\left[1 + \left(L_w \frac{\omega}{V}\right)^2\right]^2} \tag{4.13}$$

where Φ_i describes the PSD function, σ_i represents the RMS gust velocity, L_i signifies the scale of turbulence and V is the aircraft velocity. The gusty wind was generated using a combination of a several discrete gusts and a white noise as it is shown in the Fig. 4.7.

4.3.3 Venturi effect

The **Venturi effect** applies to confined flows and refers to the increase in fluid speed or flow rate due to a decrease of the flow section, where the flow rate and flow cross-sectional area are inversely proportional. Since the increase in fluid speed is generally accompanied by a decrease in pressure, the Venturi effect is also used to refer to Bernoulli's principle. Venturi effect means the increase in speed due to flow constriction. The vicinity of bridges is an ideal environment to the appearance of Venturi effect due to its structural design. In fact, the passages between pillars can be responsible for increased wind speed. Venturi effect consists of:

- An increment in wind speed magnitude.

- A divergence and a convergence of air flow around the obstacle (pillar).

In order to represent mathematically the previous statement, we first introduce the following definitions

Definition 39 *A Gaussian function is a continous function having the following form*

$$G(x) = a_G e^{\frac{-(x-\mu)^2}{2\sigma^2}} \tag{4.14}$$

where, a_G represents the height of the curve's peak, μ denotes the position of the center of the peak, and σ describes the deviation.

Definition 40 *A Sigmoid function is a continous function having an "S" shape. It is given by*

$$Sig(x) = \frac{1}{1 + e^{-a_{sig}(x-x_0)}} \tag{4.15}$$

where, a_{sig} defines the sharpness of the curve, and x_0 is the position of the switch.

Definition 41 *$E(x)$ is an enable function on some interval $\{x_1, x_2\}$ if and only if*

$$E(x) = \left\{ \begin{array}{ll} 1 & ; \quad x_1 \leq x \leq x_2 \\ 0 & ; \quad otherwise \end{array} \right. \tag{4.16}$$

A continuous approximation for $E(x)$ is given by

$$\tilde{E}(x) = Sig(x_1) - Sig(x_2) \tag{4.17}$$

Considering the presence of two pillars, supposing a horizontal plan and assuming that the wind is in the direction of x-axis. Then the wind velocity components on x and y axes are given as follows

$$\begin{aligned} W_x &= G(x) \\ W_y &= W_{y1} + W_{y2} \end{aligned} \tag{4.18}$$

where, W_{y1} and W_{y2} presents the component divergence and convergence of the air flow for the first and the second pillar respectively. These terms are defined as following

$$\begin{aligned} W_{y1} &= a_y(y - y_{p1})\tilde{E}(y_1) \left[\tilde{E}(x_1) - \tilde{E}(x_2) \right] \\ W_{y2} &= a_y(y - y_{p2})\tilde{E}(y_2) \left[\tilde{E}(x_1) - \tilde{E}(x_2) \right] \end{aligned} \tag{4.19}$$

Definition 42 *Significant meteorological information (SIGMET) is weather advisory that contains information about significant weather events like thunderstorms and severe turbulence.*

Definition 43 *Terminal area forecast (TAF) is weather report established for the five nautical miles around an airport.*

4.3.4 Effects of weather on performance

Survey of micro-meteorology and weather While wind patterns and the theories of circulation are accurate for large scale atmospheric circulation, they do not take into account changes to the circulations on a local scale. The friction of the wind blowing along the surface of the Earth actually changes its direction from 2000 feet. Local conditions, buildings and other man-made structure, geological features and other anomalies can change the wind direction and speed close to the Earth's surface as well.

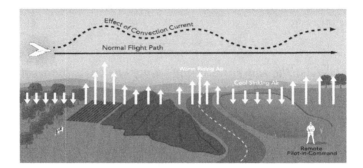

FIGURE 4.8 Wind and currents

The best way to fly in windy conditions is flying into direction of wind, i.e. when the fuselage is parallel to the wind. Flying into the wind will allow maximum wind speed on leading edge of wing airfoil, as they are designed in such a way. But this isn't always possible as the path planned may have orientation either away from or at an angle with respect to the wind direction with no choice. In such cases the aircrafts are flown with their nose pointing towards the wind instead of directly towards planned path. The angle between Aircraft heading and desired course is known as Crab angle. The calculation of crab angle depends on various factors such as wind direction, magnitude, aircraft velocity and the course it needs to follow.

Convective currents

1. Different surfaces radiates heat in varying amounts. Plowed ground, rocks, sand and barre land give off a large amount of heat; water, trees and other ares of vegetation tend to absorb and retain heat. This uneven heating of the air creates small areas of local circulation called convective currents.

2. Convective currents cause that turbulent air sometimes experienced when flying at lower altitudes during warm weather. On a low-altitude flight over different types of surfaces, updrafts are likely to occur over areas like pavement or sand and downdrafts often occur over water or expansive areas of vegetation like a group of trees.

3. This is particular true when it comes to the shores of large bodies of water. The land will heat up faster than the water so the air over the land becomes warmer and less dense. It rises and is replaced by cooler, denser air flowing in from over the water.

4. At night the opposite happens. The land cools faster thatn the water, so the warmer air over the water rises and is replaced by the cooler

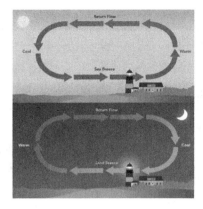

FIGURE 4.9 Wind and currents

denser air from the land. This creates an offshore wind called a land breeze.

5. Anywhere there is an uneven heating from the Earth's surface, there are convective currents.

Effects of obstructions on wind:

1. Obstructions on the ground can affect the flow of wind and this can be an unseen danger. Ground topography and large buildings can break up the flow of the wind and create wind gusts that change rapidly in direction and speed.

2. These obstructions range from man-made structures like hangars to large natural obstructions such as mountains, bluffs or canyons.

3. The intensity of the turbulence associated with ground obstructions depends on the size of the obstacle and the primary velocity of the wind.

4. It is important to map the flight environment considering large obstructions as that might affect the flight operations.

5. In a mountainous environment, wind flows smoothly up the winward side of the mountain, but on the other leeward side, the wind follows the contour of the terrain and can be quite turbulent. This is called a kabatic wind. The stronger the wind, the greater the downward pressure. A downdraft is a downward moving air.

FIGURE 4.10 Obstructions

Man-made obstruction

Wind shear and Microburst:

1. **Wind shear** is a suddent, drastic change in wind speed and/or direction over a relatively small area. Wind shear can occur at all altitudes, in all directions, and it is typically characterized by directional wind changes of 180 degreeas and speed changes of 50 knots or more (1 knot = 1.852 Km/h)

2. **Low-level wind shear** can be particularly hazardous for remote pilots, due to the proximity of the UAV to the ground. Wind shear can cause violent updrafts and downdrafts, and due to increased wind speed, it can push the aircraft around horizontally with sudden, unforeseen force.

3. Wind shear is commonly associated with passing frontal systems, thunderstorms, and temperature inversions with strong upper level winds (greater that 25 knots).

4. **Microburst** is one type of wind shear. It is associated with convective precipitation, which is shorter and more intense. A microburst typically occurs in a space of less than one mile horizontally and within 1000 feet vertically for about 15 mn. It can produce severe downdrafts of up to 6000 feet per mn (fpm). It can also produce a hazardous wind direction change of 45 degrees or more, in a matter of seconds.

5. Microbursts are often difficult to detect because they occur in relatively confined areas Many airports have wind shear alert systems to warn pilots. This system is called low-level wind shear alert system (LLWAS)

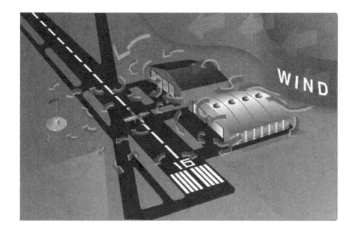

FIGURE 4.11 Man-made obstructions

6. Wind shear is particularly important when flying in and around thunderstorms and frontal systems, and whenever wind speet at 2000 to 4000 feet AGL is 25k nots or more.

7. Surface weather maps provide information about fronts, areas of high and low pressure, and surface winds and pressures for each station.

Isobars:

1. Every physical process of weather is accompanied by a heat exchange.

2. The stability of the atmosphere correlates with its ability to resist vertical motion. A stable atmosphere makes vertical moment of air difficult. An unstable atmosphere allows an upward or downward disturbance to grow on a vertical (or convective current).

3. Instability can lead to significant turbulence, extensive vertical clouds and severe weather.

Adiabatic heating and cooling:

1. When air rises, it expands and cools, and when descends, it compresses and the temperature increases. This temperature change, which takes place in all upward and downward moving air, is known as **adiabatic hearing and cooling** (no heat transfer).

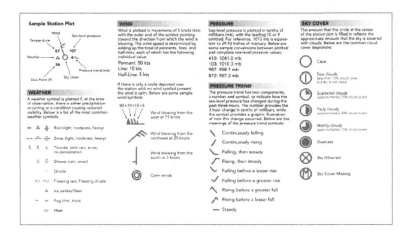

FIGURE 4.12   Weather chart

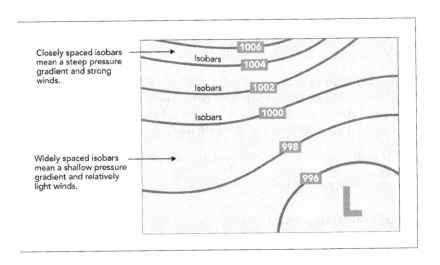

FIGURE 4.13   Isobars

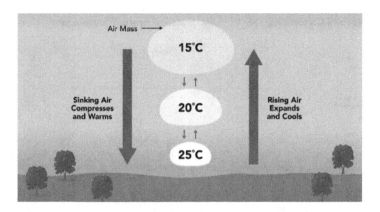

FIGURE 4.14 Adiabatic heating and cooling

2. As the air increases in altitude, the rate at which the temperature decreases is referred to as its lapse rate. As air ascends through the atmosphere, the lapse rate is 2 degrees Celsius per 1000 feet in unsaturated air.

3. This lapse rate helps in determining the stability of the atmosphere. The bigger gap between the existing lapse rate and the nominal one, the more unstable the atmosphere.

4. The combination of temperature and moisture determine the stability of the air and the resulting weather. Cool, dry air is very stable and resists vertical movement, which leads to good and generally clear weather. Stratiform clouds may be present in this case.

5. The greatest instability occurs when the air is warm and moist. Turbulence and shower precipitation are prevalent.

6. Typically thunderstorms appear on a daily basis in these regions due to the instability of the surrounding air.

Temperature Inversion:

1. As air rises and expands in the atmosphere, the temperature decreases. However, an atmospheric anomaly can occur called a temperature inversion where the opposite happens.

2. The temperature of the air increases with altitude to a certain point called the top of inversion.

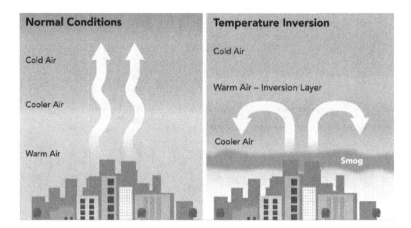

FIGURE 4.15 Temperature inversion

3. The air at the top of the inversion layer keeps weather and pollutants trapped below. If the relative humidity of the air is high, it can contribute to the formation of clouds, fog, haze or smoke, resulting in diminished visibility in the inversion layer.

4. Surface based temperature inversion occurs on clear, cool nights when the air close to the ground is cooled by the lowering temperature of the ground.

5. The air with a few hundred feet of the surface becomes cooler than the air above it.

Moisture and temperature:

1. By nature, the atmosphere contains moisture in the form of water vapor. The amount of moisture present in the atmosphere is dependent upon the temperature of the air. Every 10 degrees Celsius increase doubles the amount of moisture the air can hold. Conversely, a decrease of 10 degrees cuts the capacity in half.

2. Water is present in the atmosphere in three states: liquid, solid, and gaseous. All three forms can readily change to another, and are all present within the temperature ranges of the atmosphere. As water changes from one state to another, an exchange of heat takes place. These changes occur through the processes of evaporation, sublimation, condensation, deposition, melting and freezing. The only ways water vapor is added into the atmosphere is through evaporation and sublimation. Evaporation is the changing of liquid water to water vapor.

Sublimation is the changing of ice directly to water vapor, completely bypassing the liquid stage.

3. Relative humidity: Humidity refers to the amount of water vapor present in the atmosphere at a given time. Relative humidity is the actual amount of moisture in the air compared to the total amount of moisture the air could hold at that temperature. For example, if the current relative humidity is 55 percent, the air is holding 55 percent of the total amount of moisture that are capable of holding at that temperature and pressure.

4. Temperature/Dew point relationship: the dew point, given in degrees, is the temperature at which the air can hold no more moisture; as moist, unstable air rises, clouds often form at the altitude where temperature and dew point reach the same value. At this point, the air is completely saturated, and moisture begins to condense out of the air in the form of fog, dew, frost, clouds, rain, hail or snow. Typically, when the temperature and the dew point converge, there is fog.

UAV operation in freezing weather:

1. The pilot can be greatly affected by the cold. Numb fingers can be a very bad thing when the feel of the controls on the remote is so important. With a numb thumb one could easily bump the throttle down and not feel it. Batteries can also be greatly affected by the cold?

2. Air masses: When air masses stagnate in or move really slowly over an area with uniform temperature and moisture characteristics on a day-to-day basis, the air mass takes on those temperature and moisture characteristics. This happens in places like polar regions, tropical oceans and dry deserts. These air masses are categorized based on temperature characteristics (polar or tropical) and moisture content (maritime or continental).

3. A front is the boundary layer between two different air masses or areas of pressure. An approaching front of any type always means that weather changes are imminent. Within a front (warm or cold), there will always be a change in the wind direction (Shifting wind) and in the temperature. While warm fronts bring low ceilings, poor visibility, and rain, cold fronts can be characterized by its shifting wind conditions and violent weather.

4. Thunderstorms are produced by cumulonimbus clouds. They form when there is sufficient water vapor or moisture, an unstable lapse rate and an initial upward boost to start the process (heat). Generally, the most severe thunderstorm conditions are destructive winds, tornadoes, heavy hail, and a like. **Do not operate an UAV within 20 nautical miles of a thunderstorm since hail may fall for miles outside of the clouds.**

5. Tornadoes: Any cloud connected to a severe thunderstorm cloud could spawn tornadic activity, even if it is miles away from the main thunderstorm cloud.

6. Icing is bad for aircraft. Airframe icing would be when ice builds up on the UAV and it can no longer sustain flight and the aerodynamic qualities of the propellers change. The worst condition is freezing rain.

7. Hail: even small hailstones can damage the UAV.

8. Fog: It is not advisable to operate a UAV in fog conditions. It is tougher to maintain a direct line-of-sight of the UAV.

9. Ceiling and visibility: current ceiling information is calculated by the temperature and the dew point and is reported by the aviation routine weather report (METAR) and automated weather stations of various types. Visibility refers to the greatest horizontal distance at which prominent objects can be viewed with the eye. It is also reported in METAR.

Weather considerations for UAVs:

1. Weather is the biggest external factor that affects the performance of the UAV.

2. Manned aviation pilots have access to a number of weather resources, publications and tools to assist them in evaluating weather risks and how weather might affect their mission (Flight Services, Sirius XM weather, NOAA, National Weather Service etc.). These pilots also receive significant training on how to read, understand and use weather information during their training. There are three key differences between manned and unmanned aviation that should be considered when discussingweather for drones:

   (a) Unmanned missions are typically much shorter than their manned counterparts. This has the significant advantage of allowing operators to focus most of their pre-flight on current weather observations as opposed to forecasts.

   (b) Limited ability to divert, abort or execute an emergency landing in the event that unexpected weather conditions occur in-flight. In traditional aviation, the ability to safely execute a contigency is directly correlated the the pilots training and skills. In unmanned aviation, to safely execute a contingency is the responsibility of the UAV autopilot. The autopilot function provides self-control of the UAV during take-off, landing and desired flight phases when a UAV operator does not have control on the UAV. Using autopilot reduces the error ratio of a UAV operator during two critical times:

landing and take-off. This highlights the importance of thorough flight planning which includes detailed weather considerations.

(c) Unmanned aircraft are a lot more expendable than their manned counterparts in critical weather conditions, this presents decision-making challenges in case people, or property are endangered by the flight.

3. UAV operators do not go through the same amount of training than aviation pilots. UAV weather inputs are: MDCRS, TAMDAR, UAV weather down-link.

4. Weather severity

(a) **Moderate** with hazards such as reduced visibility, weather types: fog, haze, glare, cloud cover

(b) **Adverse** with hazards such as loss of communication, loss of control, loss of command, diminished aerodynamic performance, reduced operator effectiveness; weather types wind and turbulence, rain, solar storms, temperature and humidity, snow and ice.

(c) **severe** with hazards such as severe damage to loss of aircraft, unacceptable risk to operator and personnel, weather types such as lighting, hail, tornadoes, hurricanes.

Sources of weather:

1. **Density Altitude**: air gets thinner with altitude and heat; manned aviation uses the concept of density altitude to predict the performance of aircraft based on altitude, non-standard pressure and temperature. Flying at 6000 feet in the mountains or on a 35 degrees summer day will greatly decrease the ability of the multicopter propellers to generate lift, which will affect maximum allowable payload and flight time.

(a) The density of air is defined by both the pressure altitude and ambient temperature and can have a significant effect on the aircraft's performance. When the density altitude is high, aircraft performance is reduced. Higher density altitude occurs at higher elevations, lower atmospheric pressures, higher temperatures, higher humidity. Higher density altitude means thinner air and with thinner air, reduced aircraft performance. Lower density altitude means thicker, denser air and stronger aircraft performance.

(b) Because when the density altitude is high, the air is less dense, and the propellers become less efficient in thin air. As the density altitude increases, the performance of the UA decreases. This is VERY important in a mountainous or other high-elevation environment. Taking off to 200 feet above-ground-level (AGL) is different at sea level than it is in the mountains.

2. **Temperature**: As the temperature increases, the air molecules spread out. the propellers or motors don't have as much air to grab on to. not only do high temperatures reduce the performance of the UAV because of density altitude, low temperatures also reduce the efficiency of the LiPo batteries. At low temperatures, battery voltage can drop below the cut-off of the ESCs (Electronic Speed Control) which would cut-off the motors. Batteries also discharge faster reducing flight time.

3. Both hot and cold environments will cause adverse reactions for various components in the UAV, resulting in reduced flight performance. In hotter environments the motors will need to work harder to generate more lift, which causes shorter flight times; and the generated heat could potentially overheat the electronics and/or melt the wired connections in some instances. Allowing for longer downtimes between flights gives the electronics time to cool down to a more stable temperature before taking it up again. In colder environments the efficiency of the LiPo battery decreases. There is also a higher chance of the battery dropping below the critical voltage that will cut off the ESC's/motors.

4. **Visibility**: affects how well the operator can see his UAV in the case of line-of-sight operations, it also affects any camera-based navigation features of the UAV such as the vision positioning system.

5. **Humidity and moisture**: moisture in the form of fog, mist or rain can short UAV electronics that are not well protected. Relative humidity, when too close to 100 percent is an early warning of moisture. If the weather is not pleasant enough for the human operator to stand outside during the duration of the flight, then a visual-line-of-sight mission should be postponed.

6. **Icing**: visible moisture and freezing temperature can cause structural icing on propeller blades which can significantly reduce their ability to generate lift. Icing is one of the top killers of manned aviation and could very well become a top UAV killer as well with commercial operators forced to push safe weather boundaries.

7. In summary, there are many weather hazards that UAV operators need to be aware of and pay attention to.

8. **Take-Off**: it is essential that operators have accurate, on-demand reporting of wind-speed and direction, atmospheric pressure, humidity and visibility in the take-off area. Additionally, reporting of cloud cover and precipitation can help operators determine if conditions are favorable for a safe take-off. Depending on the climate, extreme weather during take-off conditions, such as rain, snow and dust storms can inhibit the course of a UAV. Real-time weather data acts as the eyes and ears of a pilot responsible for a plane remotely.

9. **In-Flight**: many UAVs often fly at lower altitudes, so they are directly affected by the weather. Accurate information about precipitation, cloud height and depth, and humidity can help operators make decisions about route planning and alterations, as well as fuel management. A common problem for UAVs, especially during longer flights, is ice accumulation on the wings and body of the vehicle. Operators and weather officers can use real-time reporting as well as model forecast data to determine the safety of a UAV based on current and future weather conditions.

10. **Safe Landing**: operators need accurate information on wind speed and direction (especially runway cross-winds), atmospheric pressure, temperature and humidity (used to calculate density altitude), and precipitation in the landing area. Hazardous weather conditions, such as freezing rain and thunderstorms, may be detrimental to a UAV landing if pilots are misinformed. Thunderstorm data measured by tactical lightning detectors indicate the presence of lightning strikes in the area. With accurate weather reporting, pilots can determine which approach can be used, and even in some cases whether an approach should be attempted or an alternate landing base is required.

11. **Clouds**: To UAVs, the cumulonimbus cloud is the most dangerous. It appears individually or in groups and is known either as an air mass or orographic thunderstorm. Heating of the air near the Earth's surface creates an air mass thunderstorm; the upslope motion of air in the mountainous regions causes orographic thunderstorms. Cumulonimbus clouds that form in continuous line are nonfrontal bands of thunderstorms or squall lines. Since raising air currents cause cumulonimbus clouds, they are extremely turbulent and pose a significant hazard to flight safety.

12. For example, if a small UAV enters a thunderstorm, the small UAV could experience updrafts and downdrafts that exceed 3000 fpm (feet per minute). In addition, thunderstorms can produce large hailstones, damaging lightning, tornadoes, and large quantities of water, all of which are potentially hazardous to an aircraft.

13. **Stability of an air mass** determines its typical weather characteristics. When one type of air mass overlies another, conditions change with height. Characteristics typical of an unstable and stable air mass are as follows:

    (a) stable air: stratiform clouds and fog, continuous precipitation, smooth air, fair to poor visibility in haze and smoke

    (b) unstable air: cumuliform clouds, showery precipitation, rough air (turbulence), good visibility (except in blowing obstructions).

14. Internet weather briefing and sources of weather available for flight planning purposes

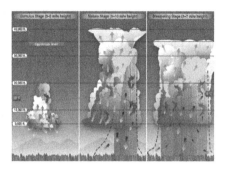

FIGURE 4.16 Life cycle of a thunderstorm

15. Aviation routine weather reports (METAR)

16. Terminal aerodrone forecasts (TAF)

17. Weather charts

18. Automated surface observing systems (ASOS) and automated weather observing systems (AWOS)

19. life cycle of a thunderstorm

4.4 AVIATION WEATHER INFORMATION SOURCES

Aeronautical advisory communications station (UNICOM) and associated communication procedures used by manned aircraft pilots: An airport may have a full or part-time tower or flight service station (FSS) located on the airport, a full or part-time universal communications (UNICOM) station or no aeronautical station at all. There are 3 ways for pilots to communicate their intention and obtain airport/traffic information when operating at an airport that does not have an operating tower: by communicating with an FSS, a UNICOM operator, or by making a self-announce broadcast.

Definition 44 *Automated surface observation system (ASOS) is a Weather reporting system that provides surface observations up to the minute via digitized voice broadcasts and printed reports.*

Definition 45 *Automatic terminal information service (ATIS) is a continuous broadcast of recorded aeronautical information of busier airports. Contains essential information such as weather information, active runways, available approaches and NOTAM.*

Definition 46 *Notices to airmen (NOTAM) are issued when aeronautical information could affect a pilot's decision to make a flight.*

Definition 47 *Automated weather observation system (AWOS) is a Weather reporting system that consists of various sensors, a processor, a computer-generated voice subsystem and a transmitter to broadcast weather data on a minute-by-minute basis.*

Many airports are now providing completely automated weather, radio check capability and airport advisory information on an automated UNICOM system. These systems offer a variety of features, typically selectable by microphone clicks, on the UNICOM frequency.

Definition 48 *Aviation routine weather reports (AWS) is a meteorological aerodrome report reporting observation of current surface weather reported in a standard international format. Issued hourly unless significant weather changes have occured.*

Automatic terminal information services (ATIS) Aircraft call signs and registration numbers: all registered aircraft will have a unique registration number, which would be pronounced in aviation terms by use fo the phonetic alphabet

   Phonetic alphabet Phraseology: altitudes, directions, speed and time

   The aeronautical information in a NOTAM (notices to airmen) is time-critical and either a temporary nature or not sufficiently known in advance to permit publication on aeronautical charts or in other operational publications. NOTAMs are issued when there is aeronautical information that could affect a pilot's decision to make a flight. It includes such information as airport or aerodrome primary runway closures, taxiways, ramps, obstructions, communications, airspace and changes in the status of navigational aids, ...

   A remote pilot is not expected to communicate with other aircraft in the vicinity of an airport and should not do so unless there is an emergency situation.

4.4.1   Hazards and in-flight weather conditions

While drones are proving to be extremely useful tools for data collection amongst a number of various industries, there are many current restrictions on the weather conditions in which drones are able to safely operate, making the link between weather and drone deployment a very important factor in UAV operations. Amidst the importance of climate, it is imperative to examine the possibility and impact of varying weather conditions that occur while preparing to utilise a commercial drone. Notable ways to track and prepare for this are through pre-planned mapping and collection of climate information. With that in mind, advanced weather data plays a critical part in establishing ideal flight times when utilizing drone technology.

   While of course precipitation is what first comes to mind, wind velocities are also a significant part of deploying uniform drone-based missions and

FIGURE 4.17 ICAO phonetic alphabet

therefore should be factored in the project planning and deployment phases. This also means that there is a demand for low-altitude wind acceleration data. Organizations in, oil and gas, government, energy, and construction will leverage high-level weather data analytics for safe site surveying, which allows for a better response to accidents and dangers.

While pre-flight planning for various conditions is a large part of successful drone deployment, information gathered during flight can also be extremely useful. Post flight, the data gathered in flight can be matched with the pre-flight weather data and can aid users in understanding how the weather has reshaped/affected areas over time. As an example, annual bridge inspections using drones can overlay weather data to recognize the effect of weather on the strength of the bridge's infrastructure year to year. Over time, through analysing data of advanced weather visualization, and utilizing drones to capture infrastructure inspection data, this technology has the potential to significantly advance analytics processes and improve the overall operations.

The terrain in most mountainous areas is highly variable. Valleys can be wide with gentle sweeping turns or very narrow with abrupt changes in direction or dead ends commonly referred to as box or blind canyons. Ridge heights can often exceed 10,000' and the rate of change in terrain elevation can vary from gentle slopes to near vertical cliffs several thousand feet in height. Terrain awareness is a critical component of safely flying in mountainous areas.

Wind is almost always a factor when operating in mountainous terrain. Dependant upon the direction and speed of the wind, its interaction with the terrain can lead to updrafts, downdrafts and turbulence which may exceed aircraft limitations or performance capability. Mountain waves are associated with strong winds blowing perpendicular to the mountain range and are generally considered a mid to high altitude risk. However, for an aircraft contour flying in the mountains, winds well below the speed required to generate mountain waves can result in very hazardous clear air turbulence conditions.

Mountain flying requires the ability to maintain good VFR conditions. Penetrating a weather front or localized phenomena such as upslope or orographic wind, Fhn Wind and dry microburst can all lead to deteriorating weather.

It is critical to understand that the threats of wind, weather, lighting, aircraft performance and situational awareness may occur in combination with one another and will always be associated with the principal threat of terrain. Shaded areas can mask the presence of a hill or outcropping that does not conform to the general slope of the rest of the valley creating a CFIT hazard. This situation is most likely to occur when flying towards the sun due to the increased glare and the additional contrast between shaded and non shaded terrain that results.

CHAPTER 5

Flight Control

5.1 INTRODUCTION

Avionics is for Aviation Electronics. This is the set of all electronic and electromechanical systems and subsystems (hardware and software) installed in an aircraft or attached to it. This includes communications, navigation and the display and management of multiple systems. UAV avionics, like those of traditional aircraft, are in charge of implementing flight control and flight navigation. However, they should also ensure a desired level of autonomy and the control of the payload (if any). Navigation systems that operate on satellite signals, enhanced and synthetic vision that is completely constructed from electrical and infrared sensors, and aircraft performance controlled by digital electronics are examples.

A new generation of unmanned aerial vehicles (UAVs) is being developed to enhance monitoring of many kinds of systems. From tracking fires to monitoring traffic, these UAVs are making the most of the latest sensor technology in various ways. For example, infrared cameras can track missing people at night, while laser spectroscopy is used to monitor pollution in the air.

Having airborne sensors can significantly enhance the quality of data that is acquired by giving more flexibility to move around and faster response times. This is coupled with a move from remotely piloted aircraft to autonomous systems that need inertial navigation sensors, combining accelerometers and magnetometers with GPS systems. All of this requires more focus on the integration of sensor systems in an aerial application that is severely constrained in power and weight.

Navigation systems, a **Traffic Collision Avoidance System** (TCAS) box, transponders are all avionics already integrated into the UAV. However, the FAA is not ready yet for TCAS and that more traditional [Federal Aviation Regulations] FAR 91 type of equipment to be adopted yet for UAVs. But they are in a passive mode to understand what aircraft is around and how the technology works on a remotely piloted aircraft

Radio Technical Commission for Aeronautics (RTCA) Special Committee 228 is developing the Minimum Operational Performance Standards (MOPS) for sense and avoid. But there are technologies available today on a smaller scale that do provide sense-and-avoid capabilities. MASPS specify characteristics that are useful to designers, installers, manufacturers, service providers and users of systems intended for operational use within a defined airspace.

In addition to the flight control and navigation part, UAV require specific autonomy means. The autonomy requirement is the main difference between UAV and manned aircraft. Autonomy is the ability to operate without direct control from a ground operator.

5.2 ARCHITECTURE

Definition 49 *An architecture is the structure of components, their relationships, and the principles and guidelines governing their design and evolution over time*

Establishing the basic architecture is the first and the most fundamental challenge faced by the designer. The architecture must conform to the overall aircraft mission and design while ensuring that the avionics system meets its performance requirements. These architectures rely on the data buses for intra and intersystem communications. Avionics Systems Control is of all of the software in the system.

Establishing the basic architecture is the first and the most fundamental challenge faced by the designer. The architecture must conform to the overall aircraft mission and design while ensuring that the avionics system meets its performance requirements. These architectures rely on the data buses for intra and intersystem communications. The optimum architecture can only be selected after a series of exhaustive design tradeoffs that address the evaluation factors.

The central computing complex is connected to other subsystems and sensors through analog, digital, synchronization and other interfaces. When interfacing with computer a variety of different transmission methods , some of which required signal conversion (A/D) when interfacing with computer.

The main challenge encountered by UAV avionics is to safely operate on-board two types of computation: flight control/navigation and flight planning/re-planning, including the reconfiguration of the avionics itself in case of mission re-planning. In order to respond to this challenge, the first generation of UAV avionics architectures were divided into three loosely coupled physical parts. The first one is dedicated to navigation and flight control; the second one offers sensors, hardware and software components ensuring the desired level of autonomy; while the third part controls the payload of the UAV. The second and third parts are generally specific to the operational role that the UAV is supposed to carry out. In most cases, each part is implemented by a monolithic dedicated platform composed of the simplest possible processor with its own resources (memory and communication bus). However, these first architectures based on the principle of separation of concerns have many limitations.

Firstly, safety is guaranteed in the final degraded mode (i.e. the mode in which the automatic flight control part is lost) by the ability to pilot the vehicle from the ground. As stated above, it assumes safe onboard mechanisms to commute from the automatic flight mode to the remote-controlled flight, a data-link between the vehicle and the group operator, which guarantees that orders and data are transmitted in real-time (in less than 10 or 100 milliseconds for flight control orders) and, a ground infrastructure able to present to the human operator the complete situation of the vehicle (position, speed, attitude, obstacles in front of the vehicle, etc.). Such requirements are not consistent with complex and faraway missions, or with missions in a hostile environment. In that case, contrarily to manned aircraft, the UAV must ensure its own safety without waiting for backup orders sent by a human pilot. However, first generation UAV avionics architectures do not offer the appropriate safety level. This is their first limitation. Secondly, the continual development of UAV applications results in an ever-increasing demand on embedded algorithms. On board computational resources must meet this demand, while at the same time providing robustness, reliability and a small footprint, both in physical size, mass and power consumption.

Initially running on different processors, the idea is to place these functions on processing modules partitioned with respect to space (resource partitioning) and time (temporal partitioning).

1. Resource partitioning. A processing module is divided into partitions. Each partition is seen as a virtual processing module. It is allocated a set of private spatial resources (memory, nonvolatile memory, I/O resources, etc.) in a static manner. Low-level mechanisms (at the operating system level) provide protection for partition data against any modification from the other partitions. They monitor function activity with reference to allowed resources, which are statically allocated through configuration tables.

2. Temporal partitioning. Each function is allocated a partition. The scheduling of partitions on each module is defined off-line by a periodic sequence of slots, statically organized in a time-frame. Each partition is allocated a time slot for execution. At the end of this time slot, the partition is suspended and execution is given to the next partition (running another function). Thus, each function is periodically executed at fixed times.

Utilizing **Controller Area Network** (CAN) in a UAV provides a versatile communications system which allows multiple avionics subsystems to communicate simultaneously between each other, and with various sensors and actuators. A properly considered CAN setup can include redundant sensors or actuators which communicate with each other and resolve contention issues transparently without any input from the autopilot. This can all be achieved while at the same time reducing the I/O burden on avionics systems because all CAN devices are connected to a multi-drop bus topology. CAN communication features hardware bus arbitration, device addressing, message checksums, and automatic retransmission of corrupted messages. Designed for the automotive industry, where reliability under all situations is vital, CAN is a robust communication standard, which is very suitable for UAV applications.

5.3 AUTO PILOT

A flight controller is an integrated circuit made up of a microprocessor, sensors and input/output pins.Certain parameters must be set in a software program, and once complete, that configuration is then uploaded to board. The drone-building community has created many software and hardware projects under open licenses that allow to build, repair, customize, and experiment with your own drone, or to supplement the use of drones in some other way. Some of the most renowned are:

1. **Ardupilot** is one of the most advanced open source autopilot for use by both professionals and hobbyist. It supports multi-copters, planes, and helicopters.

2. **Paparazzi UAV** is a project that combines both the software and hardware needed to build and fly an open source vehicle, released under open licenses. Its primary focus is autonomous flight, and is designed to be portable to allow operators to take their devices into the field easily and program their flights across a series of waypoints. Source and releases to the software components can be found on GitHub, and tutorials for adapting it to off-the-shelf or custom-built hardware can be found on the project's wiki. It is flexible enough to work with various types of flying vehicles. The autopilot software controls all avionics devices algorithms for guidance, navigation and control.

3. **Dronecode/PX4** is a Linux Foundation-sponsored project working to build a common open source platform for UAV development. They continue to host a number of different developer resources, including GitHub repositories of several useful tools.

4. **OpenDroneMap** takes aerial imagery and processes it into point clouds, digital surface and elevation models, or orthorectify the imagery (in essence, line up the imagery to a known coordinate system for further analysis).

FIGURE 5.1   Flight-controller

This is definitely an incomplete list of projects as new projects are created.

Main processor: This is the central unit that runs the autopilot firmware and performs all the calculations. Most flight controllers have 32 bit processors which are more powerful that than 8bit systems, but there are still a few popular 8 bit autopilot platforms such as ardupilot mega.

1. **8051 versus AVR versus PIC versus ARM**: These microcontroller families form the basis of most current flight controllers. Arduino is AVR based and MultiWii is the preferred code. Microchip is the primary manufacturer of PIC chips. ARM uses 16/32-bit architecture, whereas AVR and PIC tends to use 8/16-bit. As single board computers become less and less expensive, a new generation of flight controllers can run full operating systems, such as Linux or Android.

2. **Central processing unit** (CPU): is $8, 16, 32, 64$-bit and a reference to the size of the primary registers in a CPU. Microprocessors can only process a set number of bits in memory at a time. The more bits a micro-controller can handle, the more accurate the processing will be.

3. **Operating frequency**: The frequency at which the main processor operates, Hertz. This is also referred to as the clock rate. The higher the operating frequency, the faster it can process data.

4. **Program Memory/Flash** is essentially where the main code is stored. The greater the memory, the more information it can store. Memory is also useful when storing in-flight data such as GPS coordinates, flight plans, automated camera movement. The code loaded to the flash memory remains on the chip even if it power is cut.

5. **SRAM**: Static Random-Access Memory is the space on the chip, which is used when making calculations. The data stored in RAM is lost when power is cut. The higher the RAM, the more information will be available for calculations at any given time.

6. **EEPROM**: Electrically Erasable Programmable Read-Only Memory is used to store information which does not change in flight, such as settings, unlike data stored in SRAM which can relate to sensor data.

7. **Additional I/O Pins**: on a flight controller, some are used by the sensors, others for communication and some may remain for general input and output.

8. **A/D analog to digital converter**: for the sensors used on-board output analog voltage is normally 0–3.3V or 0–5V, the analog to digital converter needs to translate these readings into digital data. Just like the CPU, the number of bits which can be processed by the A/D determines the maximum accuracy. Related to this is the frequency at which the microprocessor can read the data to try to ensure no information is lost. The higher the A/D conversion, the more accurate the readings will be, but it is important that the processor can handle the rate at which the information is being sent.

Power: There are often two voltage ranges described in the specificiation sheet of a flight controller, the first being the voltage input range of the flight controller itself (most operate at 5V nominal), and the second being the voltage input range of the main microprocessor's logic (ex 3.3V or 5V).

5.3.1 Control station

It is the control center of the UAV. Mission planning, mission execution and data manipulation can be performed and most importantly, UAV is operated/remotely piloted from the control station.The control station can be mobile or stationary. Choosing the equipment and control and monitor tools is very important for the crew members. In planning and conducting flight paths, all entities operating UAS should select and adhere to those tracks and altitudes that completely minimize the possibility of UAS failing into congested areas in the event of electronic or material malfunction that could lead to loss of control. Flight levels (FL) should be determined as a part of route planning. Ground traffic management plans are required for all activities in or around a roadway that may affect operating conditions of the roadway.

UAS are especially sensitive to wind conditions while at altitude. When planning for recurring missions or surveys, historical data should be part of scheduling. Weather patterns and trends can, to a certain degree, be predicted from a weather analysis. Anenometer should be considered a critical part of the control station equipment, which should possess an instrument to measure wind speed.

The software used on certain flight controllers may have additional features which are not available on others:

1. **Autonomous waypoint navigation** allows to set GPS waypoints which the UAV will follow autonomously

2. **Orbiting** i.e. moving around a fixed GPS coordinate with the front of the UAV always pointed towards the coordinate (useful for filming)

3. **Follow me** feature can be GPS based (for example tracking the GPS coordinates of a smartphone)

4. **3D imaging**: Most 3D imaging is done after a flight using images captured during the flight and GPS data

5. **Open source** products generally allow advanced users to modify the code to suit their specific needs.

Communication

Radio Control (RC): communication involves a hand-held RC transmitter and RC receiver. A minimum four channels are associated with:

1. **Pitch** (which translates to forward / backward motion)

2. **Elevation** (closer to or farther away from the ground)

3. **Yaw** (rotating clockwise or counter-clockwise)

4. **Roll** (to strafe left and right)

5. **Arming or disarming** the motors

6. **Gimbal controls** (pan up or down, rotate clockwise or counter-clockwise, zoom)

7. **Change flight modes** (acrobatic mode, stable mode etc)

8. **Activate or deploy** a payload, parachute, buzzer or other device

Most pilots prefer handheld control. On its own, the receiver simply relays the values input into the controller, and as such, cannot control a UAV. The receiver must be connected to the flight controller, which needs to be programmed to receive RC signals.

Definition 50 *Automatic flight control system (AFCS) can be defined as the process of manipulating the inputs to a dynamical system to obtain a desired effect on its outputs without a human in the control loop. For UAS the design of AFCS consists of synthesizing algorithms or control laws that compute inputs for aircraft actuators (aileron, elevator, rotors ...) to produce torques and forces that act on the vehicle in controlling its 3D motion (position, orientation and their time derivatives). AFCS or autopilot is thus the integrated software and hardware that serve the control function as defined.*

5.4 SENSORS DEDICATED TO THE FLIGHT CONTROLLER

Without a pilot on-board, the success of UAV flights depends heavily on accurate information and reporting. In terms of hardware, a flight controller is essentially a normal programmable microcontroller, but has specific sensors onboard. At a bare minimum, a flight controller will include a three axis gyroscope, but as such will not be able to auto-level. Not all flight controllers will include all of the sensors below and may include a combination thereof.

5.4.1 Inertial navigation system

An inertial navigation system is a navigation aid that uses motion sensors to continuously track the position, orientation, and velocity (direction and speed of movement) of a vehicle without the need for external references. Initial position and velocity must be provided before computing its own position and velocity by integrating information from sensors. Rate gyros measure the components of inertial angular rate of the aircraft in the sensitive direction of the instrument.

Completely self-contained navigation system capable of providing great circle tracks over random routes without reference to external information sources.

1. The most complex and expensive flight-deck navigation system currently in use.

2. Still the navigation system of choice for many operations.

3. Accurate, reliable, not susceptible to signal jamming or erroneous signal transmission.

4. Extremely simple in concept, extremely complicated in execution.

5. Sometimes described as a very accurate dead-reckoning system.

5.4.1.1 Fundamentals

Inertia Measurement Unit (IMU): is essentially a small board which contains both an accelerometer and gyroscope (normally these are multi-axis). Most contain a three axis accelerometer and a three-axis gyroscpe, and others may contain additional sensors, such as a three axis magnetometer, providing a total of 9 axes of measurement.

Accelerometer measures linear acceleration in up to three axes X, Y and Z. The units are normally in gravity (g), which is 9.81 meters per square second. The output of an accelerometer can be integrated twice to give a position, though because of losses in the output, it is subject to drift. A very important characteristic of three axis accelerometers is that they detect gravity, and as such, can know which direction is "down". This plays a major role in allowing multi-rotor aircraft to stay stable. The accelerometer should be mounted to the flight controller so that the linear axes line up with the main axes of the UAV.

Linear accelerometers are used to measure the components of aircraft linear acceleration minus the components of gravity in its sensitive direction. Newton's Law for the aircraft is

$$F = ma = F_{aero} + F_{thrust} + mg \tag{5.1}$$

Accelerometer measures

$$a - g = (F_{aero} + F_{thrust})/m = specificforce \tag{5.2}$$

Gyroscope measures the rate of angular change in up to three angular axes. The units are often degrees per second. A gyroscope does not measure absolute angles directly, but angular velocity, it is subject to drift. The output of the actual gyroscope tends to be analog or I2C. The gyroscope should be mounted so that its rotational axes line up with the axes of the UAV.

Starts from a known point, advances estimated position based on speed, direction and time.

1. Uses acceleration (changes in speed and direction) in place of speed itself.

2. Movement detected by accelerometers mounted on a stable platform (Stabilized gyroscopically).

3. Accelerometers are like pendulums but more sophisticated, using sliding shutters with frictionless bearings and now solid state technology. Can detect velocity changes to 1000 of a G force.

4. This is the basic principal of INS.

5. Most critical element is platform stability.

6. Gyros are of primary importance.

7. Accelerometer technology fairly static; advances now are mostly in gyro technology, especially Ring Laser Gyros.

5.4.1.2 INS drift

Since each new position is a function of the last position, INS is a relative system. Any initial entry error remains as a constant but subsequent errors are cumulative and increase over time. Total of errors is called "Drift" measured in NM/hour. 2 NM/Hour is historical industry norm. Drift can be corrected by updating: reentering aircraft position over a known fix (navaid or visual checkpoint). Another way to provide redundancy is by adding a complimentary system, such as GPS. This system can be used to update the INS. GPS can provide aiding to an INS by providing an independent measurement of x, y, and z. Furthermore, certain GPS implementation can provide velocity aiding by providing independent measurements of V_x, V_y and V_z. A Kalman filter is often used to help blend the GPS measurements with the INS outputs in an optimal way. INS gives accurate estimates of aircraft orientation. GPS provides accurate estimates of aircraft position. INS solutions are generally computed 100 times per second. GPS solutions are computed once per second. GPS in subject to jamming, INS is not. Combining GPS and INS provides accurate and robust determination of both translational and rotational motion of the aircraft. Both translational and rotational motion are required to locate targets on the ground from the drone.

INS has the advantage of integration of data, however, resulting in long-wavelength errors. GPS has low data output rate in receivers, it is difficult to maintain accuracy at the centimeter level resulting in short-wavelength errors. Their benefits when coupled are precise continuous positioning of a moving platform as INS complements GPS, and aids in positioning solution in events of cycle slips and signal losses.

Single blended navigation solution from pseudorange, pseudorange rate, accelerations, gyro measurements gives more accurate solution than loosely coupled system.

Tightly integrated system continues to extract info from GNSS receiver even when fewer than 4 satellites are visible. Unaided INS have troublesome errors that grow with time or oscillate with an 84 minute period. Various aiding schemes are often implemented to stabilize the INS errors. GPS aiding of INS is an effective means to stabilize INS position and velocity errors. Integrated INS and GPS systems are useful for determining both the position and orientation of an aircraft. Such systems are, therefore, helpful in locating of targets on the ground.

5.4.2 Compass / Magnetometer

An electronic magnetic compass is able to measure the Earth's magnetic field and used it to determine the UAV's compass direction (with respect to magnetic north). This sensor is almost always present if the system has GPS input and is available in one to three axes. Magnetometers point to the magnetic north. the magnetic north is constantly changing in location and strength. It even changes strength depending on the time of day! Magnetometers are not subject to drift. The readings will be consistent throughout the flight

Tables are published that correct from magnetic north to true north. The tables need to be constantly republished because the magnetic north and the flux lines move around so much.

Remark 51 *The main difference between accelerometer and gyroscope vs magnetometer is that first two give only relative information. As both gyroscope and accelerometer give only accelerations values, calculation of pose and heading basing on their readings is incremental. That means that pose estimation error increases over time. Magenetometer can be used to correct these data.*

A magnometer lets the drone control its geographical heading. It is really the accelerometer that tells direction and, in this case, the direction is down-wards. This provides feedback to manipulate the drone's pitch-and-roll positions. A magnometer tells another direction—feedback used to manipulate the angular yaw position. A magnometer senses magnetic flux density across the pitch-, roll-, and yaw-axis. A system could use this data, combined with data from the accelerometer and gyroscope, to estimate the aircraft's orientation relative to the Magnetic North Pole and use this feedback to manipulate angular velocity such that a desired angular position is maintained in the yaw-axis.

5.4.3 Pressure / Barometer

Since atmospheric pressure changes, a pressure sensor can be used to give an accurate reading for the UAV's height. Most flight controllers take input from both the pressure sensor and GPS altitude to calculate a more accurate height above sea level. It is preferable to have the barometer covered with a piece of foam to diminish the effects of wind over the chip.

5.4.4 GPS

Global Positioning Systems use the signals sent by a number of satellites in orbit around the earth in order to determine their specific geographic location. A flight controller can either have onboard GPS or one, which is connected to it via a cable. The GPS antenna should not be confused with the GPS chip itself, and can look like a small black box or a normal duck antenna. In order to get an accurate GPS lock, the GPS chip should receive data from multiple satellites, and the more the better.

A GPS module measures your drones location by measuring how long a signal takes to travel from a satellite. A GPS modules is also able to give an estimation of your drones altitude. However, GPS modules are rather inaccurate and will only give you a position to within 5m. However, as discussed before, by combining measurements fro other sensors the flight controller can get a better picture of what the drone is doing. The main feature used by the GPS module is that you can autonomously fly your drone to way-points, so your drone can potentially fly on its own from takeoff to landing.

Since the GPS module needs to see the sky, it is often mounted on the top of your drone. When flying on a multi rotor most drone builders will use a GPS mast to mount the GPS module high up away fro all the other electronics to ensure it gets a solid GPS signal.

5.4.5 Distance

Distance sensors are being used more and more on UAVs since GPS coordinates and pressure sensors alone cannot tell how far away from the ground the UAV is (hill, mountain or building) or if it will hit an object. A downward-facing distance sensor might be based on ultrasonic, laser or lidar technology (infrared has issues in sunlight). Very few flight controllers include distance sensors as part of the standard package.

5.5 SENSE AND AVOID TECHNOLOGIES

Definition 52 *Detect and avoid technology is the capability of the drone to remain at safe distance from, and to avoid collisions with other aircraft.*

The RTCA document contains Phase 1 **Minimum Operational Performance Standards** (MOPS) for Detect and Avoid (DAA) systems used in Unmanned Aircraft Systems (UAS) transitioning to and from Class A or special use airspace (higher than 500' Above Ground Level (AGL¿¿. traversing Class D. E. or G airspace in the National Airspace System (NAS). It does not apply to small UAS (sUAS) operating in low-level environments (below 500") or other segmented areas. Likewise, it does not apply to operations in the Visual Flight Rules (VFR) traffic pattern of an aiiport. These standards specify DAA system characteristics that should be useftil for designers, manufacturers, installers and users of the equipment.

These Phase 1 MOPS focus on Unmanned Aircraft (UA) in order to fly in airspace normally frequented by commercial transport and general aviation aircraft. Aircraft operating in all classes of airspace van-from operation under Instrument Flight Rules (IFR) in Reduced Vertical Separation Minimum (RVSM) airspace to VFR operations with minimal onboard equipage. The technology needed to detect this range of aircraft as defined in these Phase 1 MOPS at sufficient distance to prevent the nsk of collision may limit the size of the UA in which tins equipment can be integrated. The UAS will need to cany relatively large and length-power sensor systems, which could weigh 200 pounds or more. Therefore, these MOPS are unlikely to be applicable to smaller size UAS, but such aircraft are not prohibited from installing equipment that meet the standard and have a need to transit to Class A airspace. Future revisions of this document are expected to address other operational scenanos and sensors better suited to smaller UAS needs, as well as other DAA architectures, including ground-based sensors.

Sensors dedicated to the mission can be optical (high-definition optical imaging, infrared (IR)/enhanced IR), chemical/ radiological/ toxicity specific sensors, atmospheric (temperature/pressure/humidity, wind direction/speed, turbulence/ride quality).

Sense and avoid capability is to detect ground or flying obstacles that determine a potential threat of collision in the immediate future and to provide adequate maneuvers in order to prevent the threat itself. This capability can be integrated on-board the UAV by providing a specific setting composed by a series of sensors and systems with relevant integration and computing units. Two types of on-board sources of information can be used to assess a collision threat as:

1. Cooperative sources of information, i.e. performing, broadcast of aircraft status information in terms of position, velocity and intent, such as automatic dependent surveillance broadcast (ADS-B). By collecting data from these external sources, each aircraft is capable of assessing

the status of surrounding traffic and to check if any collision threat has been issued.

2. Non-cooperative approach of information, i.e. sensors that collect physical data by scanning a proper field of the UAV environment. The most commonly adopted sensors include electro-optical sensors and radars.

A collision threat is defined when two aircraft fly closer than a safety distance S. Prediction of a collision in the near future can be defined as conflict detection or conflict declaration. This happens when the relative velocity vector between these two UAVs crosses the buble safety, i.e. a sphere that is centered on an instantaneous position of the intruder aircraft and has a radius equal to S. Within this framework, the two main quantities of interest are the time-to-go or time to the closest point of approach and the distance to the closest point of approach.

This is a system that will basically generate a predictive bubble in the ground-based pilot's display much like a cloud. It shows him a cloud, with vertical and horizontal dimensions predicting zones where, if they keep flying, they will end up colliding with another aircraft. So, basically, the UAV has to avoid those yellow clouds. They are predictive zones and, the closer the object, the larger that cloud is going to grow because it indicates a reduced possibility that the operator has to maneuver around that aircraft.

Remark 53 *The ASTM F-38 Committee has issued a published standard for DSA collision avoidance, that requires a UAV to be able to detect and avoid another airborne object within a range of + or −15 degrees in elevation and + or −110 degrees in azimuth and to be able to respond so that a collision is avoided by at least 500 ft. The 500 ft safety bubble is derived from the commonly accepted definition of what constitutes a Near Mid Air Collision. This gives airframe and avionic / DSA electronics manufacturers a target for certification.*

Search, detect and avoid technologies: TCAS, ADS-B, laser ranging, sonar, radar, electro-optical devices.

1. **Ground based sense and avoid** systems are means of detecting airborne traffic and providing the necessary intelligence to the UAS to mitigate the inability for a UAS pilot to directly see and avoid other aircraft or to provide an alternate means of compliance to see an avoid regulations.

2. **Airborne sense and avoid** is a capability on-board the UAV to perform both separation and collision avoidance functions to mitigate the inability for a UAS pilot to directly see and avoid other aircraft or to provide an alternate means of compliance to see and avoid regulations.

3. **Separation** maintains a specific minimum distance between an aircraft and another aircraft or terrain to avoid collisions, normally by requiring

aircraft to fly at set levels or level bands, on set routes or in certain directions, or by controlling an aircraft's speed.

Reliable and redundant safety system, parachute. Safety is the state in which the risk of harm to persons or property is reduced to, and maintained at or below, an acceptable level through a continuing process of hazard identification and risk management.

The requirement for a **collision avoidance** or sense and avoid (SAA) capability on-board the UAV has been identified as one of the most significant challenges facing the routine operation of UAS in the national airspace. Two architectures have been proposed for implementing the collision avoidance function on-board the UAV:

1. A system that is fully based on the integration of one or more non-cooperative information sources, such as radar and EO sensors.

2. A system that exploits information from mixed sources, such as cooperative and non-cooperative information sources.

As more than one sensor is used, appropriate data fusion techniques are adopted. One of the most known is the **Kalman filter**.

5.6   CAMERA AND VIDEO

The key challenges associated with the use of machine vision include

1. the need to properly account for unpredictable lighting and atmospheric conditions in an airborne environment.

2. compensating effectively for image jitter and sensor ego-motion

3. processing high-resolution image data on-board the UAV in real-time

4. extracting appropriate situational awareness and determining appropriate collision avoidance strategies.

One key aspect of inspections is not only the collection of appropriate images in the correct locations, but the catalogue and presentation of the data too. The most important applications are:

1. Land Survey Data: Development and planning; Flood risk analysis Volume calculations: Quarries / Stock Piles; Coastal erosion

2. Agricultural Survey Data: Crop health monitoring; Multispectral imaging; Species identification

3. Forestry Survey Data: Disease monitoring; Species counting

4. Inspections Survey Data:Building roof surveys; Bank / river course surveys; Road and rail network infrastructure

UAV-based data acquisition is another "tool in the toolbox" for many different industries professions. It does not solve every problem that exists for 3D measurement, but it does solve many of them more efficiently than was previously possible. Passive sensors (Imagery/video) : visible (RGB), near infrared (NIR), thermal (far infrared, multispectral, hyperspectral Active sensors: Lidar, Radar The most common and cheapest type of sensor is a high-resolution camera, which takes visible wavelength images (VIS). Several of these cameras can also take near-infrared images (NIR) when equipped with the right filters. The minimum image resolution required for agriculture applications is 12 megapixels. A camera with a wide-field, wide-angle, or fish-eye lens is needed as these lenses tend to capture more area in a single shot. About the image distortion, quality image processing software eliminates this during processing.

Questions around what can and should be done with all this data are ones that professionals of all sizes and types are struggling with. It represents a big problem that is starting to become more apparent as the drone industry matures and companies scale up in their capabilities. UAV-based data collection is "Big Data". If the drone is flying 3–5 times/week and averaging 500 images per flight, tens of gigabytes of data is assembled each week and specific choices in this area depend on the mission. Those choices will impact the present and future of the project. Most operators prefer to keep everything, provided the cost is within reason.

5.6.1 Camera types

1. **Charge-Coupled Device** (CCD): This goes back to the first digital cameras which used CCD sensors which were made to have high quality images due to the intense care taken to produce the sensors. They produce less noise (which is especially good in low light situations) over their CMOS counterparts. However, the CCD sensor requires lots of power when put in comparison to the CMOS sensor and thus it needs to be charged more frequently.

2. **Complimentary Metal Oxide Semiconductor** (CMOS): These sensors are cheaper than CCD sensors due to the fact that they are not produced in the same way. They have one main advantage, which is that they use far less power consumption than the CCD sensors.

3. **National Television Systems Committee** (NTSC): NTSC is a very common type of television broadcasting system that can be found in some parts of Asia and Africa. NTSC has a nice smooth video as it has a high frame rate of 30 frames per second (well 29.97 fps to be exact!) However, it has a lower resolution image than PAL.

4. **Phase Alternating Line** (PAL):PAL is not very common in America and Asia, but is much more prominent in Europe. As explained above,

it has a higher resolution that NTSC but has a frame rate of just 25 fps (which is lower than it's counterpart.)

5.6.2 Video

5.6.2.1 First Person View

First Person View (FPV): currently involves mounting a video camera to the UAV which sends video in real-time to the pilot or an assistant. An FPV drone is an UAV with a camera that wirelessly transmits video feed to goggles, a headset, a mobile device or another display. The user has a first-person view (FPV) of the environment where the drone flies and may capture video or still images. FPV drones may be remotely controlled or may be programmed to fly autonomously through software-controlled flight plans accessing data from onboard sensors and GPS. From the user's perspective, an FPV drone is like a flying telepresence robot, enabling virtual presence wherever the device can fly, often in environments that a human could not physically access safely. In contrast to humans, personal drones can access smaller spaces and tolerate harsher environments – in addition to having the ability to fly. Sensor Type—FPV Cams typically have either a CMOS or CCD image sensor inside. Typically CMOS cameras are cheaper and lighter but lack the ability to react quickly to changes in lighting. This Is quite necessary in FPV flight as we often face the bright sun followed by the darker ground, any lack of visibility could result in a crash!

You can get away with flying a cheap CMOS camera, however a CCD will give you better results. Almost all CCD cameras use the Sony Super HAD II sensor, which is the gold standard in FPV drones. Examples of this include the RunCam Swift or HS1177 variants.

There are also some special cameras that make better use from CMOS, such as the higher resolution Monster or Eagle cameras and the low light cameras, such as the Owl or Night Wolf.

Resolution and Latency—I've grouped these two together as they go hand in hand, the higher resolution you run the more latency you are likely to see! Analogue cameras are rated in TVL, which is the number of horizontal lines across the screen.

Due to the added latency I would recommend sticking with a camera the same resolution as your goggles (typically 600tvl). Another consideration is weather you want 4:3 or 16:9 resolution with 4:3 being the most common.

Camera Features - Some cameras have special feature, such as the ability to monitor your battery voltage and display it on screen. Other options are low light cameras that can see in nearly total darkness. Mini and even micro cameras are available that may be a better choice for smaller builds whilst some cameras offer a microphone for audio feeds.

Lens—Different sized lenses give a different **field of view** (FOV) which allow the pilot to see more around them. The higher the field of view the more fisheye effect you will also have to deal with.

1. 2.8 mm—The old standard, very narrow FOV

2. 2.5 mm—A great all rounder lens

3. 2.1 mm—A wide angle lens.

5.6.2.2 Video Camera

Video Camera: Almost any video camera which can be connected to a video transmitter can be used for FPV, though it is important to consider weight. Video cameras come in a wide range of shapes and sizes, as well as video resolution. Most of these cameras have a composite video out and power input, or analog output and power input via a 3 or 4 pin connector (GND, PWR, analog video signal and optional audio). Larger cameras such as DSLRs or larger video cameras tend to be used by professionals, but because of their weight, the UAV required tends to be quite large.

5.6.2.3 Video Antennas

The best way to improve your video range or clarity isn't necessarily increasing the VTX output power but is actually getting a good pair of antennas. Those black dipole antennas you get with cheap goggles or VTXs referred to as "rubber duckies" really don't perform well and are often binned and replaced with a high end antenna. An FPV setup requires two antennas, one to send out the video and another to receive it.

Things to consider:

Antenna Type—Different antenna designs have different performance, without going into too much detail dipoles perform poorly where as circular polarized antennas perform well. More innovative recent antennas, such as TBS Triumph or Pagoda push video range even further. A patch antenna can be used to increase range but only in one direction and should only be used as a receiving antenna.

Connector Type—Antennas come with two connector types SMA and RP-SMA both can talk to each other fine but you need to make sure they match your VTX or goggles connectors. Failing that adaptors are available.

Polarization—The antenna itself can come in tow flavors RHCP and LHCP both work the same but they must match in order to get a signal. By having different polarizations it is possible to get more pilots in the air at once.

Robustness—Obviously the antenna on the drone will be subject to a lot more abuse than the one on your goggles! For this reason I recommend using your best/most delicate antenna as a receiver and using a durable protected antenna on the drone.

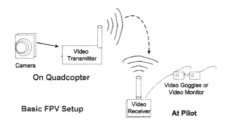

FIGURE 5.2 FPV block

5.6.2.4 FPV Glasses

FPV Glasses: 2D glasses are widely used in FPV because of their lower price, compatibility with a single video source (from a single video camera) and ease of use with an external battery pack. Certain models include a video receiver, and kits are available with camera, video transmitter, FPV glasses (with built-in video receiver) and external battery, as well as both antennas.

5.6.2.5 Head tracking

Head Tracking is essentially the same as motion tracking, but specifically measuring 3D orientation / angles as opposed to linear motion. Head tracking sensors are made up of MEMS accelerometer chips, gyroscopes or **inertial measurement units** (IMUs). The sensors are mounted (or built into) FPV / VR (virtual reality) glasses and send data to a microcontroller to interpret the sensor data as angles, which then sends the data either via the RC remote system (for higher end models) or via a separate wireless transmission system.

5.6.2.6 Video Transmitter

Video Transmitter (VTX): Currently very few flight controllers have an integrated video transmitter, meaning a separate video transmitter is normally needed. Video transmitters used for RC systems are currently popular since they are lightweight and small. The most common type of frequency is the 5.8GHz frequency. The video transmitter takes the signal from your camera and sends it out through your antenna.

Things to consider:

Power Output—Different VTX's pump out your video at different power levels. These often range from 25mW to 800mW with some offering a means of switching power output.

Channel Options—Most modern VTX's can run the majority of channel bands including Raceband. As long as the VTX channel list is compatible with your receiver you should be fine!

VTX-Video Signal Quality—This one really comes down to who you'll be flying with, you'll notice that some VTXs offer the same power and channel options yet cost up to four times as much! The reason for this is that the cheaper VTXs spit out noise over a much wider range than the selected channel which can lead to interference in other pilots video feeds.

If you intend to fly on your own a cheap VTX will work great for you however, if you intend to fly in larger groups or at race events you really need a clean transmitter like the TBS Unify Pro or the IRC Tramp.

Switching Options—If you do intend to fly with other people or at race events then you'll often have to change channel to ensure everyone can get clean video. Traditionally VTXs have a small push button you can use to cycle through video channels, bands and power levels, the channel is then shown via a LEDs on the VTX itself.

The more race friendly transmitters actually connect up to your flight controller and allow channel changing via an OSD or a Taranis Transmitter. Although it sounds like a little feature it makes a huge difference when flying in groups of over three pilots and is one I cannot go without anymore.

5.7   RADIO COMMUNICATIONS

Implement redundant communications if possible.

Definition 54 *Command and control link* *is the data link between the drone and the remote pilot station which manages the flight*

Data link is a term referring to all interconnections, to, from and within the remotely piloted aircraft system. It includes control, flight status, communication, and payload links. The UAV is controlled from the ground control station by line of sight (LOS), relay and/or satellite communication (SATCOM) data link. LOS is used for low range distances, while relay and SATCOM help to extend the range and also are good for low altitude flights or flights in mountainous areas. A datalink element is necessary for communication between the UAV and the ground control station (GCS). Commands to the UAV, payload and sensors via uplink, while real-time information from sensors, telemetry and video images from downlink. If the communication links are broken, the UAV must follow autonomous, pre-planned instructions if it is to recover and land.

5.7.1   Equipment

Transmissions from aircraft stations operating in Class G airspace are generally of three types.

1. The first is an advisory broadcast (for which an acknowledgement is not expected) when — for traffic separation purposes — a pilot informs the other stations in the vicinity who are listening-out, of her/his whereabouts and intentions.

2. The second type is a station-to-station call, where a pilot requests specific information from the Airservices flight information service, another aircraft station or an aerodrome ground station.

3. The third type is a response to another aircraft or ground station where specific information is supplied in response to a request, or in response to an advisory broadcast when a potential traffic conflict is perceived.

Most transmissions by aircraft in Class G will be made when in the vicinity of non-controlled airfields and usually in the form of broadcasts made in accordance with the requirement that pilots "must make a broadcast ... whenever it is reasonably necessary to do so to avoid a collision, or the risk of a collision, with another aircraft ..." operating in the vicinity. Transmissions to avoid collision, or the risk of a collision, are mandatory. Other broadcasts are discretionary, but their format should conform with a standard broadcast structure.

WiFi control is normally achieved using a WiFI router, computer (latop, desktop, tablet or smartphone). WiFi is able to handle both data transmission as well as image transmission, but is much more difficult to set up/implement. As with all WiFi devices, the range is limited by that of the WiFi transmitter.

The range/max wireless range of an RC system is almost never provided from the manufacturers because it involves many factors, such as obstructions, temperature, humidity, battery power and more. Some RC systems have a receiver which also has a built-in transmitter for transmitting sensor data (GPS coordinates for example) which are shown on the RC transmitter's LCD display. Not all RC transmitters can provide the full RC signal range of 500ms to 2500ms.

Bluetooth: Bluetooth, and BLE (Bluetooth Low Energy) products are intended to be used to transfer data between devices without the complexity of pairing or matching frequencies. Certain flight controllers on the market can send and receive data wirelessly via Bluetooth connection, making it easier to troubleshoot issues in the field.

SmartPhone: Almost all smartphones include integrated Bluetooth as well as WiFi either of which are used to control the UAV and/or receive data and/or video.

Infrared (IR): Infrared communication is rarely used to control UAVs as there is so much IR interference present even in a normal rooms that it is not very reliable.

Radio Frequency (RF) control refers to sending data from a computer or microcontroller wirelessly to the aircraft using an RF transmitter/receiver (or two-way transceiver). Using a normal RF unit connected to a computer allows for long range two-way communication with a high density of data (normally in serial format).

Frequency spectrums and associated limitations: a UAS typically uses radio frequencies link between the control station, also referred to as the transmitter and the UAV. The **2.4 GHz and 5.8 GHz** are the unlicensed radio frequency bands that most UAS use for the connection. These frequencies are also used for computer wireless networks and the interference can cause problems when operating an UAV in an area that has many wireless signals.

Loss-of-control and fly-aways are some of the reported problems with small UAV frequency implications. To avoid frequency interference, many UAS operate using a 2.4 GHz system to control the UAV and a 5.8 GHz to transmitt video and photo to the ground. Both RF bands (2.4 GHZ and 5.8 GHz) are considered line-of-sight and the command and control link between the control station and the UAV will not work properly when barriers are between the UAV and the control station.

5.7.2   Radio communications procedures

Radio communications are an important aspect for the safe operation of aircraft in the NAS. It is through radio communications that pilots give and receive information before, during and at the conclusion of a flight. This information aids in the flow of aircraft in highly complex airspace areas as well as in less populated areas. Pilots can also send and receive important safety issues, such as unexpected weather conditions, and inflight emergencies. Although small UAV pilots are not expected to communicate over radio frequencies, it is important the remote PIC understand aviation languae and the different conversations they will encounter if the UAV pilot is using a radio to aid them in situational awareness when operating in the NAS. Although much of the information provided here is geared toward manned aircraft pilots, the UAV pilot needs to understand the unique way information is exchanged in the NAS.

Understanding proper radio phraseology and procedures contribute to a pilot's ability to operate safely and efficiently in the airspace system.

Airport operations with and without an operating control tower: although a remote PIC is not required to communicate with manned aircraft when in the vicinity of a non-towered airport, safety in the NAS requires that remote pilots are familiar with traffic patterns, radio procedures and radio phraseology. When a remote PIC plans to operate close to a non-towered airport, the first step in radio procedures is to identify the appropriate frequencies.

Description and use of a common traffic advisory frequency (CTAF) to monitor manned aircraft communications.

Recommended traffic advisory procedures used by manned aircraft pilots, such as self-announcing of position and intentions. It is essential that pilots be alert and look for other traffic when operating at an airport without an operating control tower. This is particular important since other aircraft may not have communication ability ,or in some cases, pilots may not communicate their presence or intentions when operating into or out such airports. To achieve the greatest degree of safety, it is essential that all radio-equipped aircraft transmit/receive on a common frequency and small UAV pilots monitor other aircraft identified for the purpose of airport advisories.

5.8 GROUND CONTROL SYSTEM

A **ground control station** (GCS) is a land- or sea-based control center that provides the facilities for human control of drones.

1. GCS hardware refers to the complete set of ground-based hardware systems used to control the UAV. This typically includes the Human-Machine Interface, computer, telemetry, video capture card and aerials for the control, video and data links to the UAV. GCS software is typically runs on a ground-based computer that is used for planning and flying a mission. It provides a map screen where the user can define waypoints for the flight, and see the progress of the mission. It also serves as a "virtual cockpit", showing many of the same instruments as in manned aircraft.

2. A ground station is typically a software application, running on a ground-based computer, that communicates with your UAV via wireless telemetry. It displays real-time data on the UAVs performance and position and can serve as a "virtual cockpit", showing many of the same instruments that you would have if you were flying a real plane. A GCS can also be used to control a UAV in flight, uploading new mission commands and setting parameters. It is often also used to monitor the live video streams from a UAV's cameras.

3. There are at least ten different ground control stations. On desktop there is Mission Planner, APM Planner 2, MAVProxy, QGroundControl and UgCS. For Tablet/Smartphone there is Tower (DroidPlanner 3), MAVPilot, AndroPilot and SidePilot that can be used to communicate with ArduPilot (i.e. Copter, Plane, Rover, AntennaTracker).

4. The decision to select a particular GCS often depends on your vehicle and preferred computing platform:

5. Ready-to-fly users may prefer the portability and ease of use of Tower (Droid Planner 3), or another GCS running on a tablet or phone. DIY/Kit users and developers often have to access configuration and analysis tools, and would, therefore, need (at least initially) Mission Planner, APM Planner 2 or another more full-featured GCS.

6. UgCS - Universal Ground Control Station:

    (a) Universal and easy to use ground control station with a 3D interface. Supports APM, Pixhawk as well as drones from other manufacturers, such as DJI, Mikrokopter and more. Intended for enthusiasts as well as professional users.

(b) It is capable of communicating with and controlling multiple drones simultaneously.

(c) UgCS supports multiple map layers as well as different map providers. Some of the features of UgCS include—DEM Import, ADS-B transponder and receiver support, Click and Go mode, Joystick mode, image geotagging and video recording. UgCS also comes with a telemetry player, allowing the replay of all flights.

(d) UgCS comes with in-built no-fly zones around all major airports as well as the ability to create custom no-fly zones.

(e) Supports multi-node installation, meaning that it is possible to connect multiple pilots with UgCS laptops in the field to a central ground control server.

7. The Ground Control Station software is mainly designed for the use with multiple types of flight control modules fixed on a wide range of UAV platforms. The GCS uses Mavlink and STANAG 4586 type messages to cover the flow of all the important procedures and parameter between airborne aircraft and ground control segment. According to GCS modular architecture, there is a separate communication module already implemented.

8. This module is responsible for GCS-UAV communication. Depending on user preferences and autopilot type, the module can be modified easily for any requested communication standard. With this advantage, the end-user receives the GCS software with dedicated communications protocols support which can be updated within a short period of time. Payload capabilities like multisensor observation gimbal control or other dedicated equipment service is also implemented in the same application. Considering this advantage, no additional specialized software is needed for payload management.

5.9   FIRST PERSON VIEW (FPV)

First person view (FPV):

1. First person viewer flight (FPV), video transmitter power, frequencies, connectors, antenna. It is the ability of the user of some technology to see from a particular visual perspective other than one's actual location, such as the environment of a character in a UAV. First-person-view drone flying is the closest thing to being a bird. The difference between being the pilot rather than passive viewer is the direct connection between visual input and your manual control of the quadcopter. If you're about to bang into a wall, but micro-adjust to avoid it, it feels real and comes with a spike of adrenaline. FPV cameras have the potential to be mishandled, but the same is true for all technology.

2. First Person View provides you with a true pilot's eye view while flying your airplane or copter. A video camera and transmitter are placed in your plane or copter and a receiTBSDiscoveryver and video display are used on the ground. An OSD (On Screen Display) can be connected to your flight controller to provide an aircraft instrument overlay on your FPV monitor. The video display can be either an LCD screen display or a head mounted display (video goggles). This system is smaller, lighter and less expensive than you would think and can provide a wonderful true pilot flying experience. All the FPV copters described on this page are small providing increased agility, performance, pilot experience, survivability, and safety.

3. Very Important Safety Warning Relating Specifically to FPV Flight:

   (a) In normal radio control flight you are continuously watching your plane in the sky and can easily spot hazards.

   (b) In First Person View flight you are looking at a video screen or wearing a set of vision blocking goggles.

   (c) The AMA requires that there be a second person acting as spotter in their rules for all FPV flights.

   (d) It is very important to keep in mind that your perception of the area surrounding your vehicle is limited to the FPV view.

   (e) Whether you use a spotter or not it you must fly in a safe manner that does not endanger people or property.

   (f) Do not fly higher than 400 feet above ground level and fly your vehicle so it always stays in line of sight (without FPV).

   (g) You can fly beyond your FPV transmitters range or you can get radio signal or visual interference from structures.

   (h) You need to learn the FPV signal loss warning signs and be ready to shed the FPV and retake manual control at all times.

   (i) It is not necessarily difficult to fly in FPV but there is a learning curve, take your time and be safe.

4. An FPV drone is an unmanned aerial vehicle (UAV) with a camera that wirelessly transmits video feed to goggles, a headset, a mobile device or another display. The user has a first-person view (FPV) of the environment where the drone flies and may capture video or still images. FPV drones may be remotely controlled or may be programmed to fly autonomously through software-controlled flight plans accessing data from onboard sensors and GPS. From the user's perspective, an FPV drone is like a flying telepresence robot, enabling virtual presence wherever the device can fly, often in environments that a human could not physically access safely. In contrast to humans, personal drones can access smaller spaces and tolerate harsher environments – in addition to having the ability to fly.

5. The capacity of FPV drones to enter environments that are unsafe for humans makes them effective for search and rescue missions. Drones can be remotely piloted to locate people in dangerous situations, avoiding much of the need for physical presence. Similarly, drones can be used to inspect physical infrastructure that is difficult to access, such as bridges and high buildings.

6. In agri-tech (agricultural technology), an FPV drone allows a farmer to survey crops and livestock much more quickly than is possible with ground-based inspection and much more closely than is possible from a plane. A drone can also be equipped with sensors to capture environmental data for more sophisticated analysis. Drone-based inspection can facilitate precision agriculture, the application of information technology to ensure that the crops and soil receive exactly what they need for optimum health and productivity, while also optimizing the efficient use of resources.

5.10   DATA FUSION

Although UAS use has skyrocketed, the photogrammetric processing of associated data has remained highly intensive and requires expensive, complex and stationary desktop software environments. Data capture and transfer of the sensor information, filtering of data sensors, Data fusion. Data fusion is fusing the information coming from different sensors to get a better estimation of the attitude. There are several algorithms that perform data fusion, among them the Kalman filter in its different versions (linear KF, extended KF, unscented KF) and the complementary filter in its linear LCF and nonlinear NCF version. Example include: SLAM (simultaneous localization and mapping) of vehicles, targets, landmarks; Introduction to GIS (Geospatial information systems): aerial photography and videography, aerial ground control and land mapping; Image processing, visual image interpretation; Thermal radiation principles and thermal sensing; Post-flight analysis with system performance evaluation and optimization; If a UAS does not analyze data during in-flight collection or if the analysis requirement is too complex for that sort of automated analysis, the organization must often employ staff and other computational resources to process the data.

5.10.1   Kalman Filter

Kalman filter is a linear, discrete-time finite dimensional time-varying system that evaluates the state estimate that minimizes the mean square error. The Kalman filter dynamics results from the consecutive cycles of prediction and filtering. The dynamics of these cycles is derived and interpreted in the framework of Gaussian **probability density functions** (pdf). Under additional conditions on the system dynamics, the Kalman filter dynamics converges to a steady state filter and the steady state gain is derived. The innovation process associated with the filter, that represents the novel information conveyed to the state estimate by the last system measurement, is introduced.

The drone is driven by a set of controls and its outputs are evaluated by sensors, such as the knowledge on the system's behavior is solely given by the inputs and the observed outputs. The observation conveys the sensor noise on the UAV errors in the process. Based on the available information, it is required to obtain an estimate of the system's state that optimizes a given criteria.

The model for propagating the covariance matrix of estimation uncertainty is derived from the model used for propagating the state vector. The following formulation is used:

$$X_k = \Phi_k X_{k-1} + \vartheta_{k-1}$$
$$Z_k = \mathbf{H}_k X_k + \nu_{k-1}$$
$$(5.3)$$

The noise process ϑ_k, ν_k are white, zero mean uncorrelated and have known covariance matrices respectively $\mathbf{Q}_k, \mathbf{R}_k$. In the following derivation, $\hat{X}_k^-$ represents the a priori estimate, $\hat{X}_k^+$ represents the posteriori estimate, $\mathbf{P}_k^-$ represents the a priori covariance, $\mathbf{P}_k^+$ represents the posteriori covariance.

Algorithm 1 presents the main steps of the Kalman filter.

Algorithm 1 Essential Kalman Filter Equations

---

1. Predictor (Time Updates)

   (a) Predicted state vector

$$\hat{X}_k^- = \Phi_k \hat{X}_{k-1}^+ \tag{5.4}$$

   (b) covariance matrix

$$\mathbf{P}_k^- = \Phi_k \mathbf{P}_{k-1}^+ \Phi_k^T + \mathbf{Q}_{k-1} \tag{5.5}$$

2. Corrector (Measurement Updates)

   (a) Kalman gain

$$\bar{\mathbf{K}}_k = \mathbf{P}_k^- \mathbf{H}_k^T \left(\mathbf{H}_k \mathbf{P}_k^- \mathbf{H}_k^T + \mathbf{R}_k \right)^{-1} \tag{5.6}$$

   (b) Corrected state estimator

$$\hat{X}_k^+ = \hat{X}_k^- + \bar{\mathbf{K}}_k \left(Z_k - \mathbf{H}_k \hat{X}_k^- \right) \tag{5.7}$$

   (c) Corrected covariance matrix

$$\mathbf{P}_k^+ = \mathbf{P}_k^- - \bar{\mathbf{K}}_k \mathbf{H}_k \mathbf{P}_k^- \tag{5.8}$$

5.10.2   Data capture and processing

UAVs are especially useful for capturing a large amount of data very quickly, collecting data from large areas that must be covered in a short amount of time. These large-area data will be analyzed later. They are particularly useful for hard-to-reach places. They provide a safer alternative to collecting that data than sending an actual person. Another advantage of a UAV is the ability to carry a wide variety of external sensors to remote locations.

Because of the fact that they are able to cover large amounts of land quickly without the use of extensive manpower, drones have become increasingly more attractive to entities that have a need for regularly monitoring large amounts of infrastructure. These entities include, but are not limited to, construction companies, emergency services, and agricultural organizations.

UAV data capture can be utilized within many areas of the construction industry. The UAV can capture data for a quick and easy overview of the site progress. Aerial images are a way to see what is happening on the site or to send to the client as part of the progress report. Vertical or oblique imagery of the whole site can be provided as well as concentration on a certain area as a hard to reach areas. Defects can be detected earlier with high definition images. Aerial photography is also a way to get images for all the promotional and marketing needs.

Introduction to GIS (Geospatial information systems): aerial photography and videography, aerial ground control and land mapping. UAV technology allows GIS professionals to work more efficiently. With an easy-to-deploy mapping UAV, accurate aerial imagery can be captured and transformed into 2D orthomosaics (maps) and 3D models of small- and medium-sized sites. In terms of resolution, systems, such as the eBee can achieve orthomosaic-3D model accuracy of roughly 1-3x GSD, or down to 4.5 cm per pixel, significantly higher than current satellite and manned aircraft can attain. Plus, due to the altitudes at which UAVs typically fly, cloud cover is not an issue, meaning fewer weather delays and less unusable imagery. Morphology algorithms play an important role in high-resolution land cover mapping, not in terms of accuracy, but in terms of improving the cartographic representation. Morphology algorithms are often integrated into an automated feature extraction project. To improve the appearance of the buildings, a series of morphology steps are applied that included smoothing, generalization, and finally orthogonalization.

UAV LiDAR is a relatively new land surveying technique, which is based on high precision laser scanners, the Global Positioning System (GPS) and Inertial Navigation Systems (INS). Combined, they allow the positioning and orientation of the footprint of a laser beam as it hits an object, to a high degree of accuracy. Airborne lidar is unmatched in its ability to provide high-resolution data over broad areas along with the capacity to measure the terrain. Digital Elevation Model (DEM) can be improved using a combination

UAS photogrammetric and airborne lidar elevation models. A DEM is defined as a surface model in which above-ground features are removed.

Image processing, visual image interpretation: UAV software is designed to capture hyper-spectral, thermal and RGB images and processes it applying machine learning and cloud-based architecture for data storage and scalability. Object-Based Image Analysis (OBIA) techniques are applied.

Thermal radiation principles and thermal sensing. Thermal imaging camera offers radiometric thermal imagery, heat loss from a building can be quickly spot, it will highlight damp areas in roofs and show defects in solar panels. Images captured are radiometric which allows to take temperatures from the image and create reports of hot spots, cold spots and minimum, maximum temperatures.

Post-flight analysis with system performance evaluation and optimization: Availability and reliability of the data underlying environmental management support tools is essential, whether it is collected directly on the ground or using remote sensing technology.

Extraction of vector data: GPS recording; Geodatabases; Manual data collection; Digitization; Web services; UAV point cloud.

Import, layering of vector and raster data: GIS software.

Analysis and decision making: Progress tracking, feature identification, flood simulation, project planning .

5.10.2.1 Data Processing challenges

1. It is important for the operator to make sure that all of the project specifics are laid out in detail before data collection. What is the turnaround time on the deliverable/s? What are the accuracy requirements? Who is the end user of the deliverables?

2. Being able to effectively and concisely identify what a deliverable for a project is going to look like can eliminate a number of headaches for everyone, but that means expectations around the needs and capabilities of a process and system have to be effectively communicated. It is important to communicate as often as possible, even if it means admitting a mistake, even if asking simple questions. It's always better to ask a dumb question than be put in a dumb situation.

3. Processing drone data quickly: Processing a single aerial photo is a time-consuming task as it is. Processing several aerial photos in a short period of time can be next to impossible. In order to do so, a concrete and structured workflow is necessary.

4. Processing drone data accurately: In order for data to have meaning, it has to be collected and processed accurately. There are several factors that could skew the accuracy of an aerial drone image during processing. It's important to take these factors into account and handle them as delicately as possible.

5. Understanding how to use the correct software: While software that automatically processes drone data does exist, it is not a be-all, end-all solution. Automated processing is typically very general, lacking in accuracy and nuance. It takes an experienced GIS specialist with a keen eye and analytical mind to process data adequately, even when using software.

5.10.2.2 Data Processing Management

1. There are a number of existing software on the market that can do a lot of the work for you, but none of them are perfect. While the use of this software is wise, it is important that the people operating them know the difference between correctly processing data, and incorrectly processing data. Quality control is key.

2. The first order of business in processing data is to calibrate the data. In the case of drone data, data calibration refers to the syncing up of points on an aerial image with geographical points on physical land. Ideally, pre-calibration is done on the land itself to ensure maximum accuracy. However, it has been proven that self-calibration after the fact is accurate enough for most uses.

3. Once data points have been created to correlate with physical points, these data points will be placed in a point cloud. A point cloud is a set of data points in a coordinate system that allows for the visualization and analysis of the geographical area it represents. From a point cloud, it is possible to create Digital Elevation Models, 3D models, and more. These visualizations as well as the statistics rendered from the processed data will help in making informed decisions about monitored infrastructure.

4. While it is possible to process drone data without the use of a GIS specialist, it does take a lot of work and know-how. If your organization only makes use of drone data every now and then, contacting a third party could help make this process painless. Similarly, if your organization makes use of drone data on a regular basis, but doesn't want to take the time to find and train GIS specialists, you'd be best served by hiring a third party to process it.

5. In order to get maximum use out of data, it needs to be processed as quickly as possible. As time passes after an aerial photo has been taken, existing physical conditions are prone to change. Hiring an outside company with GIS expertise will ensure that data is processed consistently, accurately, and efficiently.

6. The accuracy highly depends on the ground resolution (GSD) of the input imagery. When chosen appropriately this mapping solution can

compete with traditional mapping solutions that capture fewer high-resolution images from airplanes and that rely on highly accurate orientation and positioning sensors on board.

5.10.2.3 Data Processing Software

1. *Pix4D* desktop software is a complete mapping and modeling solution that automatically converts aerial images into 2D mosaics and 3D models.

2. DroneDeploy offers powerful cloud-based drone software that is compatible with any drone. It allows to map and create 3D models and analyze and share the data right from the device.

3. PrecisionMapper was created by Precision Hawk, and automatically processes aerial data into 2D and 3D products. One noteworthy feature of this software is that it is now free .

4. SiteScan is 3D Robotics' flagship data processing platform. It enables pilots to quickly generate a survey of any site quickly and cost effectively. With a few taps on a tablet, any pilot can generate orthophotos, point clouds, and meshes, which can be used to build design surfaces and contours.

Flight operations management software

1. Skyward is a flight operations management platform designed for drone operators. Their platform can be used for solopreneurs to plan and track flights, and also for large teams to coordinate efforts.

2. Flyte is a platform to help pilots manage their operations. In addition to planning, logging, and reporting support, Flyte provides full and up to the minute information on digital NOTAMS/TFRs and ground hazards, as well an airspace integration through AIRMAP, which enables pilots to integrate into national airspace and communicate with ATC.

3. Kittyhawk is a one-stop shop for flying, logging, and coordinating UAV operations. They have a strong focus on providing value for their pilots, which manifests in the usability of their platform and the fact that they allow for unlimited logging of hours.

4. DroneLogbook is a flight management platform for UAV Pilots. They focus on automating log collections, by supporting more than 20 different UAV log file types. They also have features to manage equipment, battery, maintenance, incident, location, pre-flight documents. DroneLogBook supports a spectrum of UAV pilots, from hobbyists to large companies.

Pre-flight inspection: the pilot should make sure to follow the pre-flight guidelines found in the owner's manual concerning all protocols for pre-flight inspections. These protocols may vary from one drone to another.

Flight Operations Best Practices: When starting the flight, the pilot should hover in the air for 30 seconds before starting the mission. This will give the pilot the chance to detect any potential issues with the drone before starting.

The pilot should make sure to keep the drone in sight at all times. If using a Visual Observer, the pilot should make sure to have agreed on terminology and communication procedures during flight beforehand, and use them faithfully while in the air.

The pilot should always make sure to follow CAA regulations, including the prohibition against flights over people not directly involved in the mission. If someone walks into the site of operation, alert them to the ongoing mission and ask them to move on. Also, the pilot should must remember to have the Return Home Function set up, and keep the path home clear in case you need to use it.

5.10.3 Geospatial information systems

A geographic information system (GIS) is a system designed to capture, store, manipulate, analyze, manage, and present spatial or geographic data. In general, the term describes any information system that integrates, stores, edits, analyzes, shares, and displays geographic information. GIS applications are tools that allow users to create interactive queries (user-created searches), analyze spatial information, edit data in maps, and present the results of all these operations. Geographic information science is the science underlying geographic concepts, applications, and systems. GIS can refer to a number of different technologies, processes, and methods. It is attached to many operations and has many applications related to engineering, planning, management, transport/logistics, insurance, telecommunications, and business. For that reason, GIS and location intelligence applications can be the foundation for many location-enabled services that rely on analysis and visualization.

Drones are one of the newest and most innovative tools to be considered for commercial use. They survey data in less time, using fewer natural resources than manned aircraft. While UAVs offer advantages of utilizing superior reach and dexterity in data collection, they usher in their own set of hurdles. Drones' own physical limitations, a consideration often overlooked, pose a limit to their technical scope.

Current UAS Activity in GIS:

1. Agriculture : With precision agronomics on the rise, more farmers are adopting technology and methods to decrease cost, increase yield, and ultimately increase the return on their investment. Drones give famers the convenience of being able to inspect crops from new perspectives and with frequency never before possible. Because they are able to pinpoint problem areas in the field, they're able to remedy diseases and

defects before they become costly. Farmers are on the forefront of UAS in agriculture.

2. Emergency Services: There have already been success stories that credit drones with playing a large role in search and rescue missions. Drones don't get tired or distracted. The data collected by UAVs can be reviewed easily, unlike human observations. In law enforcement, drones play mainly a surveillance role. They are the eyes for monitoring infrastructure and pursuing suspects.

3. Geospatial Services: Geospatial technology is what gives UAS the ability to be autonomous. Without the capability of following a GPS-guided flight plan, a drone is just a glorified radio controlled aircraft. In addition to autonomous operation, certain drones carry a myriad of sensors. The convenience of inspecting vast infrastructure without significant time and manpower invested is enough of a reason for surveyors, construction firms, and power companies to deploy drones.

5.10.4   Image processing

The accuracy of aerial data is directly related to the spatial resolution of the input imagery. The high resolution images from UAV can compete with traditional aerial mapping solutions that bank on highly accurate alignment and positioning sensors on board. The advancement of computing practices resulted in vigorous and fully automatic production practices and coupled with high-end computing machines and viewing mechanisms will deal with positional inaccuracies and imagery orientation information which are characteristically challenging with customary techniques.

Processing of UAV images has its own challenges. SBL used to receive post-processed UAV images along with inertial measurement unit (IMU) and ground control points (GCP) as input. Aerial Triangulation is the first step performed. During this stage GCP and Actual Check Point (ACP) reports have been generated. This is an iterative step until we get the desired accuracy. The following will explain in brief some of the critical steps in the processing of UAV data.

1. The software examines for matching points by analyzing all images. The software may use an improved version of the binary descriptors, which are very powerful to match image points quickly and accurately.

2. Those matching points as well as estimated values of the image position and orientation provided by the UAV autopilot are used in a bundle block adjustment to reconstruct the exact position and orientation of the camera for every acquired image.

3. Based on this restitution the matching points are corroborated and their 3D coordinates calculated. A proper projection system is selected based

on the requirements, and also GPS measurements from the UAV autopilot during the flight.

4. 3D points are interpolated to form a Triangulated Irregular Network (TIN) in order to obtain a DEM. The spatial resolution of the TIN is moderated as per the need of 3D model requirements.

5. This DEM is used to project every image pixel and to calculate the georeferenced ortho-mosaic. The orthoimages will be cleared of positional and terrain displacement inaccuracies.

5.10.4.1 Air monitoring

Air monitoring:

1. This wireless radiation monitoring system is capable of detecting beta radiation (electrons), gamma radiation (photons) and X-rays from a safe distance. The sensor unit is battery powered with customizable reporting intervals and low power modes that can enable long-term battery powered operation up to many months. Radiation Sensor Features : Detects beta and gamma radiation and X-rays; Battery powered with customizable reporting intervals and low power modes that can enable long-term battery powered operation (months); Wireless communication between one or more monitors and the communication bridge or PC based data collection; 24/7 remote monitoring and threshold based alerting; Data can be exported to GIS or other custom mapping systems; Data can also be exported from our large-scale data warehouse via API and analyzed by other programs; High immunity to RF and electrostatic fields. Radiation Monitor Specifications: Detector sensitivity: 5.8 cpm $\pm$ 15 percent for 1 μSv/h radiation dose; Linear response over wide temperature range (-30 to 50 degree Celsius); Measurement range of radiation dose equivalent rate (Cs-137 and Co-60): 0.1μSv/h to 100mSv/h.

2. Air quality data collection near pollution sources is difficult, particularly when sites are complex, have physical barriers, or are themselves moving: Particle Number Concentration (PNC) monitor, Gas sensors are classified according to their operational principles with the most common being thermal, mass, electrochemical, potentiometric, amperometric, conductometric, and optical sensors. PM sensors differ in terms of monitoring PM in the range of PM10 (mass concentration of particles with aerodynamic diameter$< 10\mu$m) and PM2.5 ($< 2.5\mu$m) and the ultrafine fraction of PM ($< 0.1\mu$m). Many built in devices, with a sensor incorporated as an integral part of the device itself, already exist for PM10 and PM2.5, Ozone sampling using a KI ozone sampling system. The gas sensing payload includes three Alphasense gas sensors (Alphasense, B4 type, Great Notley, Essex, UK) and one SprintIR CO2 sensor. The Alphasense sensors are electrochemical cells that operate in

the amperometric mode and generate a current that is linearly proportional to the fractional volume of the measured gas. They are used to measure CO, NO, and NO2. The SprintIR CO2 for CO2 concentration measurements is based on Non-Dispersive Infra-Red (NDIR) technology.

5.10.4.2 Water monitoring

Water monitoring

1. Traditional water quality monitoring comprises a series of observations, measurements and samples to be collected and analyzed. The most common parameters that affect water quality can be physical, chemical or biological, in nature.

    (a) Physical properties of water quality include temperature, turbidity, flow, sediments, and erosion;

    (b) Chemical characteristics involve parameters, such as pH, dissolved oxygen, nutrients, oils, metals, pesticides and other pollutants.

    (c) Biological indicators, on the other hand, include algae and phytoplankton.

2. METHODOLOGY: Hyperspectral or multispectral sensors are used and differ in the number of bands and how narrow the bands are. Multispectral imagery generally refers to 3 to 10 bands that are represented in pixels, whereas hyperspectral imagery can have hundreds or thousands of bands. Total Organic Carbon (TOC); Dissolved Organic Carbon (DOC); Chemical Oxygen Demand (COD); Biochemical Oxygen Demand (BOD); Nitrates (NO3); Nitrites (NO2) 190-350 nm Turbidity (NTU); Chlorophyll 500-600 nm; Total Suspended Solids (TSS) 780-900 nm.

    (a) collecting remotely sensed UAV and in-situ data simultaneously;

    (b) analyzing data from all available sensors and in-situ measurements, through big data analytics.

    (c) using image processing and pattern recognition techniques to analyze the images and obtain spectral signatures for the water constituents, using several software packages available on campus for this purpose, such as MATLAB, ENVI, and Geomatica;

    (d) conducting laboratory analysis on in-situ water samples;

    (e) using statistical methods to try and correlate the remotely sensed data with the water quality parameter concentrations measured in the laboratory;

    (f) verifying if the resulting model can predict water quality parameter concentrations, within acceptable error levels;

(g) proving the feasibility of monitoring water quality parameters in remote locations using UAVs;

(h) reporting findings;

(i) extending the study to other river systems.

3. Small instrument technology is developing quickly, with promising methods for both gas measurements, including tunable diode lasers, cascade quantum lasers and fiber chemical sensing , and Particulate Matter (PM) measurements. For example, a pulsed differential adsorption LIDAR (DIAL) system has been proposed as a potential UAV payload for atmospheric CH4 detection. Light Detection and Ranging is used to detect and measure the distance of an object or surface from an optical source. LiDAR differs from photogrammetry in that photogrammetry uses passive light and LiDAR employs an active laser system. LiDAR yields an intensity with the XYZ data to provide a black and white-like image. One of the revolutionary aspects of LiDAR—as opposed to photogrammetry, which involves synthesizing the data from a large collection of photographs—is that it allows surveyors to cut through foliage and other intervening debris to create a detailed topographical map of a landscape, without having to take the time to walk it on foot.

4. Photogrammetry is the science of making measurements from photographs. The output of photogrammetry is typically a map, a drawing or a 3D model of some real-world object or land mass. To create 3D maps from aerial photogrammetry, the camera is mounted on the drone and is usually pointed vertically towards the ground. Using photogrammetry to create 3D models of monuments or statues, the camera is mounted horizontally on the UAV. Multiple overlapping photos (80 to 90 percent overlap) of the ground or model are taken as the UAV flies along an autonomous programmed flight path called a waypoint. To overlap photos of an object or land by 80 to 90 percent would be impossible to complete accurately by pilot navigation. It is essential to have a UAV which has waypoint Navigation technology.

5. Lidar (Light Detection And Ranging) is a surveying method that measures the distance to a target by illuminating that target with a pulsed laser light, and measuring the reflected pulses with a sensor. The differences in the amount of time it takes for the laser to return, and also in the wavelengths, are then used to make digital 3D-representations of the target. UAV Lidar involves mounting a laser scanner on a UAV to measure the height of points in the landscape below the UAV. Doing aerial data collection using LiDAR with drones instead of airplanes is a relatively new land surveying technique, which is based on high precision laser scanners, the Global Positioning System (GPS), and Inertial Navigation Systems (INS). These three things combined allow for incredibly precise 3D mapping.

6. Sonar works in a similar manner, with sound waves bouncing off an object and returning to their source indicating the distance to different points on the object, and thus allowing for a 3D visualization of it.

Through the use UAV photogrammetry and lidar mapping, there are many products which can be extracted from the aerial imagery. These products include:

1. DEM / DTM / DSM (surface models)

2. Orthophoto's (geospatially corrected aerial images)

3. 3D Building Models

4. Contour Maps

5. Planemetric features (road edges, heights, signs, building footprints, etc.)

6. Volumetric Surveys

Lighting is always important in photography. Bright, even lighting will allow you to have a small aperture to reduce the image's depth of field. Shallow depth-of-field is actually a bad thing for photogrammetry, because blurred details confuse the software.

5.10.4.3 Agriculture monitoring

1. Plant counts such as corn counting will give an idea of yield from those plants. Plant health monitoring, differentiating species of agricultural farms/plants and plantation estimation are the major task performed for agriculture. Growth stages of the farms can also be monitored using ortho images acquired through UAV process. UAV image processing is also helpful for the site selection for solar farms.

2. Most agriculture UAV depend on multi-spectral imaging to spot problems with a crop's health; specifically, they look at changes over time in visible light (VIS) and near-infrared (NIR) light reflected by crops. These images are taken over time by drones, manned aircraft or satellites. It is possible to detect plant health from these images because plants reflect different amounts of visible green and NIR light, depending on how healthy they are. By measuring the changes in visible and NIR light reflected from a crop, we can spot potential health issues. Multi-spectral imaging sensors allow you to see things you cannot see in the visual spectrum, such as wet patches on the ground. To monitor changes in plant health over time, drone images are processed to calculate a tracking index called NDVI (normalized difference vegetation index), which is a measure in the difference between light intensity reflected by the

field in two different frequencies: NDVI is the ratio of **near infrared reflectivity** (NIR) minus **visible red reflectivity** (VIS), divided by NIR plus VIS:

$$\text{NDVI} = \frac{(\text{NIR} - \text{VIS})}{(\text{NIR} + \text{VIS})} \tag{5.9}$$

3. Some of the more popular indices include:

   (a) **crop water stress index** (CWSI): measures temperature differentials to detect/predict water stress in plants. Requires a thermal imaging sensor and the use of a nearby weather station.

   (b) **canopy chlorophyl content index** (CCCI): detects canopy nitrogen levels using three wavebands along the red edge of the visible spectrum. Requires visible and near infrared cameras.

4. **Airborne thermal sensors** can see hotspots and measure changes in land and plant temperature over time. Thermal sensors can also detect the presence of water due to its cooling effect, which can be helpful in spotting crop damage due to drought and/or seasonal issues.

5. **LIDAR** is a precise remote sensing technology that measures distance by illuminating a target with a laser and analyzing the reflected light. LIDAR is commonly used to measure buildings and land masses with precision, and to develop an accurate 3D model of an area. LIDAR is very accurate and precise technology which uses laser pulse to strike the object. Regular photogrammetry or other survey technology can miss the surface elevation value that is hidden by vegetation or forest canopy. But LIDAR can penetrate through the object and detect the surface value.

6. Popular Image Processing Software for Agriculture:

   (a) Pix4D: this popular and expensive image processing platform converts a series of aerial images into 2D orthomosaics, 3D point clouds and 3D mesh models. Pix4D can also calculate NDVIs, DVIs, SAVIs and custom indices as needed.

   (b) senseFly's Postflight Terra 3D: based on Pix4D, this is senseFly's software for converting aerial imagery into 2D orthomosaics, 3D models and differential indices. Terra 3D is provided free with all eBee drones.

   (c) PrecisionMapper by PrecisionHawk: now called Data Mapper, this is a cloud-based application that gives anyone the ability to upload, store, process, and share their aerial image data. Works with some, but not all, UAS platforms.

   (d) Trimble: designed for professional land surveyors, Trimble's Photogrammetry Module office software to create detailed orthophotos, digital elevation models, point clouds, volume calculations and 3D models. Trimble's general-purpose Inpho UASMaster Module can be used for advanced photogrammetric processing.

(e) DataMapper by PrecisionHawk: a 100 percent cloud-based platform that supports image capture, differential processing and algorithmic analysis for many industries. Their Algorithm Marketplace lets you pick and apply specific algorithms to extract useful data, such as NDVI, DVI, plant counts, scouting reports, and more.

(f) Correlator3D^{TM} by SimActive: advanced photogrammetric processing client software for use on high-end PCs. Performs aerial triangulation (AT) and produces dense digital surface models (DSM), digital terrain models (DTM), point clouds, orthomosaics and vectorized 3D models.

7. The 3D sonic anenometer has a 10 cm vertical measurement path and operates in a pulsed acoustic mode. The three orthogonal wind components (u_x, u_y, u_z) and the speed of sound (c) are measured and output at a maximum rate of 60 Hz. Analog outputs and two types of digital outputs are provided.

8. Meteorology: LIDAR has been used for study of the cloud and its behavior since it was invented. It uses its wavelength to strike small particles in the cloud to understand it. There are different kinds of LIDAR presents which does typical task in the cloud.

(a) Elastic backscatter LiDAR: It is the simplest type of LiDAR and is typically used for studies of aerosols and clouds.

(b) Differential Absorption LiDAR (DIAL): It is used for the measurements of a gas like ozone, carbon dioxide, or water vapor.

(c) Raman LiDAR: It is also used for measuring the concentration of atmospheric gases but also to take the quantity of aerosol parameters present.

(d) Doppler LiDAR: It is used to measure wind speed.

9. LiDAR helps farmers to find areas where costly fertilizer is being overused, and also helps to create elevation maps of farmland that can be converted to create slope and sunlight exposure area maps. Layer information provided via LiDAR can be used to create high, medium, and low crop production area maps, and extracted data can help farmers to save on fertilizer, and generally optimize their efforts.

10. LiDAR data, including derivatives like contour maps, digital elevation models, hillshade projections, and others are assisting with a wide range of natural resource conservation applications.

FIGURE 5.3   Lidar image from VELODYNE

5.10.4.4   Best practices for UAS use by the electric utility industry

The prospect of obtaining an aerial view of transmission and distribution (TD) lines, towers and poles without deploying a line crew is very attractive to many utilities for the savings in money and time it offers. Transmission and distribution utilities have traditionally performed line inspections and maintenance, storm damage assessments and vegetation management using line crews, manned aircraft, and third party inspection service companies. Working on TD is cost-intensive, difficult and highly dangerous.

As a tool, UAS can be used to conduct efficient electric TD infrastructure inspection, effectively detect problems with electric equipment, access equipment in difficult terrain and provide direct support for electric utility vegetation management. The ability to sense in 3D, take thermal readings and detect metal strain will greatly improve the results of infrastructure inspection.UAS that can hover can get close enough to provide a new level of detail, improving support to maintenance, operations and overall performance.

UAS can fly at a low altitude and enter into isolated or remote areas that are typically inaccessible via foot or by manned aircraft. When operating close to energized systems, UAS can be affected by electromagnetic interference (EMI), especially when high voltages are involved. Unlike certified manned aircraft, UAS are not required to implement standard engineering practices, such as shielding to minimize risk from EMI. Further, the sensor package may very well be affected by EMI to a greater extent than the aircraft. Each combination of UAS, sensor and infrastructure, electromagnetic (EM) fields may have unique characteristics that could impact the mission profile.

In the event of a compass error on the ground, the UAS should be moved away from the energized system before takeoff. In the event of an in-flight compass error, the UAS should be moved to a safe distance from the electric infrastructure and landing procedures executed.

UAS electric utility mission planning:

1. Aircraft marking and painting with bright colors create better contrast for overall visibility and the visual tracking of the UAS during flight operations.

2. Aircraft speed less than $180Km/h$: Installing a GPS device on the UAS that reports ground information to the remote PIC who takes into account the wind direction and speed, crosswind, wind shear ... and calculates the UAS airspeed for a given direction of flight. Timing the ground speed of the UAS when it is flown between two or more fixed points, taking into account wind speed and direction between each point, then noting the power settings of the UAS to operate at the maximum velocity.

3. Altitude and altimeter: To comply with the maximum altitude requirements, there are multiple ways to determine a UAS altitude above the ground or structure: installing a calibrated altitude reporting device (MSL, AGL) or using the know height of local rising terrain and/or structures as a reference.

4. Autopilot should provide for heading, altitude and speed allowing for safe **return to base** (RTB) and obstacle avoidance. Programming prebuilt flight paths before mission potentially assists in ensuring data from the needed geographic areas are collected and enables assigned staff to maximize their time in the field.

5. Communications are vital to ensuring mission status and ultimately mission success: use transmit and receive radio communications able to communicate on aviation bands, deconfliction should be accomplished through the local **common traffic advisory frequency** (CTAF) when possible, ensure communications checks are accomplished before launch.

6. Fuel planning: all aircraft should carry sufficient usable fuel and/or battery life, considering all meteorological factors and mission requirements. At mission end, 20 percent of the fuel, beyond that required for the mission, should remain for contingencies and maintain at least 5 minutes power reserve.

7. Standardized hand signals should be used when situations dictate.

8. **Human factors**: UAS pilots should use situation awareness SA to accomplish the tasks at hand. Although the choice of whether or not to fly is normally dictated by weather and mission considerations, sound judgment plays a most important role.

9. **Aircraft lighting** is for both safety and navigation. The lighting allows for more rapid location of the UAS visually, and depending on the

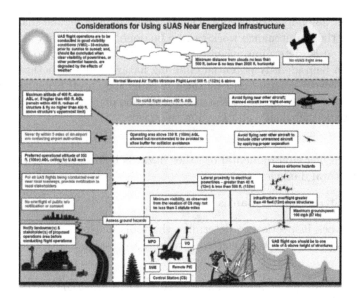

FIGURE 5.4   Mission planning considerations

lighting configuration, the lights will indicate the direction in which the aircraft is traveling.

10. **Mission brief**: in addition to having a weather brief, scheduling a mission brief before flight operations is always an effective tool for coordination among crew members. A positive mission brief is one that is interactive and establishes open communication.

11. **Navigation**: maintain SA with incoming or outgoing air traffic from airport runway approach and departure routes. A compass is used as direction and heading indicator and should be considered an essential part of the navigation equipment needed to fly safely.

12. **NOTAM**: is a notice filed with an aviation authority to alert pilots of potential hazards along a flight route or at a location that could affect the safety of the flight.

13. **Payload and weight** are a key factor in the type of UAS to be used. Once the payload is determined and it falls within the acceptable flight weight, it must be balanced. Balance is key to flight stability and stability is essential for safe operations.

Guide to surveying a tower   Communication companies with cell and radio towers, cities with water towers, and other industries that use towers as part of their daily operations—all of these towers require regular maintenance, and before the maintenance work can be be done, a preliminary survey must be conducted to determine where to work.When it comes to tower surveys, a drone can help identify potential climbing hazards, find structural damage, and help tower inspectors understand the tools they need prior to climbing. Drone surveys serve to reduce the amount of time personnel are on the tower, increasing their efficiency and keeping them safe.

Some Use cases are given:

1. Identifying environmental or other hazards before climbing (bee, birds, structural damage, etc.)

2. Identifying damaged areas

3. Pre-work inspection to determine the tools and parts needed ahead of a climb, to avoid time wasted returning to the ground to find the right tool

4. In the case of a structural emergency, you can investigate the structure's integrity before you climb, and find out if it's safe to climb at all.

Case Study: Telecommunications Tower Survey for Designing New Tower Mount

1. **Project Goal**: Identify, analyze, and design a new antenna mount for the tower.

2. **Mission**: A professional drone service company is hired to survey a telecommunications tower and create a high-definition 3D point cloud that could be used as a model for designing a new antenna mount for the tower.

3. **Timeline**: It took only one day to capture the images and process them into a precise 3D point cloud (shown below), which focused on the upper rad center mounts, wireless-panel style antennas, and associated mounts.

4. **Project Deliverable**: A 3D densified point cloud created on Pix4Dmapper (shown below).

Case Study: Cell Tower Inspection

1. **Project Goal**: Collect highly detailed visual data regarding the condition of a cell phone tower.

2. **Mission**: The Unmanned Vehicle Technologies team used a drone to collect clear, accurate visual data on the state of a cell phone tower. Using a camera that allows for high accuracy while zooming, they were able to fly at a significant distance from the cell tower and still collect clear, usable images. Skip to 1:07 in the video below to see how the pilot

uses the "point of interest" flight mode to circle the cell phone tower, maintaining an equal distance from the tower while collecting detailed visual data.

3. **Timeline**: The timeline is unclear, but it seems that all of the data needed was collected in a single flight.

4. **Deliverables**: Visual data that can be used to analyze the condition of the cell tower.

5. Zoom is a crucial feature for cameras used in tower inspections, since, due to guy wires and elctromagnetic fields, you want to avoid flying close to the tower you're surveying. Note that the pilot switches from digital zoom to optical zoom at 1:36, providing a clearer resulting image.

Setting Flight Goals: Before conducting the mission it is important to have the objectives clearly defined. There are three general examples of tower surveying flight goals:

1. Pre-work inspection. Use data collected via drone to determine what types of tools will be required for tower inspector to do his or her job.

2. Hazard and obstacle analysis. Use data collected via drone to determine potential biological (i.e. bees or birds) or structural hazards (i.e. weak areas in the tower) or obstacles. The presence of a bird's nest may not always be a danger to the tower inspector, but if it's an endangered species it could present other legal and ethical concerns.

3. Structural analysis. Use data collected via drone to find degradations in the tower's structure, and identify areas where work is required.

Wind: Wind speed can be a huge factor for tower surveys, especially for extremely high flights. The conditions near the ground, or at 30 feet in the air, will be nothing like the conditions at 1,200 or 1,900 feet. If it's breezy on the ground, it might be incredibly windy once you get to the top of the tower. Pilots should be cautious, and cancel a mission if the conditions are not safe. Better to come back another day than to risk a crash that could ruin the drone or injure someone.

Electromagnetism and Distance from the Tower: AM towers, FM/TV antennas, and even cellular and microwave antennas, can all emit powerful electromagnetic fields at close range. These fields could interfere with your control signal, and can cause your drone to malfunction and crash. The pilot should stay a safe distance away from the tower throughout the flight.

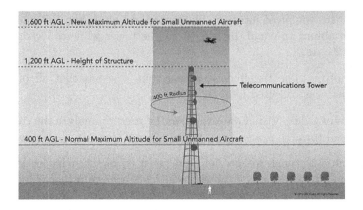

FIGURE 5.5 Surveying a tower

5.11 LABS

5.11.1 Inertial navigation systems

In this simple two-dimensional example, two linear accelerometers and one rate gyro are used. To provide a tutorial overview of inertial navigation systems (INS). Illustrate ideas with a 2-D navigator.

1. Discuss inertial sensors (simple rate gyros and linear accelerometers).

2. Discuss characteristic errors in the INS.

3. To demonstrate the need by the INS for altitude aiding.

4. To show how GPS aids the INS and leads to far superior navigation accuracy. Altitude-aided

5. Altitude and X-aided

6. Heading-aided

7. GPS aided

5.11.2 Wiring the flight controller

The hardest part of wiring the flight controller is knowing what goes where since all flight controllers have a slightly different layout. The very first thing I suggest you do is search for a pinout diagram of your board, it should look something like this.

Some manufactures such as Matek have even started giving users full wiring diagrams such as the one below. This shows you exactly what pads you are looking to solder making things much easier for you. Note that all the red and black power wires we have already soldered! The following diagram is for the boards that I am using, it is, however, a little unique as there is a ribbon cable connecting the PDB to the flight controller.

Typically you will be looking to connect the following wires to their respective pads:

Power—As with all other components we need to power them, almost all flight controllers require 5V however, some have there own regulator and will run off battery voltage. You will need to check what input your flight controller requires for this.

Vbat—If your flight controller runs off of 5V it will still need to read the main battery voltage if you want to make use of features, such as the OSD or beeper. You will often have a positive and negative wire to do this connecting to the Vbat and ground pads.

Motors—Each of the four motors will have one signal wire (typically white) and one round wire (black). Refer to the motor layout diagram for the order!

Receiver—You'll have one signal in wire to connect to either an UART RX port or a dedicated SBUS port, etc. You may also have a telemetry wire which will connect to a different UART TX!

OSD—If you have an OSD you will have connectors for video in, video out and then grounds for both signals. It is important that you use these grounds for both your camera and VTX if you want clean video.

Some extras you could also include could be

Buzzer—This works as a mean to find your lost drone in a crash or to warn you if the battery gets low. Flight controllers typically have a + and - buzzer pad to use here.

LEDs—You can run all kinds of LEDs with all kinds of patterns on your drone which are great for distinguishing your drone whilst racing. LED strips are typically powered by any + and −5V pads with a signal wire connecting to the flight controller. As with most components I would recommend powering your LEDs off of the PDB if possible.

Software Configuration Software configuration is a huge article in itself with a massive amount to get through depending on your components and preferences that will be different for almost every build. All I can recommend is a basic checklist of things to set until we have completed a full article. Make sure you have installed a software configurator, such as Betaflight on your computer and connect up to the drone via a USB cable (you may need to install the relevant drivers for your flight controller)

Flash your firmware - Just like a computer runs Windows, OSX or Linux a flight controller runs different software versions. It's always best when setting up a new flight controller to update to the latest release of your firmware of choice. This is often done from the main screen of the configurator. Set up your Peripherals—When you wired up our flight controller you may of connected things to one of the UART connections, your receiver will be connected to one of these that has been labeled as SBUS. We need to set up these ports in order to tell the flight controller what it's communicating with. Drone configuration—We want to tell the drone which angle with mounted the flight controller at, which receiver we are using, how to talk to ESCs and set various limits, such as the minimum throttle. There's a lot to set here which will be better explained in a future video. Set up your flight modes—These modes need to be allocated to switches on your transmitter. For a beginner I would recommend setting an Arm switch and then a separate switch for Auto level and acro mode. Additional switches can be used for features, such as buzzers. Set your rates—Rates determine how sensitive your transmitter sticks are, for a beginner I would recommend leaving them at default and adjusting as your confidence grows.

5.12   CONCLUSION

Some well-known techniques of classical linear and nonlinear control methods were presented in this course. Other techniques have been used for flight control of UAV, but mostly for some particular missions.

CHAPTER 6

Theory

6.1   INTRODUCTION

Flight requires control of position, attitude and velocity. Control law design can only be performed satisfactorily if a set of design requirement or performance criteria is available. Control theory provides a standard approach:

1. Model the dynamics of the aircraft.

2. Represent the task in terms of a state error.

3. Design a control algorithm to drive the state error to zero.

4. Measure all the states if possible.

5. Estimate the system state online.

6. Input the state/output estimate into the control to close the loop.

Existing UAS flight controllers can be classified into three main categories:

1. Linear flight control system

2. Model-based nonlinear controllers

3. Learning-based control methods.

In the last decades, control for these systems was developed using the linearization approach. A lot of work has been devoted to the control and state estimation of these linear systems. In guidance system, in point-mass models, attitude control systems are incorporated and attitude is assumed to be quickly controlled. Only translational motion is considered. A flat Earth model is assumed. In a coordinated flight, the flight direction is confined to the plane of symmetry leading to a zero side force.

PID Control Loop and Tuning: Proportional Integral Derivative control allows to change the UAV's flight characteristics, including how it reacts to user input, how well and how quickly it stabilizes and more. The PID

DOI: 10.1201/9781003121787-6

settings and how the software uses the various sensor inputs are important. Manufacturer which produce ready to fly kits are able to fine tune the PID settings and equations for their specific platform, which is why most RTF multirotors fly quite well out of the box. Builders of custom UAVs, however, need to use flight controllers which are designed to be suitable for almost any type of multirotor aircraft, and as such it is up to the end-user to adjust the values until they are satisfied with the flight characteristics.

First approach, guidance and control design problems separated into:

1. An outer loop controller: to track the given position commands and reach the desired positions given the thrust, the lift and the bank angle as the inputs (or thrust, angle of attack, bank angle): results in the aircraft's navigation relative to a fixed frame. The desired position and velocity are stored online at discrete times serving as nominal values.

2. An inner loop controller: to follow the desired attitude generated from the outer loop, using the control surface of the aileron, elevator and rudder: results in control of aircraft's orientation.

Continuous control laws using Euler angles cannot be globally defined; thus, these representations are limited to local attitude maneuvers:

1. Local attitude control: changes in the attitude and angular velocity in the open neighborhood of the desired attitude and angular velocity.

2. Global attitude control: when arbitrary changes in the attitude and angular velocity are allowed. No a priori restrictions are placed on the possible rotational motion.

Second approach, guidance and control problems addressed together: flight controller designed to stabilize the attitude by holding a desired orientation and position, by tracking a desired trajectory/path:

1. Path following: an aircraft converges to and follows a desired spatial path, while tracking a desired speed profile that may be path dependent. The temporal and spatial assignments can be separated.

2. Trajectory following control system: guiding the aircraft to stay on a given reference trajectory. Due to unconsidered disturbances and simplifications made in the model used for guidance, a control system for trajectory error reduction must be designed.

In an atmospheric flight, aircraft can encounter a wide range of flight conditions, disturbances can be as strong as it's own control forces.

The main challenges of flight control and planning include:

1. Generation of a feasible trajectory with respect to dynamics and capabilities.

2. Integration between guidance and control to ensure safety, maximizing performance and flexibility.

3. Satisfaction of performance criteria and terminal state constraints.

Drones with obstacle detection and collision avoidance sensors are becoming more prevalent in both the consumer and professional sectors. This obstacle detection and avoidance technology started with sensors detecting objects in front of the drone. Stereo Vision, Monocular Vision, Ultrasonic, Infrared, Time-of-Flight and Lidar sensors being used to detect and avoid obstacles. Manufacturers are fusing these various sensors together to create the obstacle detection and collision avoidance systems.

Flight control must account for changing weather and possible collision avoidance, while achieving optimal fuel consumption. Depending on the mission, a set of design requirements may be different.

1. In a dynamic maneuvering situation, the autopilot is mainly concerned with the control forces that must be exerted and the resulting 6 dof translational and angular accelerations.

2. In a task requiring precision tracking, the evaluation of the control system is more influenced by landmarks and the response of the aircraft to turbulence.

6.2   LINEAR CONTROL METHODS

Linear control methods are generally divided to:

1. PID (one of the most successful linear controller)

2. Linear time invariant (LTI) (linearization around an operating point)

3. Linear time variant (LTV) (linearization around a trajectory)

4. Linear parameter variant (LPV) (multi-model approach).

6.2.1   PID controller

The PID controller is widely employed because it is very understandable and because it is quite effective. One attraction of the PID controller is that all engineers understand conceptually differentiation and integration, so they can implement the control system even without a deep understanding of control theory. Further, even though the compensator is simple, it is quite sophisticated in that it captures the history of the system (through integration) and anticipates the future behavior of the system (through differentiation). We will discuss the effect of each of the PID parameters on the dynamics of a closed-loop system and will demonstrate how to use a PID controller to improve a system's performance.

1. Generally, a hierarchical two-loops architecture is used, assuming a time-scale separation between the inner-loop and the outer-loop subsystems.

2. The inner loop controls the attitude using single-input-single-output (SISO) PID for each axis.

3. The outer loop is responsible for translation motion control using decoupled PID controllers.

4. These PID-type flight controllers were implemented and are still in use in most projects.

5. The model may not be used and controller gains can be tuned empirically by trial and error. This is a time-consuming process that can be improved by identifying dynamic model from flight data and then tuning PID controllers in simulation using the identified model.

PID necessitates three direct feedback gains:

1. P: On the measurement deviation (error to be minimized), high P: fast (the nominal value is reached early) but not precise (important oscillations around the nominal value), low P: slow (the nominal value is reached late) but precise (few oscilations);

2. I: On its integral (to counter any disturbances), high I: slow, but precise (at the beginning, the farthest value is quite close to the nominal value), low I: fast, but not precise (at the beginning, the farthest value is quite away from the nominal value);

3. D: On its derivative (to provide damping). high D: slow (it takes a long time until the values stay in the acceptable range) but precise (the range becomes narrow), low D: fast (the value get fast in the acceptable range) but not precise (the range stays quite wide).

The output of a PID controller, which is equal to the control input to the plant, is calculated in the time domain from the feedback error as follows:

$$U(t) = \mathbf{K}_P e(t) + \mathbf{K}_I \int_0^t e(\tau)d\tau + \mathbf{K}_V \frac{de(t)}{dt} \tag{6.1}$$

error $e(t) = R(t) - Y(t)$, $R(t)$ being the reference signal and $Y(t)$ is the measured signal; $\mathbf{K}_P, \mathbf{K}_I, \mathbf{K}_V$ are the gain diagonal matrices.

The transfer function of a PID controller is found by taking the Laplace transform of equation (6.1)

$$G(s) = K_p + \frac{K_i}{s} + K_d s = \frac{K_d s^2 + K_p s + K_i}{s} \tag{6.2}$$

Increasing the proportional gain (K_p) has the effect of proportionally increasing the control signal for the same level of error. The fact that the controller

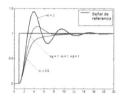

FIGURE 6.1 Landing-gear

will "push" harder for a given level of error tends to cause the closed-loop system to react more quickly, but also to overshoot more. Another effect of increasing K_p is that it tends to reduce, but not eliminate, the steady-state error.

The addition of a derivative term to the controller (K_d) adds the ability of the controller to "anticipate" error. With simple proportional control, if K_p is fixed, the only way that the control will increase is if the error increases. With derivative control, the control signal can become large if the error begins sloping upward, even while the magnitude of the error is still relatively small. This anticipation tends to add damping to the system, thereby decreasing overshoot. The addition of a derivative term, however, has no effect on the steady-state error.

The addition of an integral term to the controller (K_i) tends to help reduce steady-state error. If there is a persistent, steady error, the integrator builds and builds, thereby increasing the control signal and driving the error down. A drawback of the integral term, however, is that it can make the system more sluggish (and oscillatory) since when the error signal changes sign, it may take a while for the integrator to "unwind."

The advantages of PID law are that tuning is easily linked to physics and objectives, while the drawbacks are lack of optimization and filtering must be in series.

6.2.2 Properties of Linear Systems

General formulation

$$\dot{X} = \mathbf{A}X + \mathbf{B}U$$
$$Y = \mathbf{C}X$$

(6.3)

X, U, Y state variable, input or control variable and output or measure variable. $\mathbf{A}, \mathbf{B}, \mathbf{C}$ state matrix, control matrix and output matrix.

Controllability iff the controllability matrix $\mathbf{Co} = \begin{bmatrix} \mathbf{B}, \mathbf{AB}, \mathbf{A}^2\mathbf{B} \dots \mathbf{A}^{n-1}\mathbf{B} \end{bmatrix}$ has rank n. The pair $(\mathbf{A}, \mathbf{B})$ is said to be controllable.

Observability iff the Observability matrix $\mathbf{Ob} = \begin{bmatrix} \mathbf{C} \\ \mathbf{CA} \\ \mathbf{CA}^2 \\ \vdots \\ \mathbf{CA}^{n-1} \end{bmatrix}$ has rank n.

The pair $(\mathbf{A}, \mathbf{C})$ is said to be observable.

The system is stable if the eigenvalues of $\mathbf{A}$ have negative real parts, it is Hurwitz.

6.2.3 Linear Approaches for LTI Models

Traditional methods for flight control design typically use nested single-input-single-output (SISO) control loops and strongly structured control architectures. These methods are based on detailed aircraft system analysis. Autopilots have been designed using these methods.

However, multivariable methods, such as optimal control and robust control design methods are state of the art for more complex flight control tasks under coupled and/or uncertain system dynamics.

Three large groups of control design methodologies are optimal, adaptive and robust control design methods.

Robustness is a property that guarantees that essential functions of the designed system are maintained under adverse conditions in which the model no longer accurately reflects reality.

6.2.4 Classical methods: Direct approach

Many state-space methods have been used for the design of the autopilots, such as the direct approach, the pole placement, the eigenvalue assignment by output feedback, the linear quadratic regulator and the adaptive approach. Direct approach where a static control law can be proposed:

$$U(t) = \mathbf{K}_r R(t) + \mathbf{K}_x X(t) \tag{6.4}$$

$\mathbf{K}_x$ is the feedback gain matrix and $\mathbf{K}_r$ is the feed-forward gain matrix, to be determined so that the closed-loop control system:

$$\begin{aligned} \dot{X} &= \mathbf{A}_d X + \mathbf{B}_d U \\ Y &= \mathbf{C}X \end{aligned} \tag{6.5}$$

$\mathbf{B}$ being generally not invertible, the following gain matrices can be proposed:

$$\mathbf{K}_x = \mathbf{B}^T \left(\mathbf{B}\mathbf{B}^T \right)^{-1} \left(\mathbf{A}_d - \mathbf{A} \right) \tag{6.6}$$

$$\mathbf{K}_r = \mathbf{B}^T \left(\mathbf{B}\mathbf{B}^T \right)^{-1} \mathbf{B}_d \tag{6.7}$$

This method is seldom used because of the difficulty of the choice of the matrices $\mathbf{A}_d, \mathbf{B}_d$.

6.2.5 Classical Methods: Pole placement

If the pair $(\mathbf{A}, \mathbf{B})$ is completely controllable, then for any set of eigenvalues $\lambda_1, \lambda_2, \ldots, \lambda_n \in \mathbb{C}$ symmetric wrt the real axis, there exists a matrix $\mathbf{K} \in \mathbb{R}^{n \times n}$ such that the eigenvalues of $\mathbf{A} + \mathbf{BK}$ are $\lambda_1, \lambda_2, \ldots, \lambda_n$.

In this method, the following control law is proposed

$$U(t) = -\mathbf{K}_x X(t) \tag{6.8}$$

$\lambda_1, \ldots, \lambda_n$ given then using the characteristic polynomial:

$$\lambda(s) = \det\left(s\mathbf{I} - A + \mathbf{BK}_x\right) \tag{6.9}$$

Identification or other methods, such as Bass-Gura method allow to solve n equations giving the elements of the matrix $\mathbf{K}_x$.

If only $m < n$ eigenvalues are imposed, the matrix $\mathbf{K}_x$ can be decomposed into the product of two vectors:

$$\mathbf{K}_x = bd^T \qquad b \in \mathbf{R}^m \qquad d \in \mathbf{R}^n \tag{6.10}$$

The closed-loop system is then given by:

$$\dot{X} = \mathbf{A}X - \mathbf{B}(bd^T)X = \mathbf{A}X - \varphi\varpi \tag{6.11}$$

with $\varphi = \mathbf{B}b$ and $\varpi = d^T X$ with the pair $(\mathbf{A}, \varphi)$ controllable:

$$U = -b\left(k_1\varpi_1^T + k_2\varpi_2^T + \cdots + k_m\varpi_m^T\right)X \tag{6.12}$$

with

$$k_j = \frac{\prod_{i=1}^{m}\left(\lambda_i^d - \lambda_j\right)}{\varphi\varpi_j \prod_{i=1,i\neq j}^{m}\left(\lambda_i - \lambda_j\right)} \tag{6.13}$$

It imposes the pole placement λ_i^d while the other eigenvalues remain unchanged. The ϖ_j are the m eigenvectors of $\mathbf{A}^T$ associated with the eigenvalues $\lambda_1, \ldots, \lambda_m$.

6.2.6 Gain Scheduling

To extend the capabilities of linear flight controllers, nonlinear dynamics can be modeled as a collection of simplified linear models, with each model representing a particular operating regime. Gains scheduling is the most used technique.

1. In the design of aircraft control systems, it is important to realize that the rigid body equations are only an approximation of the nonlinear aircraft dynamics. An aircraft has also flexible modes that are important at high frequencies, being potentially destabilizing.

2. Changing equilibrium flight conditions, the linearized model describing its perturbed behavior changes. Suitable controller gains must be determined at several design equilibrium points to guarantee stability for actual flight conditions near that equilibrium point.

3. Thus, it is important to design controllers that have stability robustness, which is the ability to provide stability in spite of modeling errors due to high frequency unmodeled dynamics and plant parameter variations.

4. Gain scheduling is the process of varying a set of controller coefficients according to the current value of a scheduling signal. Given a set of flight condition variables, such as Mach number, angle of attack, dynamic pressure, center of gravity location ..., Linearization at several design points throughout the flight envelope:

$$\delta \dot{X} = \frac{\partial f}{\partial X}|_i \delta X + \frac{\partial f}{\partial U}|_i \delta U = \mathbf{A}_i \delta X + \mathbf{B}_i \delta U \qquad (6.14)$$

where i represents the evaluation at the ith design points and $\delta X, \delta U$ are perturbations in the system from the design point.

5. Gain scheduling is performed between the design points by interpolating the gains to effect a smoothly varying set of gains throughout the flight envelope. Simple curve fitting approaches are used. In fact, linear interpolation seems to be the standard approach.

6. Gain scheduled controllers are effective for tackling the changes of aircraft dynamics. The classical method selects the design points, designs LTI controllers at the design points and connects all the LTI controllers to cover the admissible envelope. The provided airspeed data include some uncertainties because they are calculated from the measured dynamic and static pressures by using pitot tubes and the measurements are affected by the hull of the aircraft, inaccuracies due to the limited resolution of onboard sensors. Thus the gain scheduled controller should have robustness against uncertainties.

7. The onboard actuators have large uncertainties and the flight controller should have robustness against them. One objective is to design a flight controller that realizes a model-matching property under wind gusts as well as the uncertainties related to the onboard sensors and actuators in the admissible speed range.

Designing and implementing linear flight controllers is straightforward and there are many available tools to tune their gains and to analyze their performance and robustness. Moreover, they have been successfully used in UAV to achieve wide range of tasks and maneuvers. However, it is well-known that these linear controllers suffer from performance degradation when the UAV leaves the nominal conditions or performs aggressive maneuvers. From the theoretical point of view, ,it is also difficult to prove the asymptotic stability of the complete closed-loop system. Despite these limitations, PID and gain scheduling are the most widely accepted methods of flight control.

6.3   TRIM TRAJECTORY GENERATION

The aircraft is accelerated under the action of non-zero resultant aerodynamic and gravitational forces and moments, balanced by effects such as centrifugal and gyroscopic inertial forces and moments. Under the trim condition, the motion is uniform in the body fixed frame. The aerodynamic coefficients become stationary. Trim trajectories are characterized by the stationarity of the body-fixed velocity components and the controls.

$$\dot{V}(t) \equiv 0 \qquad \dot{\Omega}(t) \equiv 0 \qquad \forall t \in [0, t_f] \tag{6.15}$$

Focusing on the angular velocity kinematics transformation:

$$\Omega = J(\eta_2)^{-1}\dot{\eta}_2 \tag{6.16}$$

All forces and moments depending on the velocity vector are constant except the aerostatic forces and moments τ_s which depends on the attitude variables, the roll ϕ and the pitch θ angles. The roll angle ϕ_e and pitch θ_e angle must be constant.

$$\begin{aligned} p_e &= -\dot{\psi}_e \sin\theta_e \\ q_e &= \dot{\psi}_e \sin(\phi_e)\cos(\theta_e) \\ r_e &= \dot{\psi}_e \cos(\phi_e)\cos(\theta_e) \end{aligned} \tag{6.17}$$

The components of the body-fixed angular velocity vector depend on the roll angle ϕ_e, pitch angle θ_e and the yaw rate $\dot{\psi}_e$.
Geometry of the trim trajectories:

$$\dot{\eta}_1 = R(\eta_2)\begin{pmatrix} u_e \\ v_e \\ w_e \end{pmatrix} = R_z(\psi)\begin{pmatrix} a \\ b \\ c \end{pmatrix} \tag{6.18}$$

where $\begin{pmatrix} a \\ b \\ c \end{pmatrix} = R_y(\theta_e)R_x(\phi_e)\begin{pmatrix} u_e \\ v_e \\ w_e \end{pmatrix}$

Flight path angle $\gamma_e = acos\left(\frac{\sqrt{a^2+b^2}}{V_e}\right)$ Translational kinematics, $V_e = \|V\|$
Navigation velocity, ψ_0 initial heading angle

$$\dot{\eta}_1 = \begin{pmatrix} V_e\cos(\gamma_e)\cos(\dot{\psi}_e t + \psi_0) \\ V_e\cos(\gamma_e)\sin(\dot{\psi}_e t + \psi_0) \\ -V_e\sin(\gamma_e) \end{pmatrix} \tag{6.19}$$

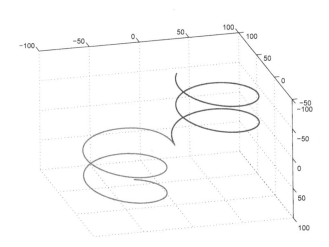

FIGURE 6.2 Helix

Geometric characterization of trim trajectories:

$$\eta_1 = \begin{pmatrix} \frac{V_e}{\dot{\psi}_e}\cos(\gamma_e)\sin(\frac{\dot{\psi}_e}{V_e}s + \psi_0) \\ -\frac{V_e}{\dot{\psi}_e}\cos(\gamma_e)\cos(\frac{\dot{\psi}_e}{V_e}s + \psi_0) \\ -\sin(\gamma)s \end{pmatrix} + \begin{pmatrix} x_1 \\ y_1 \\ z_0 \end{pmatrix} \quad (6.20)$$

where $x_1 = x_0 - \frac{V_e}{\dot{\psi}_e}\cos\gamma_e\sin\psi_e$, $y_1 = y_0 + \frac{V_e}{\dot{\psi}_e}\cos\gamma_e\cos\psi_e$, $(x_0, y_0, z_0)^T$ the initial position.

Parametrization of the trim trajectory by $\mathcal{T}_e = (\phi_e, \theta_e, \dot{\psi}_e, u_e, v_e, w_e)$ and the curvilinear abscissa s is for a uniform motion: $s = V_e t$.

Curvature and torsion are constant for trim trajectories

$$\begin{aligned} \kappa(s) &= \chi_1\cos(\gamma_0) \\ \tau(s) &= \chi_1\sin(\gamma_0) \end{aligned} \quad (6.21)$$

Depending on γ_e and $\dot{\psi}_e$, the trajectories can be represented by a helix, a circle arc or a straight line. Their geometry depends on V_e, ϕ_e, θ_e, $\dot{\psi}_e$, satisfying the dynamic equations, the controls saturation and envelope protection constraints.

6.4 CONCLUSION

Some well-known techniques of classical linear and nonlinear control methods were presented in this course. Other techniques have been used for flight control of UAV, but mostly for some particular missions.

CHAPTER 7

Flight Operations

7.1 INTRODUCTION

UAVs come in all shapes and sizes and have been optimized to perform numerous functions including, but not limited to environmental monitoring, reconnaissance and surveillance, communications relay, cargo delivery,

Airspace classification and operating requirements, and flight restrictions affecting small unmanned aircraft operation

7.2 SITUATIONAL AWARENESS

Situational awareness includes in general:

1. High level state model of the whole system: agents, vehicles, environments

2. Real-time assessment and prediction of situations: nominal, disrupted, unreachable

For UAS, Situational awareness involves:

1. Ground risk (accidents/incidents involving persons on the ground or sensitive areas)

2. Air risk (collision risk, air proximity, accidents and incidents with manned aircraft)

3. Violation of privacy, data protection and security

4. Barriers to the market, burden for industry, locked potential for innovation and development.

DOI: 10.1201/9781003121787-7

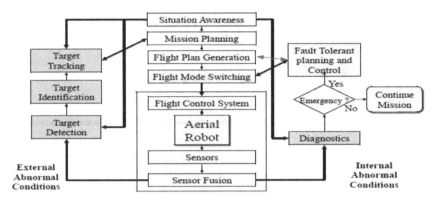

FIGURE 7.1   UAS sequence diagram

7.3   FLIGHT OPERATIONS

Architecture diagram of the avionics architecture, includes the location of all air data sensors, antennas, radios and navigation equipment and any redundant system. Sequence diagram is an interaction diagram that shows how processes operate with one another and what is their order.

7.3.1   UAV Piloting techniques

UAS flight operations are to be conducted in good visibility conditions (VMC), 30 minutes prior to sunrise to sunset and should be conducted when good visibility of powerlines or other potential hazards are degraded by the effect of weather. The minimum distance from clouds should be greater than 500 ft below and no less than 2000 feet horizontal.

Definition 55 *Geo-fencing is the software using GPS signals to stop drones flying into certain areas*

7.3.1.1   Supervision

1. Online control of the execution of planned actions

2. Reactions trigger depending on current and predicted situations

3. Execution of elementary actions: move, perception, communication, replanning

Flight planning and operations:

1. Planning a mission implies generating a flight plan, ordered list of dated actions

2. Plan: sequence of actions or policy

3. Offline preparation and online repair or replanning

4. Flight planning preparation: The first step is to receive details of the flights. This will contain a map of the area, details of what is required from the flight as well as any potential risks. To determine the operating site location, check type of airspace, other aircraft operations, hazards, local bylaws, obstructions, extraordinary restrictions, weather conditions. Digital data (scanned maps and aerial photographs) can be used as planning background. With some software, calculations such as fuel consumption (based on selected configuration), time and range of flight can be done automatically.

5. Risk management should be assessed prior to the operation.

6. On-site procedures: selection of operating area, landing zones and checking of ground risks;

7. Flight procedures: start, take-off, fligh then landing, and finally shutdown

In the future, UAVs are expected to operate with a higher level of autonomy to carry out complex tasks, while efficiently coordinating with other unmanned systems. There is a need for systematic mission planning processes.

Mountain flying: when planning a flight over mountainous terrain, gather as much preflight information as possible on cloud reports, wind direction, wind speed, and stability of the air. Satellites often help locate mountain waves. Wind at mountain top level in excess of 25 knots suggests some turbulence. Wind in excess of 40 knots across a mountain barrier dictates caution. Stratified clouds mean stable air. Standing lenticular and/or rotor clouds suggest a mountain wave; expect turbulence many miles to the lee of mountains and relative smooth flight on the windward side. Convective clouds on the windward side of mountains mean unstable air; expect turbulence in close proximity to and on either side of the mountain.

Line of sight: The pilot can see their UAV during flight.

FPV (First Person View): The pilot can see where they are flying through the UAV's camera. The capacity of FPV drones to enter environments that are unsafe for humans makes them effective for search and rescue missions. Drones can be remotely piloted to locate people in dangerous situations, avoiding much of the need for physical presence. Similarly, drones can be used to inspect physical infrastructure that is difficult to access, such as bridges and high buildings. In agri-tech (agricultural technology), an FPV drone allows a farmer to survey crops and livestock much more quickly than is possible with ground-based inspection and much more closely than is possible from a plane. A drone can also be equipped with sensors to capture environmental data for more sophisticated analysis. Drone-based inspection

WFT06X-A Transmitter Features (Front)

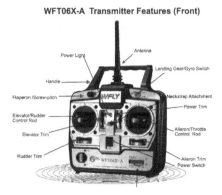

FIGURE 7.2 Remote controller

can facilitate precision agriculture, the application of information technology to ensure that the crops and soil receive exactly what they need for optimum health and productivity, while also optimizing the efficient use of resources.

Remote control/transmitter: A transmitter is a hand-held controller that lets pilot the quadrotor and control its flight pattern.

7.3.2 Checklists

7.3.2.1 PreFlight checklist

PreFlight checklist must be carried out before each flight:

1. Visual condition inspection of the UAS components.

2. Airframe structure and undercarriage, all flight control surfaces and linkages.

3. Registration markings, for proper display and legibility.

4. Moveable control surfaces, including airframe attachment points.

5. Servo motors including attachment points.

6. Propulsion system: power-plants, propellers, rotors, ducted fans, ...

7. All systems such as aircraft and control unit must have an adequate energy supply for the intended operation and must functioning properly.

8. Avionics, including control link transceiver, communication and navigation equipment and antennas.

9. Display panel, if used, is functioning properly.

10. Ground support equipment, including takeoff and landing systems.

11. Check that control link correct functionality is established between the UAV and control station (CS).

12. Check for correct movement of control surfaces using the CS.

13. Check on-board navigation and communication data links.

14. Check flight termination system, if installed.

15. Check fuel for correct type and quantity.

16. Check battery levels for the UAV and control station.

17. Check that any equipment, such as camera, is securely attached.

18. Verify communication with UAS and that the UAS has acquired GPS location from at least four satellites.

19. Start the UAS propellers to inspect for any imbalance or irregular operation.

20. If required by flight path walk through, verify any noted obstructions that may interfere with the UAS.

21. At a controlled low altitude, fly within range of any interference and recheck all controls and stability.

7.3.2.2 Pre-launch checklist

Pre-launch checklist must also be carried out:

1. Inspect local weather condition, local airspace and any flight restrictions and the location of people, animals, or other objects and ground hazards.

2. Communication within the crew concerning operating condition, emergency procedures and contingency procedures.

3. Necessary documentation available for inspection, including the remote pilot certificate, aircraft registration.

   (a) Make sure your flight path is clear of any people or airports.

   (b) Is the weather and wind providing safe flying conditions? Some days are not meant for flying.

   (c) Make sure the UAV has fresh batteries.

   (d) Make sure the propellers are correctly attached and spin smoothly without obstruction.

   (e) Configure the camera settings.

(f) If you have any object attached or carried out by the UAV, make sure that it is secure and does not adversely affect the flight characteristics or controllability of the aircraft. Even a small shift in the center of gravity of the UAV can significantly affect flight operations.

(g) Be sure that your area is clear of crowded Wifi signals.

(h) Determine the takeoff and landing surface to be level and clear of obstacles.

(i) If you are keeping a flight log, note the date, time, flight path, and weather conditions.

(j) Turn on the transmitter.

(k) If your UAV needs to calibrate and get satellite lock, wait until it finishes.

(l) Make sure there is enough room for launch and flight.

(m) Make sure the throttle (left stick) is all the way down.

(n) Turn on the transmitter.

(o) Back away 3 or 4 steps (or to a safe distance).

(p) Keep facing the quadrotor the entire time.

(q) Keep a direct line of sight at all times when flying, so you can always see your quadrotor. You want to keep a direct line of sight so you know when you're about to crash. Also, sometimes, quadrotors can fly out of the range of the transmitter's signal, which can cause your UAV to fly off on its own. Keep the transmitter's range in mind, and don't let your quadrotor fly out of that range.

4. Important safety precautions: quadrotors can be dangerous if not operated carefully.

(a) If you're about to crash into something, turn the throttle down to zero, so you don't potentially destroy your quadrotor, injure somebody, or injure yourself.

(b) Keep your fingers away from the propellers when they're moving.

(c) Unplug/take out the battery of the quadrotor before doing any work on it. If it turns on accidentally and the propellers start spinning, you might have a tough time doing future flights with missing fingers.

(d) If you are a beginner learning to fly indoors, tie the quadrotor down or surround it by a cage.

7.3.2.3 Post-flight checklist

Post-flight checklist:

1. The pilot will make sure that the immediate area is clear of hazards before taking off.

2. The pilot will follow the flight procedures to ensure a safe flight.

3. If the requestor wishes to alter the task while the UAV is in flight, the pilot must first land. The task will then be discussed to see what is required and if there will be additional hazards associated with the change.

4. If there are any changes to the weather, ground conditions or potential hazards then the pilot will decide whether or not to continue the flight.

5. The pilot will make sure that the landing site is clear from hazards before landing the UAV.

6. After the flight, the pilot will dis-assemble the UAV, checking for any damage or wear and tear.

7. The pilot will place the UAV and any accessories back into the carry case.

8. In the case of any accidents or collisions, the pilot will report the occurrence.

7.3.3 Loading and performance

The environment is the aggregate of operational and ambient conditions to include the external procedures, conditions and objects that affect the development, operation and maintenance of a system. Operational conditions include traffic density, communication density, workload. Ambient conditions include weather, EMI, vibration, acoustics etc. In any aircraft system, there are hazards introduced by equipment failures.

Important medical factors that a pilot should be aware of include: hyperventilation, stress, fatigue, dehydration, heatstroke, the effects of alcohol and drugs.

Before any flight, the remote PIC should verify the UAV is correctly loaded by determining the weight and balance condition of the UAV. An aircraft's weight and balance restrictions established by the manufacturer should be closely followed. Compliance with the manufacturer's weight and balance limits is critical to flight safety. The remote PIC must consider the consequences of an overweight aircraft if an emergency condition arises:

1. Although a maximum gross takeoff weight may be specified, the aircraft may not always safely takeoff with this load under all conditions Conditions that affect takeoff and climb performance, such as high elevations, high air temperatures, and high humidity (high density altitudes) may require a reduction in weight before flight is attempted. Other factors to consider prior to takeoff are runway/launch area length, surface, slope, surface wind and the presence of obstacles. These factors may require a reduction in weight prior to flight.

2. Weight changes during flight also have a direct effect on aircraft performance. Fuel burn is the most common weight change that takes place during flight. As fuel is used, the aircraft becomes lighter and performance is improved, but this could have a negative effect on balance. In small UAV operations, weight change during flight may occur when expendable items are used on board (example a jettisonable load).

Effects of loading changes: Before any flight, the operator should verify that the UAV is correctly loaded by determining the aircraft's weight and balance condition. Although a maximum gross take-off weight may be specified in the flight manual, the UAV may not always be able to take off with this load under all conditions. At higher density altitudes (higher elevations, temperatures and humidiy), the maximum gross take-off weight, must be reduced. Other factors to consider prior to take-off are the runway/launch area length, the launch surface and slope, the surface wind and the presence of obstacles. Any of these factors may require a reduction in weight prior to flight. Additionally, the operator should consider that the load factor on the wings may be increased any time the airplane is subject to maneuvers other than straight-and-level flight. Weight changes during flight can have a direct effect on the UAV performance. In UAV operations, detachable load, like a package that is being delivered, can affect the weight and flight performance.

With the structural design of aircraft planned to withstand only a certain amount of overload, a knowledge of load factors has become essential for all pilots. Load factors are important for a two reasons:

1. It is possible for a pilot to impose a dangerous overload on the aircraft structures.

2. An increased load factor increases the stalling speed and makes stalls possible at seemingly safe flight speeds.

Payload placement: To assist with payload placement, some aircraft have indicators on the frame showing the proper center of gravity (CG) location. Aircraft manuals usually publish an acceptable CG range, longitudinally and laterally, away from the ideal CG. When using an aircraft that can accept different payloads and batteries, it is important to check that the CG is correct before every flight. The typical payload is in a fixed position in front of the aircraft while the battery slides back and forth to achieve the correct

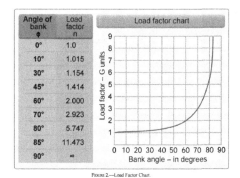

Angle of bank ϕ	Load factor n
0°	1.0
10°	1.015
30°	1.154
45°	1.414
60°	2.000
70°	2.923
80°	5.747
85°	11.473
90°	∞

FIGURE 2.—Load Factor Chart.

FIGURE 7.3 UAS traffic management

CG. Improper placement of the CG results in the motors on the heavy end of the vehicle working harder than the others. If the CG is too far off, the motors on the heavy end can reach 100 percent power in flight, leading to a loss of altitude or loss of control of the vehicle. For airplanes, improper CG can lead to the control surfaces not be able to control the aircraft. **Load factor**: Anytime an aircraft is an attitude other than straight and level flight (unaccelerated), load is imposed on it. This is very noticeable in airplanes while in turns. The greater the bank angle, the higher the load factor. It is the total load supported by the aircraft's wings divided by the actual weight of the aircraft and its contents.

Balance, stability and center of gravity: The location of the center of gravity depends on the distribution of weight in the UAV. For example, the CG is going to change if adding camera or other electronic payloads or adding a parachute recovery system. The changing of the CG may affect the UAV's performance.

Aircraft performance: Performance is a term used to describe the ability of an aircraft to accomplish certain things that make it useful for certain purposes. The primary factors most affected by performance are the takeoff and landing distance, maximum altitude, endurance, range, rate of climb, rate of descent, bank angle and turn rate limits; minimum visibility conditions.

1. Since weight, altitude and configuration changes affect excess thrust and power, they also affect climb performance. Climb performance is directly dependent upon the ability to produce either excess thrust or excess power.

2. Weight has an important effect on UAV performance. If weight is added to an aircraft, it must fly at a higher angle of attack (AOA) to maintain a given altitude and speed. This increases the induced drag of the wings, as well as the parasite drag of the airplane. Increased drag means that additional thrust is needed to overcome it, which in turn, means that less reserve thrust is available for climbing.

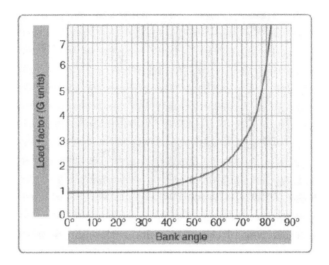

FIGURE 7.4 Bank angle changes load factor in level flight

3. A change in an aircraft's weight produces a twofold effect on climb performance. An increase in altitude also increases the power required and decreases the power available. Therefore, the climb performance of an aircraft with altitude

Terminal aerodrome forecasts (TAF):

The importance and use of performance data to predict the effects on the aircraft's performance of a small UAS: The major change in weight for an sUAV would be the size and weight of the payload being picked up or dropped off. It can have an effect on the weight, center of gravity and aerodynamic principal of the UAV.

7.4   AERONAUTICAL DECISION-MAKING

Definition 56 *Aeronautical decision making (ADM) is a systematic approach to the mental approach used by pilots to consistently determine the best course of action in response to a given set of circumstances.*

Aeronautical decision-making A UAV pilot uses many different resources to safely operate an sUAV and needs to be able to manage these resources effectively. It is estimated that approximately 80 percent of all aviation accidents are related to human factors and the vast majority of these accidents occur during landing (24.1 percent) and takeoff (23.4 percent).

Two defining elements of ADM are hazard and risk. Hazard is a real or perceived condition, event or circumstance that a pilot encounters. When faced with a hazard, the pilot makes an assessment of that hazard based upon various factors. A ris is an assessment of the single or cumulative hazard facing a pilot.

Studies have identified five hazardous attitudes that can interfere with the ability to make sound decisions and exercise authority properly: anti-authority, impulsivity, invulnerability, macho and resignation.

Crew resource management (CRM) is a component of Aeronautical decision-making, where the pilot of sUAv makes effective use of all available resources: human resources, hardware and information. A remote PIC must be able to function in a team environment and maximize team performance. This skill set includes situational awareness, proper allocation of tasks to individuals, avoidance of work overloads in self and in others, and effectively communicating with other members of the crew.

Task management

Hazardous altitudes

Hazard identification and risk assessment: A risk assessment tool contains expanded information on ADM and CRM as well as sample risk assessment tools to aid in identifying hazards and mitigating risks.

Specific operations risk assessment (SORA):

1. **CONOPS**: Concept of operations is a user-oriented document that describes systems characteristics for a proposed system from a user's perspective. A CONOPS also describes the user organization, mission and objectives from an integrated systems point of view and is used to communicate overall quantitative and qualitative system characteristics to stakeholder.

2. **ConOps Description**: the operator must collect and provide sufficient technical, operational and human information related to the intended use of the UAS needed for the risk assessment. The ConOps should not only be a description of the operation but also provide insight into the operator operational safety culture. Unmanned aircraft have no historical data and technology developments far outpaces data collection effectiveness.

3. **Determination of the initial UAS ground risk class (GRC)**: It is related to the unmitigated risk of a person being struck by the UAS (in case of loss of UAS control) and can be represented by eleven ground risk classes (GRC):

   (a) VLOS over controlled area, located inside a sparsely populated environment;

   (b) BLOS over sparsely populated environment (over-flown areas uniformly inhabited;

   (c) VLOS over controlled area, located inside a populated environment

   (d) VLOS over populated environment

    (e) BVLOS over controlled area, located inside a populated environment

    (f) BVLOS over populated environment

    (g) VLOS over gathering of people

4. A controlled area is defined as the intended UAS operational area that only involves active participants (if any)

5. An operation is defined as occurring over gathering of people if the intent of the UAS operation is to operate continuously over open-air assembly of people in which it is reasonable to assume that loss of control of the operation will result in direct hit of non-active participants.

6. In order to establish the GRC, the operator only needs the max aircraft characteristic dimension (wingspan for fixed wing, blade diameter for rotorcraft, max dimension for multicopters) and the knowledge of the intended operational scenario.

7. When evaluating the typical kinetic energy expected for a given operation, the operator should generally use airspeed, in particular V_{cruise} for fixed-wing aircraft and the terminal velocity for other aircraft: *https://www.grc.nasa.gov/WWW/K-12/airplane/termv.html*

8. **Harm barriers and GRC adaptation**: this step of the process allows for adaptation of the GRC based on the harm barriers available for the operation.

9. **Lethality determination**: different aircraft might have different lethality characteristics. The lethatlity is defined with three qualitative descriptors: high, average or low.

10. **Specific assurance and integrity levels (SAIL)**: the likelihood of losing control of the UAS operation is commensurate with the proposed ConOps.

11. **Determination of the airspace encounter category (AEC)**: AEC is a grouping of airspace types that best reflect perceived levels of collision risk. It is grouped by operational altitude, airport environment, controlled airspace, uncontrolled mode C, and in uncontrolled airspace over rural and/or urban populations into 12 categorizations.

12. **Initial assessment of the air-risk class (ARC)**: it is a qualitative classification of the rate at which a UAS would encounter a manned aircraft in typical generalized civil airspace. It is based on the assessment of the following three parameters: rate of proximity or encounter rate, geometry, Dynamics.

13. **Establish strategic and tactical mitigations**: strategic mitigation is applied to reduce the ARC while tactical mitigations are applied to meet residual risk of the ARC. Examples of strategic mitigations: restriction by time, by space, by time-of-exposure, strategic separation by procedure. Examples of tactical mitigations: Traffic collision avoidance system (TCAS), air traffic control (ATC), airborne collision avoidance system (ACAS-X), Mid-air collision avoidance system (MIDCAS), detect and avoid (DAA), airborne-based sense and avoid (ABSAA), ground-based sense and avoid (GBSAA), see and avoid, visual line of sight (VLOS).

Definition 57 *Extended visual line of sight (EVLOS): an UAS operation whereby the pilot in command maintains an uninterrupted situational awareness of the airspace in which the UAS operation is being conducted via visual airspace surveillance, possibly aided by technology means. The remote-pilot has a direct control of the UAV at all time.* **Situational awareness** *is key to the ability to mitigate problems.*

Definition 58 *Beyond visual line of sight (BVLOS or BLOS) operations; means flying an unmanned aircraft without the Remote Pilot having to keep it in visual line of sight at all times. Instead, the Remote Pilot flies the aircraft by instruments from a Remote Pilot Station (RPS). BVLOS operations require higher pilot qualifications. BVLOS flights are important because they can allow UAVs to cover much greater distances thereby improving the economics and feasibility of most commercial operations.*

7.5 AIRPORT OPERATIONS

The types of airports, such as towered, uncontrolled towered, heliport ad seaplane bases. An airport includes an area used or intended for airport buildings, facilities, as well as right of way together with the buildings and facilities. There are two types of airport: towered and non-towered (an operating control tower). Air traffic control (ATC) is responsible for providing the safe, orderly and expeditious flow of air traffic at airports where the type of operations and/or volume of traffic requires such a service.

Definition 59 *Segregated airspace: is the airspace of specified dimensions assigned for exclusive use to specific users*

ATC towers, such as ensuring the remote pilot can monitor and interpret ATC communications to improve situational awareness

Runway markings and signage

Traffic patterns used by manned aircraft pilots

Security identification display ares (SIDA)

Sources for airport data: aeronautical charts and charts supplements, Notices to Airmen (NOTAM) and automated terminal information service (ATIS). The chart supplement provides the most comprehensive information

Terminal Velocity
(gravity and drag)

Glenn
Research
Center

Forces	Net Force equals Drag minus Weight.

$$F = D - W$$

Drag Equation:

$$D = Cd \; \frac{\rho \, V^2 A}{2}$$

V = velocity
ρ = gas density
A = frontal area
Cd = drag coefficient

Drag
D

Drag increases with the square of the velocity.

When Drag is equal to Weight there is no net force on the rocket.

$$F = D - W = 0$$

Weight
W

Then: $\quad Cd \dfrac{\rho \, V^2 A}{2} = W$

Terminal Velocity: $\quad V = sqrt\left(\dfrac{2\,W}{Cd\,\rho\,A}\right)$

Comparing two objects, the higher velocity occurs for greater weight, lower drag coefficient (more steamlined), lower gas density (higher altitude), or smaller area.

Objects do <u>not</u> fall at the same rate through the atmosphere.

FIGURE 7.5 NASA terminal velocity

on a given airport. NOTAM information is time-critical aeronautical information, which is of temporary nature or not sufficiently known in advance to permit publication on aeronautical charts or in other operational publications, that receives immediate dissemination by the NOTAM system. A pilot can use this information to help them make an informed decision about where and when to operate their small UAV. Prior to any flights, pilots should check for any NOTAMs that could affect their intended flight. The automated terminal information service (ATIS) is a recording of the local weather conditions and other pertinent non-control information broadcast on a local frequency in a looped format It is normally updated once per hour. An aeronautical chart is the road map for a pilot. The chart provides information that allow remote pilots to obtain information about the areas where they intend to operate. The 2 aeronautical charts used by VFR pilots are sectional and VFR terminal area. Avoiding bird and wildlife hazards and reporting collisions between aircraft and wildlife

7.5.1 Airspace classification

1. The primary purpose of air traffic control (ATC) is to prevent a collision between aircraft operating in the national airspace system (NAS) and to organize the flow of aircraft traffic. ATC is responsible for ensuring

that the necessary coordination has been accomplished before allowing an aircraft under their control to enter another pilot/controller's area of jurisdiction.

2. There is a need to provide both vertical and horizontal separation between UAS and UAS; UAS and manned aircraft flying under IFR; and UAS and manned aircraft flying under VFR.

3. **Class B controlled airspace**: Generally, that airspace from the surface to 10,000 feet MSL surrounding the nation's busiest airports in terms of IFR operations or passenger enplanements. The configuration of each Class B airspace area is individually tailored and consists of a surface area and two or more layers (some Class B airspace areas resemble upside-down wedding cakes), and is designed to contain all published instrument procedures once an aircraft enters the airspace. An ATC clearance is required for all aircraft to operate in Class B Airspace, and all aircraft that so cleared receive separation services within the airspace. The cloud clearance requirement for VFR operations is clear of clouds.

4. **Class C controlled airspace**: Class C Airspace is generally that airspace from the surface to 4000 feet above the airport elevation (charted in MSL) surrounding those airports that have an operational control tower, are serviced by a radar approach control, and have a certain number of IFR operations or passenger enplanements. Although the configuration of each Class C airspace area is individually tailored, the airspace usually consists of a 5 NM radius core surface area that extends from the surface up to 4000 feet above the airport elevation, and a 10 NM radius shelf area that extends no lower than 1200 feet up to 4000 feet above airport elevation.

5. **Class D controlled airspace**: Class D airspace is generally that airspace from the surface to 2500 above the airport elevation (charted in MSL) surrounding those airports that have an operational control tower. The configuration of each Class D airspace area is individually tailored and when instrument procedures are published, the airspace will normally be designated to contain the procedure

6. **Class E controlled airspace**: Generally, if the airspace is not Class A, B, C, or D, and is controlled airspace it is Class E airspace. There are no specific pilot certification or equipment requirements to operate in Class E airspace. Special VFR operations are permitted but clearance must be obtained from the controlling facility. For VFR operations basic VFR visibility and distance from clouds must be maintained. Below 10000 MSL feet this is 3 statute miles visibility and 500 feet below, 1000 feet above, and 2000 feet horizontally. Above 10,000 feet MSL this increases to 5 statute miles visibility, 1000 feet above, 1000 feet below and 1 mile horizontally.

FIGURE 7.6 Airspace

7. **Class G uncontrolled airspace**: Uncontrolled airspace or Class G airspace is the portion of the airspace that has not been designated as Class A, B, C, D, or E. It is, therefore, designated uncontrolled airspace. Class G airspace extends from the surface to the base of the overlying Class E airspace. Although ATC has no authority or responsibility to control air traffic, pilots should remember there are visual flight rules (VFR) minimums that apply to Class G airspace.

8. **Special-use airspace**, such as prohibited, restricted, warning areas, military operation areas, alert areas and controlled firing areas. Special use airspace or special area of operation (SAO) is the designation for airspace in which certain activities must be confined, or where limitations may be imposed on aircraft operations that are not part of those activities. Certain special use airspace areas can create limitations on the mixed use of airspace. The special use airspace depicted on instrument charts includes the area name or number, effective altitude, time and weather conditions of operation, the controlling agency, and the chart panel location. On National Aeronautical Charting Group (NACG) en route charts, this information is available on one of the end panels.

9. **Other airspace areas**, such as airport advisory services, Military training routes (MTR), Temporary flight restrictions (TFR), Parachute jump operations, Terminal radar service areas (TRSA), National security areas (NSA), and Visual flight rules (VFR) routes.

10. General airspace.

7.5.2 UAS traffic management

UAS traffic management (UTM) is a system of systems that will develop airspace integration requirements to enabling safe, efficient (Very low level airspace < 500ft) VLL operations. The system is in the very early stages of development and the full extent of its capabilities remains unknown. *https://www.nasa.gov/aero/nasa-drone-traffic-management-tests-take-off-in-reno* UTM is a distributed set of systems made up of hardware and software built on interoperable interfaces and protocols—similar to how

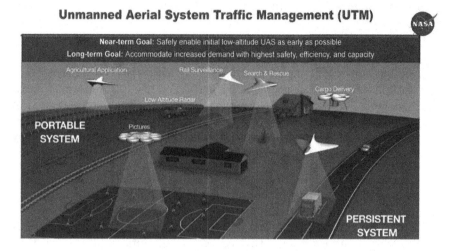

Unmanned Aerial System Traffic Management (UTM)

Near-term Goal: Safely enable initial low-altitude UAS as early as possible
Long-term Goal: Accommodate increased demand with highest safety, efficiency, and capacity

Agricultural Application
Rail Surveillance
Search & Rescue
Cargo Delivery
Low Altitude Radar

PORTABLE
SYSTEM
Pictures

PERSISTENT
SYSTEM

FIGURE 7.7   UAS traffic management

ethernet and TCP/IP create a functional Internet that all of us can access every day. UTM means that air traffic will no longer be managed via a centralized government-maintained system, as it is today. Instead a distributed set of services will provide access to the airspace through interoperable, industry-built technologies that can handle millions of aircraft in our shared airspace—all while improving on the gold standard of safety that aviation enjoys today.

the Global UTM Association (GUTMA), a non-profit consortium of stakeholders working to foster the safe, secure, and efficient integration of drones into national airspace systems. Through these groups, the drone industry is working together to provide an interoperable, distributed set of technological tools and infrastructure to bring aviation into the Information Age.

UTMs are the way of the future when it comes to drone flights, especially in populous places. NASA defines a UTM as "a cloud-based system that will help manage traffic at low altitudes and avoid collisions of UAS being operated beyond visual line of sight." By designing systems that will allow many drones to share the same airspace, drone companies, NASA, and the FAA are working to create a safer future for airspace.

Low Altitude Authorization Notification Capability (LAANC) is a threshold moment for the drone industry. This is the moment when regulated airspace becomes defined within software that is produced by industry; today is the first time that access to airspace is as easy as clicking a button. LAANC establishes a digital scaffold that will enable the growth and innovation of networked aerial robotics, and it is the first step toward a real system for UAS traffic management (UTM) in the national airspaces. Digital, automated, free access to controlled airspace, in the form of LAANC, is one of the single greatest moments we've experienced in the U.S. commercial drone industry

7.5.3   Emergency operations

Emergency operations:

1. **Emergency procedures**: When a remote pilot does experience in an inflight emergency, the pilot may take any action to ensure that there is not a hazard to other people or property. For example, if during a flight the small UAV experiences a battery fire, the remote pilot may need to climb the small UAV above 400 feet AGL to maneuver to a safe landing. In this instance, a report will need to be made only if asked to do so by the CAA.

2. **Planning for an emergency**: the remote pilot should consider many things like the different aircraft points of failure (propellers, motors, compass, ...) but also the approach of the UAV and the approach of people on the ground. A key part of emergency operations planning is understanding everything that can go wrong during a flight and then planning for the specifics of a particular flight mission.

3. **Conducting a site survey**: part of preparing for an emergency is conducting a site survey to understand the environment that you will be operating in. A good site survey might be done days in advance and could include:

   (a) A look around for local hazards such as towers, power lines, and other structures.

   (b) A check for radio interference that may compromise communication signals between the remote controller and the aircraft.

   (c) A check for magnetic interference, which could be an issue if there are steel structures close by.

   (d) A look at the traffic patterns of vehicles that may be endangere by the operation.

   (e) A look at any particpiatory by standers that may not be aware of what you are doing and be distracted or afraid by what you are doing.

   (f) A look at wind obstructions that can create turbulence.

4. **Lithium batteries** can cause fires.

   (a) Use a safety bag or fire proof containeer for charging, discharging and storage.

   (b) do NOT travel with a LiPo battery in your checked bagage but in the carry-on.

   (c) If your battery is damaged, make sure to follow proper disposal procedures and find a new battery ASAP.

   (d) Temperature matters. Cold and heat can be damaging.

5. **Maintaining your aircraft control**: If you encounter an emergency situtation while flying, rule number 1 is to maintain the aircraft control. Just because your transmitter's video feed fails, that might not necessarily mean that your control communication has failed. Many UAS come equipped with autonomous failsafe systems where the UAV will pause, auto-land or return home, depending on the situation and the emergency.

6. **Using emergency maneuvers**: Examples of situations that might trigger an emergency maneuver are: loss of orientation, loss of GPS signal, compass error, loss of direct line-of-sight, loss of video feed, flyaway, erratic movement, structures in line of flight, birds, ... After an emergency has initially occured and after you have maintained control of your UAV, you may need to conduct an emergency maneuver. Some best practices:

   (a) It might be switching from any kind of automated mode to a manual mode of flight. This could be helpful if you lose GPS signal or if you see a manned aircraft enter your flight area and need to ascend or descend as quickly as possible.

   (b) during landing, when a bystander or animal unknowingly encroaches into your landing zone: gain and hold a safe altitude and then find an alternated landing zone?

   (c) After regaining control of the UAV, the pilote should land safely as soon as possible an turn off the aircraft.

   (d) Aircraft wingtip vortices can cause an emergency if not detected. Wingtip vortices are circular patterns of rotating air left behind the wing of a large aircraft as it generates lift. They generate turbulence.

   (e) a UAV pilot has the responsibility to remain clear and yield right-of-way to all manned aircraft.

7. Accident or incident report to the authorities.

7.6 CONCLUSIONS

This chapter described flight operations, UAV piloting techniques and detailed planning and operations, risk and operation requirements as well as decision making and hazard identification. Detailed requirements for airport operations were also described and included traffic management and emergency operations.

CHAPTER 8

Safety Systems

8.1 INTRODUCTION

The UAV safety standards should aim to avoid any damage to people and the properties in the UAV's range of action. This mean to avoid in-flight collisions and uncontrolled ground impact. The aircraft should have a flight termination system FTS) capable of bringing the machine back to the ground. An FTS failure could become catastrophic. The installation of anti-collision system should be compulsory. Another peculiarity of UAV standards should be the incorporation of requirements for the grand guidance. Station have to be considered as an integral part of the flying material and should be consistent with it. Flight safety begins with the design of the aircraft. This means that the structure, system, flight performance, fight qualities, etc. must comply with the applicable requirements. Instructions also need to be provided for maintenance and repairs of the aircraft during its operational life. (F. DeFlorio (Airworthiness: an introduction to aircraft certificate, a guide to understanding JAA, EASA and FSS standards, Elvevier, 2006)).

For an aircraft, airworthiness is the possession of the necessary requirements for flying in safe conditions, within allowable limits. Safe conditions relate to the normal course and satisfactory conclusion of the flight. The aircraft is designed and built accordingly to flight qualities and performance studied and tested to be able to fly safely.

Safety is a concept generally defined as absence of danger. It is important to be able to rely on very skilled people in order to avoid errors that cause accidents or catastrophes in flight operations. The environment covers all the external factors that can have an influence on the flying of an aircraft. This includes meteorological conditions, communications, etc. Aircraft are designed for operation within a certain flight envelope which depends mainly on speed and structural load factors. In addition, the maximum weight of the aircraft can be established differently for various types of operations. Operational conditions of the aircraft are also established. Any usage outside of these requirements limits might cause an accidents. Overnight take-off, aerobatic

DOI: 10.1201/9781003121787-8

maneuvers performed with aircraft designed with load factors non-aerobatic operations, flights in icing conditions without suitable protection and exceeding the speed limits are just a few examples of flying within the allowable limits.

8.2   HAZARDOUS OPERATIONS

Failing conditions are defined as effects on the aircraft both direct and consequential, caused or contributed by one or more failure, considering relevant adverse operational or environmental conditions, failure conditions may be classified according to their severity as follows: minor, major, hazardous and catastrophic.

8.2.1   Some examples

Examples of hazardous operations include:

1. Operations that interfere with manned aircraft operations.

2. Operating a sUAS over persons not directly participating in the operation.

3. Operating a sUAS beyond its capabilities to the point of losing control.

4. Loading the sUAS beyond its capabilities to the point of losing control.

5. Failure to consider weather conditions near structures, trees, or rolling terrain when operating in a densely populated area.

6. No person may operate a sUAS in a manner that interferes with operations and traffic patterns at any airport, heliport or seaplane base

7. Flying near emergency responders, firefighters or police during a crisis.

8.2.2   What Can Go Wrong?

1. Crash due to a mechanical/electronic failure, a loss of contact between the pilot's ground control transmitter and receiver on the aircraft. It could also crash due to unsuitable weather conditions or pilot error.

2. The aircraft could fly away if control is lost between the pilot's ground control transmitter and receiver.

3. Crash into other aircraft or into into people or structures (pylons, buildings) and natural features (cliffs and trees).

4. The use of the UAV is illegal, if the operator does not comply with the strict operating conditions and limitations specified by the CAA.

5. UAS might be subject to hijacking.

8.2.3 Common aircraft accident causal factors

1. Inadequate preflight preparation and/or planning.

2. Failure to obtain and/or maintain flying speed.

3. Failure to maintain direction control.

4. Improper level off.

5. Failure to see and avoid objects or obstructions.

6. Mismanagement of fuel/battery.

7. Improper of distance and speed.

8. Selection of unsuitable terrain.

9. Improper operation of flight controls.

10. Avoid flight in the vicinity of thermal plumes, such as smoke stack and cooling towers.

11. Flying in the wire environment.

8.3 SAFETY PROMOTION

Safety promotion is a useful tool that can help to provide both the public and commercial UAS operators with a better understanding of how to use UAS safely.

System safety is a specialty within system engineering that supports program risk management. It is the application of engineering and management principles, criteria and techniques to optimize safety. The goal of system safety is to optimize safety by the identification of safety related risks, eliminating or controlling them by design and/or procedures, based on acceptable system safety precedence.

One way to mitigate risk is to perceive hazards. Hazards can be classified into three different classes:

Apparent: crashing in people or property, loss of visual sight, untrained operator, too windy, area not big enough, etc.

Detailed: autopilot settings, improper failsafe controls, improper training, powerlines or other hard to see obstructions, uncontrolled ground access, flight path clearance, etc.

Hidden: high temperature or elevation, loose screws, rolling terrain wind hazards, updrafts and downdrafts, human factors, emergency path planning, component wear, etc.

By incorporating the **PAVE** checklist into preflight planning, the pilot divides the risks of flight into 4 categories: **Pilot in command, Aircraft, enVironment, and External pressures** which form part of a pilot's decision-making process.

Air risk (collision risk, air proximity, accidents and incidents with manned aircraft): A lack of protection of aerodromes and their related airspace might lead to conflicts with other airspace users, with the potential consequence of collision. The main concern is UAS operations taking place in the whole airspace where manned aircraft operate.

UAS operators having up-to-date, accurate and easily understandable limitations information that helps them to identify restrictions or requirements in effect at the location where they wish to operate. They are responsible for identifying sensitive areas.

Geofencing and automatic performance limitations of UAS or advisory systems: This function requires position determination (for example, using GNSS or other means), a database of geo-limitation data, and control functions in order to comply with any restrictions on the time and location of UAS operation. When the unmanned aircraft takes off, or approaches a zone subject to a zone subject to UAS restrictions, the remote pilot may receive an advisory or the UAS itself may be designed not to exceed those limitations. A geofencing system should include the following functionalities and performance characteristic so as to provide

1. An interface to update data containing information on airspace limitations and requirements as well as to ensure the integrity and validity of this data.

2. Information about the airspace limitations an requirements where the UAV operates, as well as the position and movement of the UAV relative to those limitations.

3. Information on the status of the system as well as on the validity of its position or navigation data.

Emergency recovery capability is UAS safety procedure that provides for the cessation UAV flight in a manner that minimizes risk to persons on the ground, other airspace users and critical infrastructure.

Scanning techniques: to scan effectively, pilots must look from right to left or left to right. They should begin scanning at the greatest distance an object can be perceived (top) and move inward toward the position of the aircraft (bottom). For each stop, an area approximately 30 degrees should be scanned.

The structure must be able to sustain a certain number of events such as flights landing or flights hours, during which there is a low probability the strength will degrade below its design ultimate value due to fatigue cracking. The structure should be of damage-tolerance design and able to retain its required residual strength for a period of use after the structure has sustained a certain level of fatigue, corrosion, accidental damage.

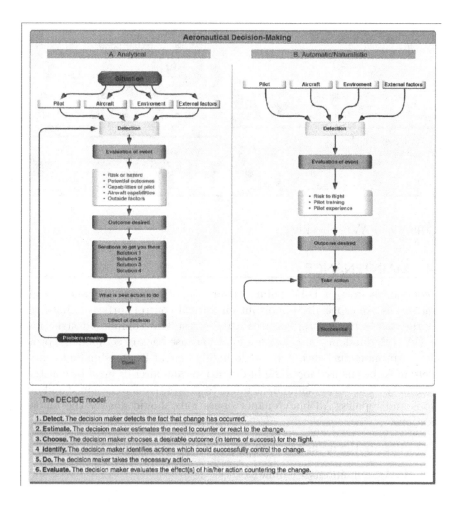

FIGURE 8.1   DECIDE checklist

Definition 60 *Crew resource management (CRM) is the management of all the resources that are available to the remote pilot in command, prior and during flight, including resources both on board the aircraft and from outside sources.*

An aircraft is subject to damage which has to be re-framed. A repair means elimination of damage and/or restoration of an airworthy condition of a product, part or applicance. These are type of damage that can be anticipated so that the repair of this damage can be studied in advance. A repair can be major or minor. Major repairs are frame, power and propeller repairs.

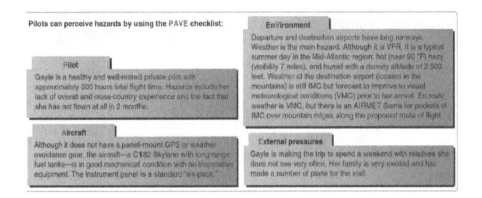

FIGURE 8.2 PAVE checklist

8.4 MAINTENANCE

A common source of UAV failure is servo malfunctions. Therefore, redundant servos are especially important on critical control surfaces. Single servo failures that drive control surfaces usually result in complete destruction of the UAV. Redundancy also satisfies FAA because backup components provide safety. Autonomous helicopters would highly benefit from redundant controls. Safety must be ensured for all flight operations and aircraft must be constantly maintained. The term maintenant refers to preventive maintenance and alterations and repairs. All maintenance operations should answer the following questions:

1. what are the items to maintain?

2. How the maintenance done?

3. Where and when to do maintenance?

4. Who can do the maintenance?

8.4.1 Inspection procedures

UAS diagnostic:

1. Detecting and diagnosing failures of Unmanned Aerial Vehicles during their mission is a key challenge for their effective deployment. On-board diagnostic systems are able to provide a huge amount of information about the state of the vehicle during the flight, by monitoring sensors, software, and hardware components. However, the ability of processing such data in an online manner is a serious obstacle to a timely detection and diagnosis of failures.

2. Drones need a large degree of tolerance towards faults. If not diagnosed and handled in time, many types of faults have catastrophic consequences, If they occur during flight. Prognosis of faults is also valuable and so is the ability to distinguish the severity of different faults in terms of both consequences and the frequency with which they appear.

3. Faults in air system sensors and in control surfaces are given special attention.

Maintenance and inspection procedures:

1. The frequency and length of time during which a drone is nonoperable due to its undergoing maintenance are significant factors in the usefulness and costs of the system. These are factors which must be addressed during the initial design of the system, involve control of the system liability to damage, system reliablity, component lives, costs and supply and the time taken for component replacement and routine servicing.

   (a) Basic maintenance: It is highly recommended that the maintenance be performed in accordance with the manufacturer's instructions. A reliable maintenance schedule must be established for the aircraft ad its components.

   (b) Pre-flight inspections.

   (c) Techniques to mitigate mechanical failures of all elements used in small UAS operations such as the battery or any device used to operate the UAS.

   (d) Appropriate record keeping: Document any repair, modification, or replacement of a system component resulting from normal flight operations and record the time-in-service for that component at the time of the maintenance procedure. Methodical maintenance and inspection data collection can be helpful in the tracking of aircraft component service life, as well as systemic component, equipment and structural failure events. Flight logging should include all components of the UAV including the remote controller, launch and recovery equipment, communications link equipment, payloa, and any other components required to safely operate the UAV.

   (e) Persons that may perform maintenance on UAS.

2. The achievement of adequate accessibility to sub-systems in both airborne and control station elements of the system must be carefully considered in the initial design and may have significance in determining the configuration of those elements.

UAV Maintenance:

1. UAS diagnostic, maintenance and inspection: composites, blade replacement, fuel, communication and instrumentation, assembly, and trouble shooting, firmware updates, batteries:

(a) Structural of skin cracking

(b) Delamination of bonded surfaces

(c) Liquid of gel leakage

(d) Strong fuel smell

(e) Smell of electrical burning or arcing

(f) Visual indications of electrical burning or arcing

(g) Noticeable sound (decibel):

(h) Control inputs not synchronized or delayed

(i) Battery causing distorted (bulding)

(j) Diminishing flight time capability (electric powered propulsion systems)

(k) Loosing or missing hardware/fasteners

2. Safety, launch and recovery, management in degraded mode.

3. Technical documents: manuals and checklists to reduce human error in order to create standardized, safe and efficient procedures: pre-flight checklist, testing, first flight.

4. Human factors, crew resource management, information transfer, problem solving.

5. Risk analysis and prevention, Evaluation and risk management, plan for emergencies.

6. It is recommended to perform maintenance after every 200 flights or 50 flight hours, unless otherwise stated in your UAS operating manual.

8.4.2   Management in degraded mode

Management in degraded mode:

1. Degraded mode (scalability): classical separation between nominal operation and faults becomes untenable; system is continuously operating under faults": Among the "faults" are – Loss of a UAV – Loss of a communication link.

2. One of the biggest challenges facing any cutting-edge Attitude and Heading Reference System/Inertial Navigation System (AHRS/INS) is the ability to perform a mission in a degraded environment. In navigation, dead reckoning is the process of calculating one's current position by using a previously determined one, and advancing it based upon known or estimated speeds (integrated) over elapsed time and course. Evidently each integration is subject to a cumulative error; the aim, therefore, is to reduce this error in order to increase precision.

3. An AHRS/INS uses a computer and a series of sensors, such as accelerometers, gyroscopes and occasionally magnetometers, which are used continuously to calculate: position, orientation and velocity of a navigation system or moving object without the need of external references, such as GNSS devices.

4. Navigation in degraded environments (e.g. with no GNSS input) is a major objective.

5. Think localy: Neither rely on communication, nor on the stability; of your neighbourhood; this is most of the time ignored; this leads to probabilistic mission sucess; Always consider other scenarios; What if?

6. Our approach: We work above the air frame level (mission oriented); Algorithms always assume degraded mode of operation; We garantee the missions are achieved; We use simulation and formal validation; We run real experiments.

7. Impact of the think localy precept – local computation based algorithms – construction of a (by nature partial/false) global view of the overall system based on local information – underlying model based on graph relabeling (or similar approach)

Health condition monitoring (HCM) allows operators to monitor the technical condition of their drones after a mission is completed. This proven procedure from manned flight is now also available for unmanned aircraft. Initially, data-driven post-flight analysis is available for such critical drone components as batteries, flight controllers, motors, and propellers.

8.5 HUMAN FACTORS

There are many different ways in which human intervention determines the success or failure of UAS operations. These include strategic, management decisions that help create the context for both the systems engineering and operations teams that monitor and control UAVs. They also include the regulatory framework that, in turn, influences every level of UAS operations. The complex nature of these applications can make it difficult to trace the different interactions between management and regulation, between operational staff and their support teams.

In case of an accident, Events and Causal Factors (ECF) diagrams must be developed. It is important to stress, however, that this is only one of several different notations that might be used to provide a similar overview.

There should be standardised form of risk assessment to consider the possible consequences and likelihood of collision with ground obstacles, including conurbations, during the planning of lost link profiles. Tthe profiles should adequately identify 'safe zones' where a UAV could ditch as it followed the lost link manoeuvres. These factors are compounded by the pilots' lack of experience and expertise in tracing the probable course of a UAV as it followed one of these profiles.

Criticality of Data Links: Probably the most pressing requirement is a system of secure, high-integrity data links between the unmanned air vehicle, the control station, and the ATC centers, plus a voice link between the UAV controller and air traffic control. The links may be line of sight or extended by satellite or other relay. Onboard video cameras may be needed for remotely piloted landings, while fully autonomous vehicles could require an ILS, microwave landing system (MLS) or transponder landing system. Navigation could be a blend of GPS, differential GPS and inertial nav.

Human intervention plays a critical role in emergency response. Organizations ranging from NATO to national civil aviation authorities (CAAs) recognize that much more work must be done to integrate UAVs with manned aircraft. Unmanned air vehicles will require sophisticated control systems with appropriate levels of autonomy, effective sense-and-avoid mechanisms, and high-integrity data links. These will be needed, in part, because neither military nor civil UAV operators will be happy to see their aircraft limited to special-use airspace or to have long-range platforms like Global Hawk and the proposed Euro Hawk be limited to cruise altitudes above 50,000 feet and to spiral climb and descent patterns.

Ask for recommendations on the certification of UAV equipment, such as situational awareness sensors and computer technology on which to base ground control stations, communication links, navigation systems and "pilot substitutes" (augmented automatic flight control systems). It also sought tools for establishing the operational viability of UAV systems and subsystems, including degraded modes.

The accuracy of onboard altimetric and other sensors will be defined according to the UAV category and stipulated flight-path accuracy. Emergency flight termination systems may be needed, ranging from parachute landing systems to explosive devices.

To locate and track UAVs on the ground, optical sensors, multilateration or tarmac-embedded induction sensors may be required. And UAV controllers may need improved human/machine interfaces featuring large-screen situational awareness displays and moving maps. They probably will have to file UAV flight plans and listen for ATC calls on emergency frequencies. Much applicable technology exists already in the military domain, says the report, but needs spinning out into the civil arena.

8.6 RISK ANALYSIS AND PREVENTION

8.6.1 Technical requirement for risk

1. **Positioning limitations** include both geographical limitations (defined using geographical coordinates) and non-geographical limitations based

on the positioning of the unmanned aircraft, such as height/altitude or range.

2. **Flight control technology**: the internal flight control loop is automatically addressed by the system, and the remote pilot does not need to have skills to stabilize the aircraft during flight.

3. **Energy limitation** refers to limiting the kinetic energy transmitted by the unmanned aircraft during a collision. In general, this may include the global energy level and/or the energy per unit of surface of the impacted element. This may leverage the used of soft/absorbing materials, special designs that facilitate the detachment of the UAV parts during a collision, blades protections, technologies that stop the rotors on impact.

4. **Collision avoidance** refers to systems that help to steer the unmanned aircraft away from an upcoming collision, with another aircraft bu also with people or infrastructure on the ground. They may provide the pilot a warnings in case of an imminent collision, or automatically steer the unmanned aircraft away through flight controls.

5. **Automatic take-off and landing** refers to the UAV automatically following a pre-established behavioral pattern when the data link connecting the control station to the unmanned aircraft is interrupted.

6. A **standard scenario** is a description of a type of UAS operation, for which a specific operations risk assessment (SORA) has been conducted and on the basis of which mitigations means have been proposed which are deemed acceptable by the competent authority.

8.6.2   Holistic risk model

1. **Risk** is the combination of the frequency (probability) of an occurence and its associated level of severity.

2. The categories of harm are the potential for fatal injuries to third parties on the ground, fatal injuries to third parties in the air; damage to critical infrastructure.

3. The **risk mitigation measures** might be implemented through various means (design and/or operations related) depending on the nature of the harm being controlled. In the case of fatal injuries on ground, for example, appropriate mitigation might be linked to the control of population density and to UAS physical characteristics concerning its lethal area such as dimensions or explosion prevention capability.

4. The **holistic risk model** (HRM) is developed to support the assessment of the risks involved in the operation of an UAS. It provides a generic

Operational Pitfalls	Description
Peer pressure	Poor decision-making may be based upon an emotional response to peers, rather than evaluating a situation objectively.
Mindset	A pilot displays mind set through an inability to recognize and cope with changes in a given situation.
Get-there-itis	This disposition impairs pilot judgment through a fixation on the original goal or destination, combined with a disregard for any alternative course of action.
Duck-under syndrome	A pilot may be tempted to make it into an airport by descending below minimums during an approach. There may be a belief that there is a built-in margin of error in every approach procedure, or a pilot may want to admit that the landing cannot be completed, and a missed approach must be initiated.
Scud running	Pilots lower their altitude to avoid clouds. This occurs when a pilot tries to maintain visual contact with the terrain at low altitude while instrument conditions exist.
Continuing visual flight rules (VFR) into instrument conditions	Spatial disorientation or collision with ground/obstacles may occur when a pilot continues VFR into instrument conditions. This can be even more dangerous if the pilot is not instrument rate or current.
Getting behind the aircraft	Allowing events or the situation to control pilot actions. A constant state of surprise of what happens next may be exhibited when the pilot is getting behind the aircraft.
Loss of positional or situational awareness	In extreme cases, when a pilot gets behind the aircraft, a loss of positional or situational awareness may result. The pilot may not know the aircraft's geographical location or may not be able to recognize deteriorating circumstances.
Operating without adequate fuel reserves	Ignoring minimum fuel reserve requirements is generally the result of overconfidence, lack of flight planning, or disregard of applicable regulations.
Descent below the minimum en-route altitude	The duck-under syndrome can also occur during the en-route portion of an IFR flight
Flying outside the envelope	The assumed high-performance capability of a particular aircraft may cause a mistaken belief that it can meet the demands imposed by a pilot's overestimated flying skills.
Neglect of flight planning, preflight inspections, and check lists	Relying on experience and memory for regular flying skills and routes instead of following procedures through planning inspections and checklists. This especially an issue with experience pilots.

FIGURE 8.3 Typical operational pitfalls requiring pilot awareness

framework to identify the hazards, threats and the relevant harm and threat barriers applicable to any UAS operation. The HRM models the risk associated to a given operation of an of an UAS through the following steps:

(a) **Harm identification**: the identification of the harms for which the risk needs to be assessed.

(b) **Hazard identification**: the identification of the hazards related to the UAS operation that may lead to the retained harm: UAS out of control. During VLOS operation, the loss of the visual contact with the UA, even when not linked to failures of the technical system (for example, wrong command correctly executed) is an example of an operation being out of control. A UAS operation could be considered out of control when a near mid-air collision (NMAC) occurs between the UAV and another aircraft. During UAS operations, especially those conducted beyond line of sight (BLOS), the situational awareness of the remote crew is highly dependent on an array of items, equipment and installations that are provided to them for that purpose. As the crew is not physically onboard the aircraft, there is an inherent increase in difficulty to maintain control of the operation, especially in abnormal operating conditions. Violation of segregated areas or altitude restrictions, issuance of incorrect commands ... are all cases of an operation being out of control, even if only temporarily.

(c) **Identification of generic threats**: the identification of the issues that can cause a hazard to occur if not kept under control. Five generic categories of threats, potentially applicable to any UAS operation can be identified: technical issue with the UAS, human error, aircraft on collision course, adverse operating conditions, deterioration of external systems supporting the UAS operation.

(d) **Human error**: The human factors analysis and classification system (HFACS) taxonomy can be used to discover the human error in UAV mishaps. HFACS focuses on historical data to determine trends in UAV system failures and human performance, to act proactively and reduce the probability of accidents and injury. While evaluating the causal factors, to achieve the best results, investigators should determine the cause of the given accident first, and then analyze the case associated with specific categories.

(e) **Harm barrier identification** is the identification of the mitigation applicable to a specific harm for a defined hazard. Harm barriers affect the likelihood that, once it occurs, the hazard can cause the harm and/or the severity of the consequences of the hazard with respect to the harm. For example, by operating over unpopulated areas, the risk of hitting third parties on the ground is mitigated by an extreme application of the harm barrier of population density. On the contrary, an operation conducted over crowded areas is likely to have a very high intrinsic risk thus requiring significant effort on reducing the likelihood of the hazard.

(f) **Threat barrier identification** is the identification of the mitigation applicable to a specific threat for a defined hazard. Threat barriers affect the likelihood that a threat can cause the hazard. Each of these threat barriers reduce the likelihood of the hazard UAS operation out-of-control by preventing the threat from developing into the hazard or reducing the likelihood of the threat.

5. The **risk model** identifies two complementary approaches to mitigating the risk of a UAS operation:

(a) To reduce the likelihood and/or mitigate the effects of the hazard (UAS operation out of control) for each category of harm. This approach is satisfied by the application of harm barriers.

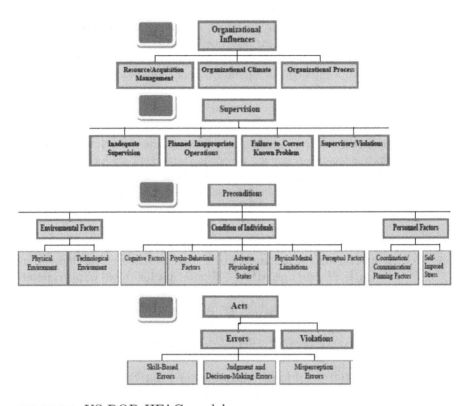

FIGURE 8.4 US DOD HFAC model

   (b) To reduce the likelihood of the UAS operation being out of control through mitigation that control the threats and/or reduce their likelihood of occurrence. This approach is satisfied by the application of threat barriers.

6. RF sensitivity of components can create flight issues with shielding needed to minimize the effects

7. UAV electronics and RF may interfere with some instruments that are not well shielded

8. Vibration effects can impact some instruments

8.6.3 Approaches to risk analysis

1. **Communication difficulties** associated with quantitative risk assessments are typically due to the fundamental differences between quantitative risks expressed in the form of probability and severity and the much

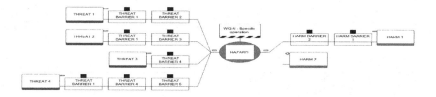

FIGURE 8.5 Bow-tie model

broader qualitative approach made by each individual in his perception of risk.

2. Whatever the limitations associated with quantitative assessments, these predictions provide valuable technical risk data to decision makers. The accuracy of the data is heavily dependent on the management of the uncertainties introduced in the risk model.

3. **Completeness uncertainties** are those introduced when attempting to model complex reality. Typical models such as Failure modes and effect analysis (FMEA) and Fault tree analysis (FTA) do not fully illustrate the complexity of real cases or scenarios. The scenarios involve interactions between the UAS, the remote crew, other traffic, air traffic control (ATC) ... both in normal or abnormal operations.

4. **Modeling uncertainties** are particularly apparent when quantitative predictions are being made of the consequences of various occurrences. It is very difficult to provide mathematical models of the impacts, considering the wide variety of shapes, materials .... Another significant

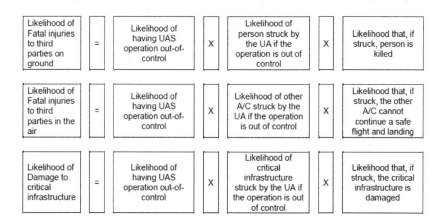

FIGURE 8.6 Likelihood estimation

Intrinsic UAS Ground Risk Class				
Max UAS characteristics dimension	1 m / approx. 3ft	3 m / approx. 10ft	8 m / approx. 25ft	>8 m / approx. 25ft
Typical kinetic energy expected	< 700 J (approx. 529 Ft Lb)	< 34 KJ (approx. 25000 Ft Lb)	< 1084 KJ (approx. 800000 Ft Lb)	> 1084 KJ (approx. 800000 Ft Lb)
Operational scenarios				
VLOS over controlled area, located inside a sparsely populated environment	1	2	3	5
BVLOS over sparsely populated environment (over-flown areas uniformly inhabited)	2	3	4	6
VLOS over controlled area, located inside a populated environment	3	4	6	8
VLOS over populated environment	4	5	7	9
BVLOS over controlled area, located inside a populated environment	5	6	8	10
BVLOS over populated environment	6	7	9	11
VLOS over gathering of people	7			

FIGURE 8.7 Ground

element of inaccuracy can be introduced when attempting to quantify human reactions to emergency situations.

5. **Parameter value uncertainties** are those related to the inaccuracy of the values to be used in the assessment. Component failure rates, atmospheric parameters, external event rates, human error rates . . . may all be subject to large uncertainties unless significant experience with these data is available.

8.6.4 United Nations call for international drone registration

1. Anything heavier than 60 grams hitting a plane in flight has the potential to cause a dangerous level of damage to the vehicle.

2. The US introduced one for non-commercial pilots in December 2015 and so far more than 770,000 people with UAVs have signed up for the scheme.

3. To minimize the potential of drones being involved in crashes, anyone who owns a UAV that weighs more than 250 g will have to register it with the government. Leisure users will also have to complete a "competency" test to ensure they are able to fly their machines safely.

4. As of September 2017, a database where drones or unmanned aircraft are required to be registered, still does not exist. Broken privacy laws as well as crashes are reasons why the pilot's information should be recorded in a global database.

5. The main concern with a global database is that the creators of drones are worried that different countries would want to create different rules

and wouldn't come together as one to create one large database. This would be mean that officers and those trying to control the registration would end up with various dispatch areas versus one single area to pull pilot information from. The ICAO (**International Civil Aviation Organization**) is trying to harmonize this since they will likely be the ones that will be in charge of the database.

6. There is also a great amount of concern that the civilians will even accept the idea of non-commercialized drones being registered. In 2015, the U.S. had decided that all non-commercialized drones would need to be registered, but the decision was overturned by Federal courts in May 2017. The FAA had to issue refunds to citizens that were compliant with the new registry.

7. Near the end of September, large companies such as Google and Amazon are expected to be at a meeting in Montreal to discuss this new registry. It likely that in addition to the pilots being registered, there will also be some geofencing in use to keep the unmanned vehicles out of airspace that they should not be flying in. This should lessen the chance of interference with jets and other smaller aircraft.

8. Once the registration database is complete, it will be easier for pilots to be identified when something like a crash happens. Drones typically crash into taller objects such as ferris wheels and large buildings and have the ability to cause a lot of damage. By having the pilot register, someone is able to be held accountable. As it currently is, it would be hard to find the person that is piloting the drone without them stepping forward in a case where an accident has occurred that caused property damage.

8.7   LABS

8.7.1   How to fly a drone

In this step-by-step guide I will assume that you've made yourself familiar with the particular model you have at your disposal. Furthermore, I will not get into the location you picked for your first flying test, as I think we've made it clear what to consider when choosing that.

1. Read the instructions first: The first thing you should do is carefully read the instructions provided with your drone. The manufacturer is responsible for providing you with all the aspects you need to know regarding the features. Don't take this part too lightly, as it may come in handy if any problems occur.

2. Charge your quadcopter battery: Before you can take off with your quadcopter, you'll have to charge the battery first. It is highly recommended to use ONLY the charger and the battery that comes with the device. If you have problems charging the battery, you should consider contacting the

manufacturer as it is not advised to use other parts for your drone than the ones provided LiPo battery.

3. Quadcopter Positioning: You have to ensure that the space you're using is clear from any danger, as we have stated before. Furthermore, be sure that the quadcopter is positioned according to the manual. You have to know where the front and the back of the model are. Position yourself behind the drone before taking off.

4. Push the quadcopter throttle down: Remember the throttle command on the left stick? Yeah, that one. Before you switch on your transmitter, push the throttle way down. Only then turn the transmitter on. After that, connect the quadcopters battery. This sequence is very important. When you are finished with your flying session, first, disconnect your drone battery, and then turn off the transmitter. Basically, the same thing in reverse order. Remember it.

5. Take off and land: The first flight maneuvering you are going to do is taking off and landing. When you did all the previous steps, you may slowly push the throttle (left stick) upwards. The quadcopter will start to take off of the ground. If the quadcopter starts leaning forward or backward, compensate this by using the pitch command (right stick up and down). The same goes for the roll control (right stick left and right). If you see that the drone is leaning to either side, compensate and hold it in balance for now.

After taking off, keep the drone in balance and try to land it as smooth as possible. This is done by pushing the throttle command (left stick) down. Attempt to land it on the same spot from where you've taken off.

6. Take off and hold quadcopter position: The next thing you're going to do is taking off with your quadcopter and holding it in position a few feet above the landing spot. It is imperative to remember that this step requires concentration in holding the position.

Keep the drone steady and hold it as still as possible over the spot you took off of. This may seem tedious at first, but learning this technique will get you a long way in getting a hang on how to start and finish your flying session. Furthermore, it will make you a safe "pilot" and will ensure a long lifespan for your device.

Without learning how to execute these basic maneuvers of taking off, landing and balancing, you'll have a hard time later when we get to the more complicated stuff. So practice this for a while first.

7. Rotate the quadcopter: One of the most important things with quadcopters is learning how to execute the rotating commands adequately. Remember, the yaw control (left and right stick) controls the rotating of your multirotor drone. If you followed all the instructions above, you would be standing behind the quadcopter for the most of the time you learned how to take off.

Now, we're going a bit more complex with our lessons. You have to take off and rotate your drone in regards to where you're standing.

Now, this might sound easy enough, but as soon as you try it you will see the problem here. You see, the quadcopter, when rotating it, will change the position in the frame of reference towards where you're standing. If you're just rotating it, the drone will not amend its position, but it will leave you wondering where its back and front are if you don't pay attention.

8. Create a mental image: Even professionals don't always have it easy in determining how the quadcopter is oriented in reference to them. But, they still have a slight advantage over the rest of us who might just begin to learn how to fly a drone. They have experience.

But, how do they do that? Simple, they create a mental image of themselves being in the drone. This way, they stay on course, regardless of how many times the quadcopter may turn and spin.

Of course, you won't be able to do this instantaneously on your first try. Maybe not even on your tenth one either. But, the more comfortable you get with the controls, the more you will get a feeling on how the drone behaves.

9. Getting to know quadcopter controls: But wait! Didn't we talk about the controls in the beginning? Yes, and no. At the beginning of this article, we discussed the concept of flying a drone using the controls for the yaw, throttle, pitch and roll. But now that we've got an actual transmitter in our hands, we must think about it for at least a second. Actually, it would be rather important to reflect on the transmitter ONLY for a second, because we need to forget it as soon as possible.

What do I mean by that? If you've ever played a video game in the past 25 years, you might be familiar with the concepts of gamepads. When we're playing an action game, we often forget that we're holding a gaming pad in our hands, but we still manage to control the character on our screen without the need for looking down on it every two seconds.

The same thing has to happen here as well. You have to get used to the transmitter as soon as possible, and then totally forget about it. If we do that, we'll have more time to concentrate on the mental image we talked earlier.

You'll have a clearer understanding of how the drone behaves, once the controls on the transmitter become as plausible to you as controlling the movement of your limbs.

10. Combine quadcopter controls: Now that I've pushed you in the right direction regarding the things you have to learn in order to become a competent pilot, it is time to combine these lessons into one coherent session. After taking off, try moving the quadcopter forward and backward (until now, we've only used these commands to stay in balance). Don't use the yaw control for now, just fly forward and backward a few times, to get a feeling of how fast your drone is.

Now, do the same thing with the roll control. Fly your drone to the sides left and right while keeping the same altitude and orientation. Good! Now, these are the first two commands we want to combine. Try moving your drone forward and to the left to see if you're going to get a parallel flying path. Repeat this for all the directions and combination on your right stick.

OK. It's time for the tricky part. You have to rotate your drone a tiny bit with the left stick and leave it like that. Now, by only using the right stick, try to control the drone forward and backwards, while you remain in the same position. In the beginning it will feel a bit weird, but eventually, you'll get used to it. Repeat this a few times, and then rotate the drone a tiny bit more.

Do the same until you arrive at 180 degrees. The drone is now turned in the opposite direction than in the beginning. Practice this and get a feeling on how to position the drone to your liking.

11. Keep the drone close: One of the biggest mistakes that happen, not only to beginners but professionals too, is not keeping the drone close enough to yourself. Of course, we all want to fly our drones through the air and not be bound by borders. That's why we bought the thing in the first place. However, we need to know what our drone limits are. The first thing we have to know before flying off into the sky is the range of our transmitter. Here comes the manufacturer's manual into play. We have to look up the recommended range and the maximum limits for the specific model we're flying.

Yes, newer models have an integrated landing mechanism that lands the drone safely as soon as it gets out of range. However, the machine cannot control the drone from being damaged due to landing on an inappropriate landing site.

The other important aspect regarding range is our capability of having an overview of our flying. The drone can stay in the range of our transmitter, but this means nothing if we can't make out the drone's orientation in reference to ourselves.

My first encounter with this problem happened as I first tried flying my new drone in the woods. The weather was perfect, the range of the transmitter was OK, but after only a few minutes, I couldn't make out how the drone was positioned above me. My view was blocked and I just couldn't position myself. Needless to say, I had to do a couple more practice rounds in an open field, before I was ready to go to the more difficult terrains.

12. Take care of your quadcopter: A thing many of us forget, so remember to take good care of your drone! We often forget how sensitive this technology still is, so be sure to clean it after every use and take good care of your device as well as the transmitter.

8.8 CONCLUSIONS

This chapter described safety requirements, risk management and procedures. The UAV safety standards aim to avoid any damage to people and the properties in the UAV's range of action. This mean to avoid in-flight collisions and uncontrolled ground impact.

CHAPTER 9

Conclusions

Remote pilots are a new category of pilots. UAS operators training should include at least: UAV components, systems, aerodynamics and flight mechanics, flight operations, mission scenarios, weather, safety, maintenance, regulations and privacy. Seven different specialized enterprise tracks at least can be considered: UAVs in Construction; Surveying and Mapping; Precision Agriculture; Mining and Aggregates; Police, Fire, and Emergency Response; Infrastructure Inspection; Videography. The number of tracks alone indicates how important training and specialization has already become when it comes to finding work in the drone industry. That trend will only continue as drones become adopted in more and more scenarios, and more and more specific skill sets are required to be paired with the ability to fly well.

The top two applications most likely to be find steady work are Agriculture / Farming Services and Utilities Inspections. That is, areas that require an extra level of professional training, in addition to simply knowing how to fly.Before launching a drone services business, it's also important to become a proficient pilot, and log the hours needed to become a proficient pilot. After this, it's important to master the skill set to be selling. If you are going to work in aerial cinematography, you have to become proficient in post production and cinematography, and the entire world of skill sets required to create sellable video footage. If you're going to work in mapping, you have to become proficient in mapping software, and in the terms and perspectives your clients will bring to the table when they request a finished product.

Bibliography

[1] Angelov, P. (2012): Sense and avoid in UAS, research and applications, Wiley aerospace series.

[2] Astrom, K. J.; Murray, R. M. (2008): Feedback systems, an introduction for scientists and engineers, Princeton University Press.

[3] Austin, R. (2010): Unmanned aircraft systems, UAVs design, development and deployment, AIAA Education Series.

[4] Bestaoui Sebbane Y. (2015): Smart Autonomous Aircraft: Flight Control and Planning for UAV, CRC Press.

[5] Cook, M. V. (1997): Flight Dynamics Principle: A Linear Systems Approach to Aircraft Stability and Control, Elsevier Aerospace Series.

[6] Corke, P. (2011): Robotics, vision and control, fundamental algorithms in matl ab, Springer www.petercorke.com/RVC OR https://github.com/petercorke/robotics-toolbox-matlab

[7] Fernandez-Rubio, J. A. (2004): Performance Analysis of an INS/GPS Integrated System Augmented with EGNOS, Universitat Politecnica de Catalunya, Barcelona, Spain.

[8] Lusk, R. M.; Monday, W. H. (2017): An early survey of best practices for the use of small unmanned aerial systems by the electric utility industry, Oak Ridge National Laboratory, ORNL/TM-2017/93

[9] Moir, I.; Seabridge, A. (2006): Civil avionics systems, aerospace series, Wiley.

[10] Moyano Cano, J. (2013): Quadrotor UAV for wind profile characterization, Univ. de Madrid, PhD thesis.

[11] Mueller, T. J.; Kellogg, J. C.; Ifju, P. G. (2006): Introduction to the design of fixed-wing micro air vehicles, AIAA Education Series.

[12] Nonami, K.; Kendoul, F.; Suzuki, S.; Wang, W.; Nakazawa, D. (2010): Autonomous Flying Robots, Unmanned Aerial Vehicles and Micro-aerial Vehicles, Springer.

[13] Oncu, M.; Yildiz, S. (2014): An analysis of human causal factors in unmanned aerial vehicle accidents; thesis, NPS, Monterey.

[14] Rogers, R. M. (2007): Applied mathematics in integrated navigation systems, AIAA Education Series.

[15] Stevens, B. L.; Lewis, F. L. (2007): Aircraft Control and Simulation, Wiley.

[16] Trips, D. (2010): Aerodynamic design and optimization of a lon range mini-UAV; Ms thesis, Delft university of technology

[17] Valavanis K. P.; Vachtsevanos, G. J., eds (2015): Handbook of unmanned aerial vehicles, Springer reference

[18] Villa, T. F.; Gonzalez, F.; Mikjevic, B. (2016): An Overview of Small Unmanned Aerial Vehicles for Air Quality Measurements: Present Applications and Future Prospectives, Sesnors.

[19] Woodman, O. J. (2007): An Introduction to Inertial Navigation. University of Cambridge.

[20] Yanushevsky, R. (2011): Guidance of unmanned aerial vehicles, CRC Press.

[21] Paul Zarchan, 'Global Positioning System: Theory and Applications Volumes I and II" AIAA, 1996.

[22] *www.nasa.gov*

[23] *www.faa.gov:* $14CFRpart47, 48, 71, 107; AC00 - 6, 150/5200 - 32, 107 - 2; AIM, FAA - H - 8085 - 2, H - 8083 - 25; SAFO09013, 10015, 10017, 15010$

[24] *www.easa.europa.eu/easa − and − you/civil − drones − rpas*

[25] *www.sesarju.eu/sites/default/files/documents/reports/*

[26] *European_Drones_Outlook_Study_2016.pdf*

[27] *http://support.identifiedtech.com/wp − content/uploads/2016/08/ID_ section3_part1_weatherEffects.pdf*

[28] *Drones − rules.eu*

[29] JARUS (joint authorities for rulemaking of unmanned systems) guidelines on specific operations risk assessment (SORA) document identifier: JAR-DEL-WG6-D.04

[30] *https://www.linkedin.com/pulse/weather − considerations − drones − cyrille − habis*

[31] *https://www.nap.edu/read/9878/chapter/6*

[32] *https://www.linkedin.com/pulse/how−do−drones−work−part−2−introduction−aerodynamics−fiorenzani*

[33] *http://www.circuitstoday.com/types−of−drones*

[34] *https://www.e-education.psu.edu/geog892/node/5*

[35] *http://mydronelab.com*

[36] *https://www.dronepilotgroundschool.com*

[37] *https://skyvector.com/*

[38] *http://edu.parrot.com/*

[39] *http://diydrones.com*

[40] *http://wiki.paparazziuav.org/wiki/Tutorials*

[41] *http:www.wired.co.uk*

[42] *https://diymodeling.appstate.edu/node/66*

[43] *http://jarus−rpas.org/sites/jarus−rpas.org/files/jar_doc_06_jarus_sora_v1.0.pdf*

[44] *http://www.flightlearnings.com/2011/03/23/atmospheric−pressure−2/*

[45] *https://aviation.stackexchange.com*

[46] *http://ardupilot.org/copter/docs/common−choosing−a−ground−station.html*

[47] *http://www.dcs.gla.ac.uk/ johnson/papers/UAV/Johnson_Shea_UAS.pdf*

[48] *https://zephyr−sim.com/?referral=uavcoach;*

[49] *http://www.techradar.com;*

[50] *http://www.realdronesimulator.com/;*

[51] *https://www.helicomicro.com/2016/02/02/real-drone-simulator/*

[52] *http://dronenodes.com/how−to−fly−a−quadcopter−beginner−guide/*

[53] *http://www.usairnet.com/cgi−bin/launch/code.cgi*

Terminology

BASIC DEFINITIONS

Definition 61 *Mass: This is a property of a body and a measure of an objects resistance to motion. It is constant and has the same value no matter where an object is located on Earth, on another planet or in space. Mass in the SI system is measured in kilograms (kg).*

Definition 62 *Force: This can be thought of as a "push" or "pull." A force can be active or reactive. The Earth's gravity pulls down on an object and this force is called weight.*

Definition 63 *Velocity: This is the speed of a body in a given direction and is measured in meters per second (m/s).*

Definition 64 *Acceleration: When a force is exerted on a mass, it accelerates, the velocity increases. This acceleration is greater for a greater force or for a smaller mass.*

Definition 65 *Center of gravity: this is the point on the aircraft where there is equal weight distributed on all sides.*

Definition 66 *Vector diagrams: In mechanics, vector diagrams are used to describe and sketch the forces in a system. A force is usually represented by an arrow and its direction of action is indicated by the direction of the arrowhead. Rectangles or circles can be used to represent masses. Force in the SI system of units is measured in newtons (N)*

Definition 67 *Couples and torques: When a force acts on an object, it produces what is known as a moment. The moment of a force about a point is the magnitude of the force multiplied by the perpendicular distance between the force and the point $T = F.d$.*

Definition 68 *Newton's laws of motion: Basic equations which can be used to work out the distance traveled, time taken and final velocity of an accelerated object*

1. **First Law:** An object will continue in its state of rest or motion in a straight line provided no external force acts on it.

2. **Second Law**: The acceleration a of a body is directional proportional to the force which caused it and inversely proportional to the mass m and takes place in the direction which the force acts $F = m.a$ for a constant mass or $F = \frac{d(mv)}{dt}$ in differential form.

3. **Third law**: For every action, there is an equal and opposite re-action.

Definition 69 *Viscous friction or drag*: *When a drone moves through the air or a vehicle moves on land, friction due to air resistance, slows them down.*

The most used derived quantities used in aerodynamics are:

$$
\begin{aligned}
velocity &= \frac{Length}{time} \\
acceleration &= \frac{length}{time^2} \\
force &= \frac{mass \times length}{time^2} \\
Momentum &= \frac{mass \times length}{time}
\end{aligned}
\tag{9.1}
$$

$$
\begin{aligned}
torque &= \frac{mass \times length}{time} \\
density &= \frac{Mass}{length^3} \\
Pressure &= \frac{force}{area} = \frac{mass}{length \times time^2} \\
energy &= \frac{mass \times length^2}{time^2} \\
massflow &= \frac{mass}{time}
\end{aligned}
\tag{9.2}
$$

Definition 70 *The **knot** is a unit of speed equal to one nautical mile (1.852 km) per hour, approximately 1.15078 mph. The ISO Standard symbol for the knot is kn. A nautical mile is based on the circumference of the earth, and is equal to one minute of latitude. It is slightly more than a land measured mile (1 nautical mile = 1.15078 statute miles). Nautical miles are used for charting and navigating.*

Glossary

AGL : Above ground level

AC : Advisory circular

ACR : Airman certification representative

ACS : Airman certification standards

ADM : Aeronautical decision making

AFS : Flight standards service

AEPL : Aviation english language proficiency

AIM : Aeronautical information manual

AKTC : Airman knowledge testing center

ASOS : Automated surface observation system

ATC : Air traffic control

ATIS : Automatic terminal information service.

AWOS : Automated weather observation system .

CRM : Crew resource management.

CTAF : Common traffic advisory frequency

FAA : Federal aviation administration

GPS : Global positioning system

IFR : Instrument flight rules

LSC : Learning statement code

METAR : Aviation routine weather reports.

MSL : Mean sea level

MTR : Military training routes

NAS : National airspace system

NOTAM : Notices to airmen.

NSA : National security areas

P-static : Precipitation static (form of radio interference caused by rain, snow or dust particles)

PIC : Pilot in command

RC : Remote control

SIGMET : Significant meteorological information

SAFO : Safety alert for operators

SMS : Safety management system

TAF : Termina area forecast.

TFR : Temporary flight restrictions

TRSA : Terminal radar service areas

UNICOM : Aeronautical advisory communications stations

VFR : Visual flight rules

VLOS : Visual line of sight

Index

Printed in the United States
by Baker & Taylor Publisher Services